The Metabolism
Miracle
Cookbook

The Metabolism Miracle Cookbook

175 DELICIOUS RECIPES THAT CAN RESET YOUR METABOLISM, MELT AWAY FAT, AND MAKE YOU THIN AND HEALTHY FOR LIFE

Diane Kress, RD, CDE

Da Capo
LIFE
LONG

A Member of the Perseus Books Group

Copyright © 2011 by Diane Kress

Design and production by Pauline Brown

Library of Congress Cataloging-in-Publication Data

Kress, Diane.
  The metabolism miracle cookbook : 175 delicious recipes that can reset your metabolism, melt away fat, and make you thin and healthy for life / Diane Kress.
  — 1st Da Capo Press ed.
     p. cm.
  Includes bibliographical references and index.
  ISBN 978-0-7382-1425-2 (alk. paper)
  1. Weight loss. 2. Reducing diets—Recipes. 3. Metabolism—Regulation.
4. Cookbooks. I. Title.
  RM222.2.K74 2010
  641.5'635—dc22

                                                            2010036693

First Da Capo Press edition 2011
ISBN: 978-0-7382-1425-2

Published by Da Capo Press
A Member of the Perseus Books Group
www.dacapopress.com

Da Capo Press books are available at special discounts for bulk purchases in the U.S. by corporations, institutions, and other organizations. For more information, please contact the Special Markets Department at the Perseus Books Group, 2300 Chestnut Street, Suite 200, Philadelphia, PA, 19103, or call (800) 810-4145, ext. 5000, or e-mail special.markets@perseusbooks.com.

10 9 8 7 6 5 4 3 2 1

CONTENTS

Introduction ix

PART ONE
The Miracle Lifestyle

1 A Different Kind of Metabolism   3

2 Do You Have Metabolism B?   11

3 Seven Simple Guidelines   17

PART II
Miracle Foods and Menus

4 Step One: Carb Rehab   31

    Reminders for Step One 33

    Step One Foods 34

    Frequently Asked Questions for Step One 47

    Sample Menus for Step One 48

5 Step Two: Transitions   55

    Don't Be Scared—Carbs Are Your Allies 56

    Reminders for Step Two 57

    Step Two Foods 59

    Frequently Asked Questions for Step Two 63

    Sample Menus for Step Two 65

6 Step Three: Keeping Weight Off for a Lifetime   71
  Counting Carbs in Step Three 71
  Step Three Foods 80
  The Slip-Up Remedy 86
  Frequently Asked Questions for Step Three 86
  Sample Menus for Step Three 90

PART III
Metabolism Miracle Recipes

7 Beverages   97

8 Appetizers   109

9 Salads   127

10 Soups   145

11 Poultry   161

12 Beef, Pork, and Lamb   177

13 Vegetarian Entrées   193

14 Seafood   207

15 Vegetables and Side Dishes   223

16 Breakfast   247

17 Snacks   263

18 Desserts   271

Acknowledgments 291
Appendix I: Shopping List 293
Appendix II: Metric Conversions 297
Index 299

INTRODUCTION

Miracle (mir-a-cle): an outstanding or unusual event or accomplishment.

Anyone who is bold enough to use the word *miracle* in a book title had better have darn good evidence to back it up. That's what I told myself as I thought about a title for the lifestyle plan that I knew could change the lives of people who kept trying and failing at losing weight.

You may find the title of this cookbook a bit over the top. I know—you've heard too many promises from too many experts who claim they've found the elusive key to weight loss. You want to believe them, so you follow their program and prepare the recommended recipes, but find yourself regaining weight in a yo-yo cycle that brings with it fatigue, irritability, and frustration. So why should this book be any different? Why should you believe in the promise of *The Metabolism Miracle* and *Metabolism Miracle Cookbook*?

This cookbook contains specially designed recipes that fit perfectly into the Metabolism Miracle program and meet the nutritional needs of the millions of people with metabolic syndrome (what I call Metabolism B). Each recipe is formulated to help you prepare great-tasting dishes that will maximize health and help keep your weight under control. The promise that comes with these recipes is one that is based on *your* unique physiology and the way *your* body responds to foods. With the help of *The Metabolism Miracle Cookbook*, you will be eating in a way that works with your metabolism, not against it.

The title of this cookbook and my first book, *The Metabolism Miracle*, starts with my own story. It's a story I saw mirrored in patient after patient as I worked as a medical nutrition specialist. About twenty-five years ago, at the beginning of my career, something changed within my body. It started with weight gain (and a roll around my middle) and as time progressed there was a definite change in my health and energy level.

Because I was a registered dietitian, diabetes educator, and weight-loss specialist following the "traditional medically recommended diet," this slow but steady increase in my weight, blood pressure, cholesterol, triglycerides, and blood sugar made no sense. I felt like a stranger in my own body. I had no energy, didn't look like myself, didn't feel like myself, and was prescribed medications for medical conditions I should not have had based on my seemingly healthy lifestyle.

Ironically, this same pattern was surfacing in nearly half the patients I saw for weight loss. Somewhere along the line, our metabolism appeared to have switched gears. I came to realize that we shared symptoms: an expanding waistline, fatigue, cravings, depression, anxiety, brain fog, decreased libido . . . and none of us could lose weight and keep it off on traditional diets!

After years of trial and error, improvement, and refinement, I was able to design a lifestyle program that enabled those of us with this "alternative metabolism" to lose weight, keep it off, and reduce the medications we took for weight-related health problems. We could finally look great, feel great, and have a new lease on our life.

More than anyone, I know the potential of this program, which is written specifically for people whose metabolism responds differently than that of the average person's. I have witnessed its overwhelmingly positive outcomes in patient after patient. And I watched it work for me.

Patients encouraged me to put the plan into book form. So I went back to them for input, asking them to choose a word that they felt most clearly described this program. The number one word they chose, all independent of each other, was *miracle*. I was sold. If the very people who lived and loved this way of life felt it was a "miracle" in their lives, then *Metabolism Miracle* was the right name.

And so, in the spring of 2009, *The Metabolism Miracle*—a comprehensive weight-loss plan for people with Metabolism B—was released. By summer, the book became a *New York Times* best seller. By autumn of 2009, it had become an international sensation.

This program has tens of thousands of devoted followers for one reason—it is the first and only scientifically based program written specifically for more than 50 percent of overweight people—people who have Metabolism B. Without this program, these people would never be able to lose weight, keep it off, and improve their cholesterol, blood pressure, and blood sugar while increasing energy. What looked like just another diet fad was a reality.

After *The Metabolism Miracle* was released, readers clamored for recipes that would match the three steps of the lifestyle. Along the same principles of the program, the cookbook had to work for busy schedules and everyday life challenges. In this cookbook, I've set out to create recipes that are quick, easy, and delicious—recipes that can work *for* your life, rather than frustrate you with tricky ingredients and long preparation times. Few of us have the time or energy to spend hours in the kitchen preparing a meal. But we do want to eat good food that keeps us healthy.

One of my goals in this cookbook was to create recipes that would entice anyone who sat down at the table, regardless of whether that individual has Metabolism B. These recipes include the same ingredients and flavors that we all love, but they've been balanced to work seamlessly for those of us who have Metabolism B.

The recipes in this book fit five criteria:

○ *They appeal to everyone.* Although they are tailored especially for your specific metabolic needs, the recipes fit any diet and appeal to most palates. After all, when you sit down to a meal with family or friends, you want to share your experience rather than eat separate dishes: "yours" and "theirs."

○ *Recipes are clearly identified so you can match them to the Step of the diet.* You don't need a degree in food chemistry to understand which of these recipes fit the various steps of the program. Each recipe is clearly labeled, indicating Step One, Two, or Three.

○ *They reflect diverse cuisines.* The dishes in this book take inspiration from around the world. *The Metabolism Miracle* has an international reader base and I wanted this companion cookbook to include recipes to help you expand your horizons while living a healthy Metabolism Miracle (MM) lifestyle.

○ *Many recipes fit people with special dietary concerns.* There are recipes tailored to match gluten-free, lactose-free, and vegetarian lifestyles.

○ *These recipes enhance the Metabolism Miracle lifestyle.* While it is true that the Metabolism Miracle can be followed without ever stepping into a kitchen, it is equally true that more and more people choose to cook in as well as eat out. These recipes make cooking enjoyable.

In addition to fitting the guidelines, the recipes are easy, flavorful, and healthful. I wish you and everyone following the Metabolism Miracle lifestyle a lifetime of health, happiness, and well-being!

PART ONE
The Miracle Lifestyle

A DIFFERENT KIND OF METABOLISM

Anthony, 46, was a well-respected and dependable office manager, having missed only four sick days in more than twenty years at the same company. He loved his job and his staff considered him fair minded, easygoing, motivated, and motivating. He was tall, lean, and the picture of health; he loved playing tennis and hiking. Because his father had a history of heart disease, Anthony steered clear of fast food, butter, fatty meats, and salty foods.

But over the past few months, Anthony hadn't felt like himself. He seemed to get plenty of sleep (lately he found himself falling asleep right after dinner), but woke up tired in the morning, dreading going to the office. His normal breakfast of coffee and a bagel left him hungry just two hours later. Even after a midmorning snack of crackers and fruit he was still anxious, irritable, and a little shaky by lunchtime. And, uncharacteristically, he found himself craving a candy bar in the afternoon.

His staff noticed and began to talk at the water cooler. "Anthony is so cranky—he really should get more sleep." "He didn't even talk about the Monday night football game at break today." "I heard him on the phone arguing with his wife. I wonder if there are problems at home."

One morning, Anthony called in sick to go to the doctor. He was genuinely concerned about how he felt: tired, cranky, irritable, dizzy, and lightheaded. His libido had tanked and he no longer cared as much about his job or anything in his life.

Dr. Jones ordered lab work for Anthony, checked his blood pressure, and asked many questions. He noted Anthony's symptoms and told him to return in one week, after the labs were back, to discuss his findings.

The next Thursday, Anthony got the shock of his life. Although he looked good on the outside, his insides told a different story. His blood pressure was 143/95 (exceeding his doctor's preference of less than 130/80). His LDL "bad" cholesterol was 149 (50 points over normal), and his HDL "good" cholesterol was 35 (15 points below normal). The most shocking finding was his fasting glucose reading at 109 (10 points over normal)—Anthony had prediabetes!

○○○

Lori is a 53-year-old woman whose last of three children left for college in the fall. She had always looked forward to the "empty nest," and even before Brian left for school, she dreamed of how she would spend some time finally caring for herself. On her first weekend "alone," she surveyed her body in her full-length mirror. When did that roll of fat around her middle grow to be that noticeable and jiggly? Did she always have a roll of fat on her back, under her bra line? Were those jowls and was that the beginning of a double chin? When did her once rosy complexion turn ashen and her hair become drab and lifeless? Lori was truly surprised at the figure that stared back at her from the mirror. Right then and there, she made up her mind. She would begin to eat right, exercise regularly, take time to relax, and make sure she got enough rest.

She thought back to the last time she looked great (wow, that was a long time ago) and remembered the tried-and-true calorie-counting diet she used to follow to lose weight, and the type of exercise that sped the weight loss along as well as toned and tightened her up. She decided to start that program again. Breathing a sigh of relief, she thought how great it would be to look and feel that good again.

On the Monday morning she was to begin her new regimen, she looked over the checklist she posted on her refrigerator:

○ Attend weekly weight-loss group meetings
○ Weigh herself daily at home and weekly at the meeting, and keep track of her weight loss

○ Attend an aerobics class three times a week
○ Use her meditation CD to help her relax and destress
○ Get to bed by 10 PM

Lori was true to her vow. For the next month she followed her "counting" diet, weighed herself daily, got her weekly group weigh-in and support, and exercised. She was shocked to find that the scale wasn't moving. She checked and rechecked her food journal. She was following her recommended program perfectly, not over- or undereating. But instead of her weight gradually decreasing, there were days when she actually gained weight! This week she was embarrassed during her weigh-in at the group meeting, when the "weight counselor" asked her to "be honest and tell her if she was closet eating or doctoring her food log." She was being honest . . . honestly! What was going on?

○○○

One Monday morning, my appointment book listed a 20-year-old woman interested in weight loss. Before meeting Theresa, I looked at her initial assessment form and fasting lab work. She was a finance major at a top university and had listed "weight loss!!!!" as the main reason for her visit. She was five foot five and listed her weight as, "Who knows this week?" Next to "activity," she had written: former athlete, current couch potato. Her family medical history included: obesity, hypertension, borderline diabetes, heart disease, and depression. Her fasting labs showed:

Glucose: 101 (normal is 65–99)
Total cholesterol: 179 (normal is less than 200)
LDL "bad" cholesterol: 129 (normal is less than 100)
HDL "good" cholesterol: 36 (normal is greater than 50)
Triglycerides: 116 (normal is less than 100)
Hemoglobin A1C: 4.9 (normal is 5.4–5.7)

Theresa entered my office without making eye contact. Even though it was 85 degrees outside and sunny, she was wearing a fleece hoodie zipped over her jeans. She sat down, made sure the hoodie covered her tummy, looked at me, and her eyes filled with tears. "I hate my body. It doesn't matter if I eat, fast, exercise, or am a couch potato. . . . I cannot lose this @#$% weight. I am slowly inflating and I don't even know who that person in the mirror is. I swear, I eat less than all my friends and I weigh more than all of them."

In just three minutes I already knew so much about Theresa. I couldn't wait to help her to get control of her weight, her health, and her life.

ooo

We've been stuck in a rut.

For more than sixty years, nutrition and medical experts have been giving misguided nutrition advice that has caused frustration, ill health, and steady weight gain in millions of people who earnestly try to stay healthy and watch their weight.

The problem stems from the fact that when it comes to weight loss, everyone is treated the same, with one set of rules and recipes for one type of metabolism. But for many of us, this "one size fits all" philosophy is wrong.

No doubt you've heard the mantra before: The calories you eat, minus the calories you burn, will equal your weight gain or loss. Traditional weight-loss programs have been built upon this rule of calories. There may be hundreds of diet books on the shelves, but underlying each diet is the "calories in—calories out" backdrop.

That's fine for anyone with a traditional metabolism. Based on the calorie formula, when you eat less and move more, you will lose weight. But this formula doesn't take into account those of us who have a different kind of metabolism— Metabolism B.

If you've been frustrated by yo-yoing weight loss, no matter how hard you've worked to stay slim, if you've been frustrated by a lack of energy and perhaps declining health, you very likely have this alternative Metabolism B (Met B for short).

And if you're overweight, it's likely that you've been trapped in the same endless cycle of earnest but frustrated dieting and declining health that I found myself in not so long ago. Take heart, it's not your fault. Guided in part by misguided nutrition advice promoted over six decades, experts in the nutrition and health fields have created an impossible task for a huge percentage of the population.

The good news is that by opening *The Metabolism Miracle Cookbook,* you just opened the key to breaking the cycle and getting your body back to optimal health and weight. With these recipes, you can get out of the rut, escape the endless cycle of frustration, and celebrate a future of excellent health.

A Personal Story

I found out about Metabolism B the hard way. During my early twenties, my body began to change. I started to gain weight around the middle and often felt fatigued and irritable, and became mildly depressed as my overall physical and emotional demeanor changed.

As the years progressed, my health began to decline. My blood pressure rose and my joints ached; an odd combination for someone so young. I became so involved in trying to decipher what was going on with my body that I even changed my college major from finance to nutrition. All I wanted were answers to my questions, the same questions you might have today.

- ○ Why am I gaining weight without eating more calories?
- ○ Why don't I lose weight when I increase exercise?
- ○ Why do I feel periods of extreme fatigue, especially in midafternoon?
- ○ Why do my joints and muscles ache?
- ○ How did I get this roll of fat around my middle?
- ○ Why can't I focus or concentrate?
- ○ Why can't I sleep through the night?
- ○ And the list went on and on and on. . . .

I had no idea then that my quest to understand these symptoms would eventually lead to a lifetime of work discovering how to treat and control Metabolism B for the millions of us who have this alternate metabolism.

It's Not Fair

When you understand Metabolism B, you will understand why some people can drop weight by cutting their calories in a small way and making a few adjustments to their diet.

Simply removing soda for a few weeks can cause a five-pound weight loss. These individuals' success perfectly illustrates the calories rule. Meanwhile, people with Metabolism B can actually gain weight when they cut calories and never see lasting weight-loss success based on a simple calorie reduction. In fact, people with Metabolism B often gain weight following the same program on which their friends have successfully lost weight. How unfair is that?

If you're not already angry about the misinformation you've been fed regarding weight loss, you have a right to be. For too long, experts have led us to believe that the "calories in–calories out" rule works for everyone. Starting in the 1970s, when the spotlight began to focus on cutting calories, fat, and cholesterol, we were urged to increase consumption of fruit, vegetables, whole grains, skim milk, and yogurt. Recipes followed the same guidelines, and fat-free crackers, fat-free ice cream, and even fat-free fat found their way onto supermarket shelves. That is when the country began its descent into an obesity epidemic. At the same time that the United States Department of Agriculture reconfigured a previously balanced diet into a pyramid shape that emphasized the increased intake of carbohydrate foods, we began to spiral into higher rates of diabetes, heart disease, cancer, and depression. The link can't be ignored.

Low-calorie, low-fat diets make absolute sense for people with "normal" metabolisms, what I call Metabolism A. But for the 50 percent of dieters with Metabolism B, this low-calorie formula is a recipe for disaster. In fact, much of what we've been told works against those of us with Met B.

The Wake-Up Call

As my own health began to decline and my weight continued to rise, I was flummoxed by the paradox of "healthy" foods flooding the market at the same time our national epidemic of weight gain and related disease began.

When I became a registered dietitian and certified diabetes educator and began to work in progressive teaching hospitals in the New York metro area, I focused on weight reduction and diabetes management, teaching the way I had been taught. You guessed it—I taught the "calories in–calories out" formula. But as I met more and more patients, something startling came to my attention. Almost half the patients I counseled for weight and health issues told life stories very similar to my own. There was a definite pattern here, and it was a much bigger issue than my own personal problem.

If close to 50 percent of overweight people could not lose weight and keep it off on traditional diets, why was no one addressing this and why were these people being taught a diet that made them sicker physically, mentally, and emotionally. All the major medical associations sanctioned the low calorie, low fat, higher carb program providing about 50 percent carb, 20 percent protein, and 30 percent fat.

Many registered dietitians, physicians, cardiologists, and endocrinologists agreed that while the present dietary guidelines did not always work, it was best to keep with the status quo because we had no proven alternative. Meanwhile, the diet we universally taught failed almost half the people who needed help. The people we counseled, the people who put their trust in us as medical professionals, were getting sicker and heavier.

My health couldn't wait for the establishment to change its advice, and neither could the health of my patients. Although we followed the "perfect diet," we continued to gain weight and watch our cholesterol, blood pressure, and blood sugar rise. So I took a different path and began to offer my patients a choice in diet style: the traditional approach, or the program I was working on tailored to "alternative metabolism." Almost all opted for this latter program.

I collected their lab data, nutritional assessments, medical assessments, and dietary and weight histories, and, after many long hours, began to see that significant areas in their medical and personal histories overlapped. They shared similar symptoms; they had similar medical histories, and took similar medications; and no matter what they had tried, none of them could successfully lose weight and keep it off.

Jumping Out of the Rut

As the patterns became clear, I developed a program based on real science, real physiology, and the latest research on obesity and weight gain. But it did not follow the old rule of the calorie. Instead, this new plan worked to reprogram metabolism that had gone haywire in so many people.

Half of my patients, and millions of others, including me, have Metabolism B, a metabolism that is 180 degrees different in nature than the more commonly recognized

Metabolism A. The root difference is an inherited imbalance of the fat-gain hormone, insulin.

With Metabolism B, traditional diet approaches only serve to fuel the insulin over-reaction, thus causing weight gain. To have lasting weight loss and good health, people with Met B need a different formula. The Metabolism Miracle is the formula—a diet and lifestyle program that lifts us all out of the rut and on the road to lasting good health. This program remedies the fatigue, cravings, irritability, and other symptoms of Met B while also helping to control and reduce fat and lower cholesterol, blood pressure, and blood sugar. For the first time in their adult lives, my patients were succeeding! Better yet, the change was permanent!

Many physicians, cardiologists, and endocrinologists referred to me patients who couldn't find success on the traditional diet plan. Incredibly, after eight weeks on the Metabolism Miracle plan, these patients returned to their physicians thinner, healthier, and happier than they had been in years. Their weight-related lab data significantly improved. Their medication for weight-related problems such as type 2 diabetes, hypertension, and high cholesterol could be decreased. They reported less depression and anxiety, and they were exercising and felt energized. In short, they got healthier!

Just Three Steps

The Metabolism Miracle is a three-step program. Step One is a "rest and rehab" period that allows your body to return to normal hormonal balance. Step One is like sending a weary friend to a spa for two months to decrease stress and wear and tear and to relax. After eight weeks of rest and rehabilitation, the program seamlessly moves to Step Two, a reprogramming period in which your body and metabolism ease back into gear until your desired weight is reached and your lab data has significantly improved. Once you are healthy and at a weight that feels right, Step Three will maintain your health and weight for life.

The Metabolism Miracle is designed to work with your metabolism instead of working against it. It was designed to help those with Met B get out of the rut that traditional diets pushed them into. The plan will help anyone lose weight, but it is the only program specifically tailored to help people with Met B achieve their optimal health and weight forever.

DO YOU HAVE METABOLISM B?

Think back. If you grew up in the '50s, '60s, even '70s, you could probably count on one hand the overweight kids in your class. It's possible that you still remember the name of the "big kid" in the class . . . the one big kid. Walk into a school today and you'll see that 50 percent of the children are overweight. Their older siblings already have muffin tops, their parents are fighting a losing battle with the bulge, and their grandparents carry a pill box with tablets to help lower their blood pressure, cholesterol, and blood sugar.

What happened? More important, how did you become one of these people?

The answer may be in your hormones. Almost 50 percent of overweight people have an inherited hormonal imbalance that slowly but surely leads to overweight and weight-related medical problems. I call this hormonal imbalance Metabolism B, or Met B for short.

The hallmark of Metabolism B is overproduction of the fat-gain hormone, insulin. Most people think of insulin in relation to diabetes, but everybody produces and uses insulin every minute of the day. It is a critical hormone.

Insulin's job is to usher excess blood sugar out of the bloodstream and into muscle cells, where it can be used for energy, and into fat cells, where it will be stored. Excess insulin promotes fat storage *on* the body (especially midline fat) and *in* the blood (cholesterol and triglycerides).

In normal metabolism, the pancreas releases an appropriate amount of insulin. People with Metabolism B over-release insulin which causes the well-designed system to go awry and leads to excess fat gain.

Let's make this concept come to life: When a person eats a carbohydrate-containing food—an apple, for example—the carbohydrate in the apple breaks down into blood sugar (the body's preferred energy source). As blood sugar rises from the apple's carbohydrate content, the pancreas begins to release the hormone insulin to normalize the blood sugar. Think of insulin as a "key," opening the muscle and fat cells' doors so that excess blood sugar can exit the bloodstream and enter the cells.

In "normal" metabolism, the *correct* amount of insulin opens the *correct* number of cells, leaving the person's blood sugar back in the normal range. In the case of Met B, the pancreas overreleases insulin and opens excess fat cells. Once a fat cell's door is opened, it will automatically withdraw sugar from the bloodstream.

Every time a person with Met B eats carbohydrate food, he or she opens more fat cell doors than does the average person, regularly "overdrawing" sugar from the bloodstream, leaving that individual's circulating blood sugar low . . . and fat cells overfed.

The excessive sugar pumped into fat cells make the cells bigger in size. The resultant low blood sugar leaves the person hungry, shaky, irritable, and craving more carbohydrate. The individual's brain actually panics, as *normal* blood sugar is the brain's preferred fuel. The brain urgently sends an emergency signal to "eat more carbohydrate and bring the blood sugar back into the normal range."

Although a low-calorie, fat-free snack (the apple) was purposely chosen, the person with Met B processed the food differently than would friends with normal metabolism (Met A), and was left feeling hungry, fatigued, and craving more to eat.

You can see that the very same apple that worked just fine to satisfy the hunger of one person, worked against the person with Met B. He or she is left craving more carbs, leading to greater and more frequent consumption of foods that will sabotage his or her ability to lose weight and stay healthy.

So how do you break the cycle? That's where these recipes come in. But first, let's take a look at the symptoms of Met B.

Recognizing the Symptoms of Met B

I specialize in weight reduction, obesity treatment, and diabetes management, but I cannot look at you and say, beyond all doubt, that you have Metabolism A or Metabolism B. The clues lie in three different areas: personal symptoms, family and personal medical history, and fasting lab numbers. Once you piece together the puzzle, you will know how your body works and choose a lifestyle that matches your body.

The first pieces of the puzzle with which you are probably the most familiar are your personal symptoms. Place a check beside any of the following symptoms if you experience them on a regular basis:

_____ Frequent fatigue, even upon awakening

_____ Late-afternoon energy slump (3:00–5:00 PM)

_____ Mild depression

_____ Apathy

_____ Mild anxiety

_____ Occasional panic attacks

_____ Cravings for chocolate, chips, bread, pasta, or other carbohydrate foods

_____ Not feeling full for any length of time

_____ Midsection fat deposits (a.k.a. "muffin top," "love handles," "back fat")

_____ Gaining weight more easily than ever before

_____ Difficulty losing weight and keeping it off

_____ Irritability causing a "short fuse"

_____ Problems with concentration and focus

_____ Racing thoughts or brain fog

_____ Trouble falling asleep or staying asleep, or restless sleep

_____ Decreased libido

_____ Caffeine has less effect than it used to (You can drink espresso and fall asleep.)

_____ Alcohol has a greater effect than it used to (You get flushed, tipsy, "weak in the knees" after a little alcohol.)

_____ Increased aches and pains

_____ Stiff joints; needing to "crack" your neck, back, fingers

_____ Sinus and eye-area headaches

_____ Mild dizziness that comes and goes

_____ Intermittent blurry vision

_____ Dry or teary eyes

_____ Difficulty with night driving (seeing halos; lights appear brighter)

_____ Increased light sensitivity (You wear sunglasses more than you used to.)

If you have checked eighteen or more of these symptoms, you may have Metabolism B.

It's a Family Thing

Now it's time to consider your family and personal medical history, another clue to your metabolism type. You don't choose your type of metabolism, you acquire it through your genetic lineage.

Put a "yes" or "no" next to the following health conditions if you or any member of your family has been diagnosed with any of these health conditions. Family members can include parents, grandparents, siblings, children, familial aunts/uncles, and cousins.

_____ High total cholesterol
_____ High LDL "bad" cholesterol
_____ Low HDL "good" cholesterol
_____ High triglycerides
_____ ADD or ADHD (attention-deficit syndrome)
_____ Alzheimer's disease
_____ Anxiety disorder
_____ Cancer (estrogen-based breast cancer, or ovarian, uterine, prostate, testicular, or pancreatic cancer)
_____ Chronic fatigue syndrome
_____ Diabetes, including:
        Gestational diabetes (diabetes of pregnancy), or you have recently borne a baby whose birth weight was close to or over 9 pounds
        Prediabetes (fasting blood glucose 100–125 mg/dl, HbA1C: 5.8–6.5)
        Type 2 diabetes (fasting blood glucose 126 or higher, HbA1C: over 6.5)
_____ Fibromyalgia
_____ GERD (gastric reflux)
_____ Heart attack/stroke
_____ Hypertension, or increasing blood pressure
_____ Hypoglycemia (low blood sugar)
_____ Hypothyroidism (underactive thyroid—are you taking Synthroid or Levoxyl?)
_____ Infertility related to hormonal imbalance
_____ Low vitamin D

_____ Metabolic syndrome (Metabolism B) (fat around the middle, with rising blood pressure, cholesterol, triglycerides, and blood glucose)

_____ Midline fat deposits (a roll around your middle) and increasing weight without a significantly increased food intake

_____ Mild depression

_____ Obesity

_____ Osteoarthritis

_____ Osteoporosis or osteopenia

_____ PCOS (polycystic ovarian syndrome). Symptoms may include irregular menstrual period, heavy menses, clotting, severe PMS, irregular endocrine-reproductive hormonal patterns, facial hair, and acne.

_____ Prediabetes

_____ Sleep apnea

If you answered yes to fifteen or more of these above health conditions for you or a family member close to you, it's possible you have Metabolism B, even if you don't yet personally show symptoms.

Your Numbers

Lab work offers the final piece of the puzzle that determines whether you have Metabolism B. If you suspect you have Met B, you don't have to obtain lab work before starting the Metabolism Miracle program. But for many people, seeing the numbers helps to clear up any doubts.

Ask your physician to consider ordering the following fasting lab tests. Try to schedule your labs for as early in the morning as possible because you'll need to fast, meaning you can eat no food and drink only water from midnight of the night before until the tests are taken the following day. A very conclusive picture of your metabolism can be painted from the following lab tests:

Metabolic panel   Lipid profile
Hemoglobin A1C   TSH (thyroid panel)
Vitamin D

People with Metabolism B often have lab numbers that are outside of the normal Met A range. Compare your lab results to these parameters for Met A and Met B. (Note that the reference ranges listed below will differ from those on your lab slip, as these are the numbers used to ascertain Metabolism A versus Metabolism B.)

	Met A*	Met B
Glucose	65–85	Less than 65 or greater than 85
Total cholesterol	Less than 200	200 and above
LDL cholesterol	Less than 100	100 and above
HDL cholesterol	Greater than 50	Less than 50
Triglycerides	50–99	Less than 50 or greater than 99
Hemoglobin A1C	5.4–5.7	Less than 5.4 or greater than 5.7
TSH	.45–4.5	Less than .45 or greater than 4.5
Vitamin D	Greater than 32	Less than 32

* These numbers apply to people in good health who have Metabolism A. Certain health conditions unrelated to metabolism can change the numbers above.

It is very important to ascertain whether you have Met A or Met B, as a mistake can be costly to your health, well-being, and success on your diet plan. By reflecting on the symptoms you feel, taking a peek at your current lab work, and considering your medical history as well as the medical history of your family, it's quite simple to determine which type of metabolism you have.

In my nutrition practice, the three legs of the stool—personal symptoms, family medical history, and lab work—make it clear whether I will teach a patient a calorie-based, low-fat diet to promote weight loss, or opt for instructing with the Metabolism Miracle. Now you, too, can make that determination—and easily apply the Metabolism Miracle to your own life.

The Metabolism Miracle Cookbook not only offers you solutions to your frustration regarding weight and health issues, but also delicious recipes to help you find your way.

The first step is to erase everything you've ever known about calories and weight loss. Your metabolism is different than textbook metabolism, and this is the plan that will work with your metabolism, not against it. Trust that this lifestyle will help you regain health, enhance your quality of life, and lose weight once and for all!

SEVEN SIMPLE GUIDELINES

Before you begin the Metabolism Miracle lifestyle, look over the following seven guidelines. It's important that you commit to taking the best care of yourself if your body is to improve in health and energy. These guidelines are the base of the program and will support you through your transformation to full health and energy.

General Guidelines for the Metabolism Miracle Lifestyle

1. STICK TO THE TIMELINE

The Metabolism Miracle is a lifetime lifestyle program that consists of three Steps:

Step One, the strictest of the steps, is designed *to rest and rehabilitate* the pancreas and liver. It lasts a minimum of eight weeks. Some people wish to stay longer in this initial Step because it is very easy to follow and quickly becomes such a habit that moving on seems like a hassle! There is no harm in staying in this Step for longer than eight weeks, but neither is there a benefit and I don't recommend "living" in Step One. You will achieve equal results by moving to Step Two after eight weeks . . . enjoying the inclusion of nutritious and delicious healthy carbs.

Step Two is known as the *transition or reprogramming* Step. It also lasts for eight weeks or more, until a person reaches his or her desired weight. After the eighth week of Step Two, you will decide how long you desire to remain on this weight-loss Step. After eight weeks, I recommend remaining in Step Two until your lab work is in the normal range with as little medication as possible *and* you love your body!

Step Three, the *maintenance phase*, is more of a lifestyle than a diet. This way of living will keep you at your desired weight and in great health permanently. You should live in Step Three as a part of your normal life.

2. HYDRATION

Over the course of the day you should drink a minimum of 64 ounces of decaffeinated fluid or water. (A person under five foot three may consume a minimum of 48 ounces/day.) You may spread your fluid intake throughout the day or drink more in the morning and less in the evening. Although coffee, tea, and sugar-free caffeinated beverages are allowed during all steps of the program, don't count them in your 64 ounces. Caffeine acts as a diuretic and dehydrates the body.

Why this emphasis on water? It's not because water will fill you up and make you less hungry. The purpose of water in the Metabolism Miracle is to keep your blood at its proper concentration and pH. Steps One and Two are pure fat-burning stages that create end products from the breakdown of fat. Without adequate hydration, waste products (ketones) build in the blood, changing its pH to become more acidic. The brain detects this change in pH and purposely slows fat-burning in an effort to help neutralize the blood. Plain and simple: Drink water to lose more fat!

3. EATING THROUGHOUT THE DAY

The Metabolism Miracle lifestyle requires consuming food throughout the day. I advise "bookend" eating: eat your first meal or snack within one hour of waking and eat a snack right before sleeping at night. Don't let more than five hours pass without eating during your waking hours. If you are awake in the middle of the night, eat an appropriate snack.

Why? If a person waits more than five hours between eating, the liver will automatically release glycogen stores. In the case of a person with Met B, that glycogen will be more than an individual would normally eat at a meal or as a snack. To prevent the liver from overfeeding, you must beat it to the punch. Blocking excess liver release of sugar is a big part of controlling insulin release.

4. EXERCISE

You must exercise. Increase your physical activity by a minimum of thirty minutes, five times per week over and above your normal activity. A variety of physical activities is better than the same exercise done for the same length of time at the same time of day. No one type of exercise is better than another. On one day, you can walk; on another, you can bike, go for a swim, work in the garden, take a yoga class, or work out at the gym. If you are in a wheelchair or are unsteady on your feet, armchair exercise is just fine. The idea is to move your muscles so they will uptake blood sugar and decrease the need for insulin release. Muscle movement will increase blood sugar uptake for hours after exercise is completed.

Some occupations, such as those of nurses, waiters, construction workers, and shelf-stockers, require lots of movement and muscle use. Other occupations are more sedentary. Assess your own norm in terms of daily physical activity and understand that this amount of daily movement does not count as part of the minimum thirty daily minutes of increased physical activity necessary for the Metabolism Miracle to work. For example, nurses may be on their feet for hours every day, but their body is accustomed to that level of movement. A nurse would need to increase physical activity over and above his or her work activity.

I like the idea of splitting exercise time up throughout the day to keep sugar uptake in high gear. You can take fifteen minutes in the morning and fifteen in the evening or perform ten minutes at three different times during the day. You can exercise for two hours, if you desire. (See "Fueling It Forward," page 28.) The idea is to move your muscles a *minimum* of thirty minutes, five times per week, over and above your norm.

5. TAKE VITAMINS, MINERALS, AND SUPPLEMENTS

I recommend the following supplements for all steps of the Metabolism Miracle, particularly during the most restrictive Step One. Check with your physician before taking supplements and consider adding them to a medications list you keep in your wallet with your identification.

Multivitamin/mineral supplement: Many excellent multivitamin supplements are available that ensure you will meet the recommended daily allowance for essential vitamins and minerals on a daily basis. Women of childbearing age need a supplement that contains iron, whereas menopausal women and men do not require added iron in their vitamin.

Calcium with vitamin D: Take 600 mg of calcium with 200 mg of vitamin D twice a day. Calcium intake must be split because the body can absorb a maximum of 600 mg at a time. People with Met B have a greater risk of developing osteopenia and osteoporosis, and recent studies have shown that many are vitamin D deficient. Have your vitamin D level checked annually to ascertain if additional vitamin D will be needed. Remember that you will be getting vitamin D in your multivitamin as well as with your calcium supplement. This supplementation will add 600–800 IUs of vitamin D3 daily. If you take antacids or have had gastric bypass surgery, make certain that you are taking calcium in the form of calcium citrate.

Fish oil: I recommend 2,000–2,400 mg per day. Some cardiologists lean toward 4,000 mg per day in patients with high cholesterol and inflammatory disease. Fish oil contains the omega-3 fatty acids DHA and EPA, known for their anti-inflammatory, anticancer, and anti–heart disease properties. It can help decrease triglycerides, blood pressure, and plaque growth, and helps act as a blood thinner. Make sure that the fish oil you purchase contains a minimum of 60% omega-3. Every 1,000 mg of fish oil should contain at least 600 mg of omega-3. Also, look for fish oil labeled "mercury free."

B complex: I recommend B complex (B-50) be taken with your second "set" of vitamins; a multivitamin is taken with the first set and B complex is taken with the second set (see below). B complex is a combination of eight B vitamins, all of which must be replenished on a daily basis because they are not stored in the body. B vitamins help prevent anemia, increase the rate of metabolism, maintain healthy skin and muscle, and enhance the immune system.

Vitamin E: Ask your physician about vitamin E supplementation. If he or she agrees that a supplement would be in your best interest, look for d-alpha tocopherol. Vitamin E has been linked to decreasing coronary vascular disease and may prevent damage to cell membranes from free radicals that can lead to certain types of cancer and inflammation. If you decide to supplement with E, add your multivitamin's vitamin E to your supplemental E and don't exceed 400 IUs.

It's often easier to remember to take supplements with a meal, and many of them will absorb more readily if you do so. Take your vitamins "on top of" your meal . . . right after you eat. I recommend taking them at two different sessions:

Meal 1: Multivitamin with minerals, fish oil, calcium with vitamin D
Meal 2: B complex, fish oil, calcium with vitamin D, vitamin E

6. DRINK GREEN TEA

Used medicinally in Asia for over three thousand years, green tea contains a powerful antioxidant that has been linked to lowering LDL "bad" cholesterol; improving the HDL/LDL ratio; decreasing the growth of breast, prostate, colon, and skin cancer; and enhancing midline fat burn. I recommend drinking a minimum of two cups a day. Green tea has about half the caffeine of black tea.

The perfect cup of green tea: Bring cold water to just before a boil, pour the water over the tea bag, let steep for 3 to 4 minutes, and remove the tea bag.

The antioxidant in green tea is most effective within a few hours of steeping, so the use of green tea capsules, green tea drops, and bottled green tea is *not* a substitute for freshly steeped green tea. Regular green tea contains more EGCG (the antioxidant) than does decaffeinated green tea.

7. REDUCE STRESS

Take a few minutes in the morning before jumping out of bed and last thing in the evening before falling asleep to think good thoughts, framing the day in a positive light. Practice deep breathing, visualize peaceful scenes, and make sure to stop and relax during the day. Stress is directly related to increasing blood sugar and therefore increases the release of insulin. Even a few minutes of deep breathing with your eyes closed and mind clear will reduce your stress level.

More on Exercise and the Metabolism Miracle

The Metabolism Miracle is not a "calories in–calories out" program. For this reason, you will never need to refer to the calories burned while you exercise. Metabolism B requires a different approach to exercise.

It's important to keep your muscles energized in order to help the Metabolism Miracle work its magic for your body. Regular physical exercise adds wonderful health improvements to anyone's life through improved cardiovascular health, digestive health, muscle toning, and increased metabolic rate. It also provides special benefits to anyone with Metabolism B.

1. Activated muscles consume blood sugar during and after exercise. Exercise helps blunt the peak rise in sugar and causes the pancreas to release less insulin. It also helps drain the muscles' glycogen stores and attracts insulin to open muscle cells preferentially over fat cells. In fact, exercise sensitizes muscle cells to attract insulin for hours *after* the workout.

2. A couch potato with Met B who does not exercise will release excess insulin that will open fat cells rather than muscle cells. If he or she had exercised, a good portion of that excess insulin would initially be sent to muscle cells, and once muscles were refilled with glycogen, any excess insulin would move on to open fat cells. But without exercise, *all* the excess insulin goes to excess fat cells!

3. Regular exercise will help preserve muscle tissue when a person is in Step One or Two of the Metabolism Miracle. Regular exercise energizes and highlights your muscle tissue, thus enabling the brain to clearly differentiate between muscle and fat. The brain will then choose to burn the inactive fat tissue rather than the active muscle tissue. Exercise stimulates fat loss and preserves your muscles.

WHEN SHOULD I EXERCISE?

The best time for someone with Metabolism B to exercise is one to two hours after the start of a meal, as this is when blood sugar is most likely at its highest. Exercised muscles will uptake blood sugar from the meal for energy. Even after exercise, sensitized muscles will attract insulin, diverting these keys from opening fat cells.

If you prefer to exercise before breakfast, make sure to take an appropriate snack (determined by the Step of the diet you are in) prior to working out. This snack will turn off the liver's self-feeding mechanism from the previous night. If you exercise in the morning without shutting down the liver glycogen release, your insulin will over-release during exercise and you will actually gain fat!

FREQUENCY OF EXERCISE TRUMPS DURATION OF EXERCISE

It is more beneficial to exercise five days of the week for thirty minutes than two days of the week for ninety minutes each day! Exercise that burns blood sugar on a daily basis will decrease the need for insulin on a daily basis. Muscle movement will increase blood sugar uptake for hours afterward.

You can divide your exercise to keep sugar uptake high throughout the day. Fifteen minutes in the morning briskly walking the dog and fifteen minutes in the evening walking around the neighborhood, or ten minutes at three different times during the day will work equally well. You can also exercise for more than thirty minutes any given day. (See "Fueling It Forward," page 28.) Again, the idea is to move your muscles a minimum of thirty minutes, five times per week, over and above your norm.

TO WEIGH OR NOT TO WEIGH?

Most dieters base their progress by weighing themselves, sometimes more than once a day. Many dieters weigh themselves first thing in the morning and last thing in the evening. During the day, your scale weight can vary by two pounds depending on that day's food and drink.

For my patients with normal metabolism who follow a calorie-based diet, I recommend limiting weigh-ins to once a week. In a "calories-in–calories-out" program, weight loss will be predictable. Pounds lost will represent a combination of muscle, fat, and water-weight loss.

If you have Met B and follow the Metabolism Miracle, I can guarantee you that your weight loss will be fat loss from your body tissues and your bloodstream. Fat tissue is light and voluminous. In the fat-burning mode of the Metabolism Miracle, you will lose fat tissue volume that shows up in visual "inches off" your body. People with textbook metabolism can plot their weight-loss progress and note that it usually amounts to one to two pounds of weight loss per week. In contrast, people with Metabolism B will never lose weight in a set pattern.

It is strongly suggested that you weigh yourself at the beginning of each eight-week period in Steps One and Two. After each eight-week period, compare your fat loss to the expected fat loss on page 25 of this book. It does not behoove you to lose more weight than is targeted, as the human body is only capable of losing a given amount of fat over an eight-week period.

Daily weigh-ins will not provide inspiration for those with Met B. Instead, look in a mirror to "see" your progress in the change in your appearance and how your clothing fits. You will feel the change in your energy level. Your lab work will show you all the progress you are making. Put away the scale somewhere that it won't tempt you on a daily basis!

After eight weeks, compare your fat loss to the following guidelines. At the end of each eight-week period in Steps One and Two, you should have met the anticipated fat-loss target. If the steps are done correctly, you will not lose muscle or water, you will lose only fat, both in the form of cholesterol and body fat. Inches lost will exceed your expectations on this plan!

The following tables show you how many fat pounds you can expect to lose after eight weeks in Step One or Two.

FAT-LOSS EXPECTATIONS DURING STEPS ONE AND TWO

WOMEN		

Find your height and start-weight in the left-hand columns to identify the number of "fat" pounds that you are expected to lose during the upcoming eight weeks during Step One or Two. Remember, you will look like you have lost twice as much weight.

4'10"	90–130 lbs.	= 3–5 lbs. fat loss	5'6"	130–170 lbs.	= 3–5 lbs. fat loss
	130–170 lbs.	= 6–13 lbs. fat loss		170–210 lbs.	= 6–13 lbs. fat loss
	170–210 lbs.	= 14–21 lbs. fat loss		210–250 lbs.	= 14–21 lbs. fat loss
	210–250 lbs.	= 22–29 lbs. fat loss		250–290 lbs.	= 22–29 lbs. fat loss
4'11"	95–135 lbs.	= 3–5 lbs. fat loss	5'7"	135–175 lbs.	= 3–5 lbs. fat loss
	135–175 lbs.	= 6–13 lbs. fat loss		175–215 lbs.	= 6–13 lbs. fat loss
	175–215 lbs.	= 14–21 lbs. fat loss		215–255 lbs.	= 14–21 lbs. fat loss
	215–255 lbs.	= 22–29 lbs. fat loss		255–295 lbs.	= 22–29 lbs. fat loss
5'0"	100–140 lbs.	= 3–5 lbs. fat loss	5'8"	140–180 lbs.	= 3–5 lbs. fat loss
	140–180 lbs.	= 6–13 lbs. fat loss		180–220 lbs.	= 6–13 lbs. fat loss
	180–220 lbs.	= 14–21 lbs. fat loss		220–260 lbs.	= 14–21 lbs. fat loss
	220–260 lbs.	= 22–29 lbs. fat loss		260–300 lbs.	= 22–29 lbs. fat loss
5'1"	105–145 lbs.	= 3–5 lbs. fat loss	5'9"	145–185 lbs.	= 3–5 lbs. fat loss
	145–185 lbs.	= 6–13 lbs. fat loss		185–225 lbs.	= 6–13 lbs. fat loss
	185–225 lbs.	= 14–21 lbs. fat loss		225–265 lbs.	= 14–21 lbs. fat loss
	225–265 lbs.	= 22–29 lbs. fat loss		265–305 lbs.	= 22–29 lbs. fat loss
5'2"	110–150 lbs.	= 3–5 lbs. fat loss	5'10"	150–190 lbs.	= 3–5 lbs. fat loss
	150–190 lbs.	= 6–13 lbs. fat loss		190–230 lbs.	= 6–13 lbs. fat loss
	190–230 lbs.	= 14–21 lbs. fat loss		230–270 lbs.	= 14–21 lbs. fat loss
	230–270 lbs.	= 22–29 lbs. fat loss		270–310 lbs.	= 22–29 lbs. fat loss
5'3"	115–155 lbs.	= 3–5 lbs. fat loss	5'11"	155–195 lbs.	= 3–5 lbs. fat loss
	155–195 lbs.	= 6–13 lbs. fat loss		195–235 lbs.	= 6–13 lbs. fat loss
	195–235 lbs.	= 14–21 lbs. fat loss		235–275 lbs.	= 14–21 lbs. fat loss
	235–275 lbs.	= 22–29 lbs. fat loss		275–315 lbs.	= 22–29 lbs. fat loss
5'4"	120–160 lbs.	= 3–5 lbs. fat loss	6'0"	160–200 lbs.	= 3–5 lbs. fat loss
	160–200 lbs.	= 6–13 lbs. fat loss		200–240 lbs.	= 6–13 lbs. fat loss
	200–240 lbs.	= 14–21 lbs. fat loss		240–280 lbs.	= 14–21 lbs. fat loss
	240–280 lbs.	= 22–29 lbs. fat loss		280–320 lbs.	= 22–29 lbs. fat loss
5'5"	125–165 lbs.	= 3–5 lbs. fat loss			
	165–205 lbs.	= 6–13 lbs. fat loss			
	205–245 lbs.	= 14–21 lbs. fat loss			
	245–285 lbs.	= 22–29 lbs. fat loss			

MEN

Find your height and start-weight in the left-hand columns to identify the number of "fat" pounds that you are expected to lose during the upcoming eight weeks during Step One or Two. Remember, you will look like you have lost twice as much weight.

5'0"	106–146 lbs.	= 3–5 lbs. fat loss	5'8"	154–194 lbs.	= 3–5 lbs. fat loss
	146–186 lbs.	= 6–13 lbs. fat loss		194–234 lbs.	= 6–13 lbs. fat loss
	186–226 lbs.	= 14–21 lbs. fat loss		234–274 lbs.	= 14–21 lbs. fat loss
	226–266 lbs.	= 22–29 lbs. fat loss		274–314 lbs.	= 22–29 lbs. fat loss
5'1"	112–152 lbs.	= 3–5 lbs. fat loss	5'9"	160–200 lbs.	= 3–5 lbs. fat loss
	152–192 lbs.	= 6–13 lbs. fat loss		200–240 lbs.	= 6–13 lbs. fat loss
	192–232 lbs.	= 14–21 lbs. fat loss		240–280 lbs.	= 14–21 lbs. fat loss
	232–272 lbs.	= 22–29 lbs. fat loss		280–320 lbs.	= 22–29 lbs. fat loss
5'2"	118–158 lbs.	= 3–5 lbs. fat loss	5'10"	166–206 lbs.	= 3–5 lbs. fat loss
	158–198 lbs.	= 6–13 lbs. fat loss		206–246 lbs.	= 6–13 lbs. fat loss
	198–238 lbs.	= 14–21 lbs. fat loss		246–286 lbs.	= 14–21 lbs. fat loss
	238–278 lbs.	= 22–29 lbs. fat loss		286–326 lbs.	= 22–29 lbs. fat loss
5'3"	124–164 lbs.	= 3–5 lbs. fat loss	5'11"	172–212 lbs.	= 3–5 lbs. fat loss
	164–204 lbs.	= 6–13 lbs. fat loss		212–252 lbs.	= 6–13 lbs. fat loss
	204–244 lbs.	= 14–21 lbs. fat loss		252–292 lbs.	= 14–21 lbs. fat loss
	244–284 lbs.	= 22–29 lbs. fat loss		292–332 lbs.	= 22–29 lbs. fat loss
5'4"	130–170 lbs.	= 3–5 lbs. fat loss	6'0"	178–218 lbs.	= 3–5 lbs. fat loss
	170–210 lbs.	= 6–13 lbs. fat loss		218–258 lbs.	= 6–13 lbs. fat loss
	210–250 lbs.	= 14–21 lbs. fat loss		258–298 lbs.	= 14–21 lbs. fat loss
	250–290 lbs.	= 22–29 lbs. fat loss		298–338 lbs.	= 22–29 lbs. fat loss
5'5"	136–176 lbs.	= 3–5 lbs. fat loss	6'1"	184–224 lbs.	= 3–5 lbs. fat loss
	176–216 lbs.	= 6–13 lbs. fat loss		224–264 lbs.	= 6–13 lbs. fat loss
	216–256 lbs.	= 14–21 lbs. fat loss		264–304 lbs.	= 14–21 lbs. fat loss
	256–296 lbs.	= 22–29 lbs. fat loss		304–344 lbs.	= 22–29 lbs. fat loss
5'6"	142–182 lbs.	= 3–5 lbs. fat loss	6'2"	190–230 lbs.	= 3–5 lbs. fat loss
	182–222 lbs.	= 6–13 lbs. fat loss		230–270 lbs.	= 6–13 lbs. fat loss
	222–262 lbs.	= 14–21 lbs. fat loss		270–310	= 14–21 lbs. fat loss
	262–302 lbs.	= 22–29 lbs. fat loss		210–350 lbs.	= 22–29 lbs. fat loss
5'7"	148–188 lbs.	= 3–5 lbs. fat loss	6'3"	196–236 lbs.	= 3–5 lbs. fat loss
	188–228 lbs.	= 6–13 lbs. fat loss		236–276 lbs.	= 6–13 lbs. fat loss
	228–268 lbs.	= 14–21 lbs. fat loss		276–316 lbs.	= 14–21 lbs. fat loss
	268–308 lbs.	= 22–29 lbs. fat loss		316–356 lbs.	= 22–29 lbs. fat loss

6'4"	202–242 lbs.	= 3–5 lbs. fat loss	6'6"	214–254 lbs.	= 3–5 lbs. fat loss
	242–282 lbs.	= 6–13 lbs. fat loss		254–294 lbs.	= 6–13 lbs. fat loss
	282–322 lbs.	= 14–21 lbs. fat loss		294–334 lbs.	= 14–21 lbs. fat loss
	322–363 lbs.	= 22=29 lbs. fat loss		334–374 lbs.	= 22–29 lbs. fat loss
6'5"	208–248 lbs.	= 3–5 lbs. fat loss			
	248–288 lbs.	= 6–13 lbs. fat loss			
	288–328 lbs.	= 14–21 lbs. fat loss			
	328–368 lbs.	= 22=29 lbs. fat loss			

How will I see progress?

- ○ Loss of inches (check monthly)
- ○ Loss of weight (check after every eight weeks)
- ○ Change in the way clothes fit and look
- ○ Increase in energy and improved quality of life
- ○ Decrease in blood sugar (if previously elevated)
- ○ Decrease in blood lipids (if previously elevated)
- ○ Decrease in blood pressure (if previously elevated)

How do I know when I've reached my ideal body weight?

There are no tables that can be used to determine *your* ideal body weight. Your ideal body weight is the weight on the scale at which:

- ○ You like your body.
- ○ Your lab work and blood pressure are as close to normal as possible on the least amount of medication.
- ○ You feel great, have energy, and enjoy life.

I "hit a wall" after forty minutes of my exercise class, bike ride, run, and so on. I am wiped out, my muscles burn or ache, and I'm very tired the rest of the day. What gives?

If you use thirty minutes of walking, treadmill walking, elliptical machine, biking, gardening, or yoga for your exercise, you will not need to make any modifications in your diet to accommodate your exercise in Step One.

If your exercise is intense, lasting more than thirty minutes, or a combination of both, you may need to "fuel it forward." In Step One, after day four, your liver was purposely emptied of glycogen stores so that both your pancreas and liver could take a much-needed rest. During that first week of Step One, your muscle glycogen was also purposely depleted to prevent blood sugar rise. There is enough carbohydrate in the neutral foods of Step One to fuel about thirty minutes of normal-intensity exercise. If you exercise more than this without adding fuel, you will "hit a wall" and end your workout with burning muscles, muscle aches, and fatigue later in the day.

FUELING IT FORWARD

To "fuel forward" at the start of your high-intensity workout, take 15 grams of fast-acting carbohydrate to fuel the *upcoming* thirty minutes of activity. Examples of 15 grams of fast-acting carb appropriate for exercise include 8 ounces of Gatorade, $\frac{1}{2}$ banana, $\frac{1}{2}$ cup of natural applesauce, three or four glucose tabs, or $\frac{1}{2}$ cup juice (can be diluted). Normally you would not eat these foods during Step One. You are using them as fuel for your upcoming exercise, leaving your blood sugar to go back to normal after those thirty minutes.

This carbohydrate will fuel the first thirty minutes and will burn off without residual. If you continue to exercise, for the next thirty minutes, you will need to take another 15 grams of carb. Repeat the fueling for any additional thirty minutes of activity. For an hour-long spin class, for example, you might drink 8 ounces of Gatorade just before class, spin for thirty minutes and drink 8 additional ounces of Gatorade before spinning for the remaining half hour of class.

At the end of high-intensity exercise lasting longer than thirty minutes, eat a quality source of protein within half an hour of the end of the activity. Choose something such as a cheese stick, a low-carb protein drink, or the protein that will be contained in your next meal.

"Fueling it forward" will power a terrific workout that will enhance your program and leave you with plenty of energy for the rest of the day.

PART II
Miracle Foods and Menus

STEP ONE: CARB REHAB
REDISCOVERING A HEALTHY YOU

> **Time commitment:** 8 weeks
>
> **Why do it?** To rest and rehabilitate the overworking pancreas and liver and dramatically decrease the release of the fat-gain hormone insulin. This step will also allow the body to burn fat on the inside (LDL cholesterol and triglycerides) and on the outside (midline or belly fat).
>
> **How you'll feel:** After day four, your energy level will increase, your carb cravings and hunger will decrease, and you'll feel less irritable. As Step One continues, your belly fat, cholesterol, triglycerides, blood pressure, and blood sugar will decrease.

If you're like most people with Metabolism B, you will begin the Metabolism Miracle in a state of metabolic mayhem. Remember, your pancreas is currently overproducing insulin, your liver is overreleasing glycogen, and your body is overstoring fat.

Whether you begin the program overweight by 10 or 210 pounds, you will need to remain in Step One for a minimum of eight weeks. The Metabolism Miracle is a program based on science and physiology and must be followed in a certain way to reinstate normal carbohydrate metabolism. The first eight weeks will work internally to rest and rehabilitate your liver and pancreas to allow for the normal metabolism of carb and glycogen release in the future.

Step One will put the brakes on your hyperactive pancreas. Think of a car speeding down the highway at 90 mph. When the driver brakes, the car can't immediately stop. It has to slow down and might even skid out of control. When you begin this program, it will take three to four days to get your pancreas to slow down. If you are severely hyperinsulinemic, it may take longer. You won't feel great during these first four days. In fact, I can predict that you will feel some combination of the following:

○ Fatigued
○ Hungry
○ Irritable and cranky
○ Craving to eat carbohydrate foods
○ Slightly headachy, dizzy, and queasy

Big changes take some adjustment. Know that you are smoothing out the roller coaster of blood sugar peaks and valleys to a normal blood sugar curve. These first few days of symptoms occur because your liver will continue to release its glycogen stores every five hours for three to four days. Once the liver has depleted its stored glycogen, your blood sugar will maintain a smooth, constant level and you will begin to feel great.

Step One is designed to keep your pancreas at rest, without demands for spikes of insulin. The way to accomplish blood sugar equilibrium: Eat foods that do *not* convert in any significant way to blood sugar by temporarily avoiding foods that raise blood sugar and keep your carb intake low enough to prevent the liver from refilling with glycogen.

Every food on earth contains nutrients that fit into one or more of three major categories: carbohydrate, protein, or fat. Foods get categorized by the nutrient that is in greatest supply. For example, milk contains carb, protein, and fat—but its greatest nutrient is carbohydrate. As a result, milk is categorized as carbohydrate.

During Step One you will eat generously from the protein, fat, and neutral vegetable categories because they have very little impact on blood sugar and insulin response. You will need to temporarily avoid carbohydrate-dense foods.

Acceptable Step One foods are as follows:

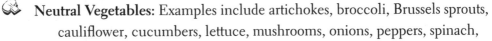

Protein Foods: Cheese, eggs, fish, meat, nut butters, poultry, soy

Fat Foods: Include avocado, butter, cream, margarine, oil, nuts, olives, salad dressing, sour cream, seeds

Neutral Vegetables: Examples include artichokes, broccoli, Brussels sprouts, cauliflower, cucumbers, lettuce, mushrooms, onions, peppers, spinach, sprouts. These vegetables are high in vitamins, minerals, and fiber, but do not contain significant carbohydrate, protein, or fat.

You should familiarize yourself with the Arrow Sheet on page 38, which lists the many foods that fit into Step One and those that are to be temporarily avoided. There are many, many choices! And better yet, all of the recipes in this cookbook that are tagged with a "Yes" for Step One will fit seamlessly into your first eight weeks. The beauty of this cookbook is each recipe's simple classification for each step: Yes or No.

It is critical during Step One to temporarily eliminate the foods that spike blood sugar and insulin. Although fruit, potatoes, lentils, and yogurt are very healthy and loaded with vitamins, minerals, and fiber, their carb content is over-working your pancreas and contributing to your weight and health woes. Sugar, candy, desserts, regular soda, and chips are not the only foods that rock the pancreas—*all* carbohydrates do that, as every carbohydrate causes your blood sugar to rise to some degree. You will eliminate the most blatantly active carbs for just two months. During Step Two, healthy carbohydrates will return in a controlled amount, at the proper time to allow for a smooth blood sugar curve. In this way you will program your metabolism to handle carbohydrate foods normally.

Reminders for Step One

TAKE YOUR SUPPLEMENTS!

Because your diet will be necessarily "unbalanced" for these first eight weeks, you should take the recommended vitamins, minerals, and supplements outlined on page 19. Think of them as insurance to keep you nutritionally balanced and healthy.

DRINK, DRINK, DRINK!

Drink water or decaffeinated, carb-free fluids, liberally! Drink at least 64 ounces of water or decaf fluid per day. During the fat-burning mode of Step One you need adequate water to flush the waste products of fat-burning away.

EAT OFTEN, BUT DON'T EAT CARBS!

Eat either a snack or breakfast within one hour of waking in the morning, an appropriate snack right before you go to bed, another in the middle of the night if you wake up, and make sure to "graze" on "Yes" foods throughout the day, without any gaps of over five hours.

MOVE!

Remember to increase physical activity above and beyond your normal daily activity by a minimum of thirty minutes, five times per week. This will allow your body to burn fat and retain valuable muscle tissue.

RELAAAAAXXXXXXX . . .

Try to "de-stress" on a regular basis. Think peaceful, positive thoughts first thing in the morning and last thing at night, and stop for a few minutes during the day to close your eyes, clear your mind, and reset your thoughts in a positive way.

EAT IT ALL!

During Step One, you may eat lean proteins, healthy fats, and neutral vegetables at any time in reasonable amounts. (See the Arrow Sheet, page 38.)

Step One Foods

NEUTRAL PROTEINS (ARROW UP)

No need to check nutrition facts for net carb grams for the following foods:

Poultry
Skinless chicken, lean ground chicken, Cornish game hen, skinless turkey, lean ground turkey, turkey bacon (nitrite/ nitrate free recommended)

Lean Beef
Such cuts of beef as filet mignon, flank steak, 85–93% lean ground beef, ground round, London broil, porterhouse (trimmed), rib roast, round chuck roast, rump roast sirloin, steak, T-bone (trimmed), tenderloin

NEUTRAL PROTEINS (ARROW UP) *(continued)*

Fish and Shellfish
All unbreaded fish and shellfish that is
    baked, broiled, browned, grilled,
    poached, or sautéed

Pork
Lean cuts such as Canadian bacon, ham,
    pork tenderloin, trimmed pork chops

Lamb
Lamb chop, leg of lamb, roast lamb

Veal
Lean veal chop, veal roast

Game
Buffalo, skinless duck and pheasant,
    ostrich, rabbit, venison

Cheese
Low-fat or light preferred: all cheeses
    such as cheddar, cottage cheese, grated
    cheese, hard cheese, mozzarella, ri-
    cotta, string cheese, swiss, etc.

Eggs
Eggs (whole), egg whites, egg substitute

Soy and Soy Products
Edamame, soy milk (unsweetened and
    unflavored), tofu, vegetarian meat sub-
    stitutes (without added carbohydrates)

**Natural Nut and Seed Butters
(containing nuts or seeds, oil, and
optional salt)**
Almond butter, cashew butter, peanut
    butter, tahini

NEUTRAL FATS (ARROW UP)

No need to check nutrition facts for net carb grams for the following foods:

Butter
Butter (light or low-fat preferred),
    butter blends ($\frac{1}{2}$ butter, $\frac{1}{2}$ oil),
    whipped butter

Margarine
Tub or stick margarine (light or
    low-fat preferred), whipped
    margarine (without hydrogenation
    or trans fats)

NEUTRAL FATS (ARROW UP) (continued)

Sour Cream and Cream Cheese
Light or low-fat preferred: cream cheese, sour cream, whipped cream cheese

Cream and Creamers
Light or low-fat preferred: cream, half-and-half, whipped cream

Oils
Canola, corn, olive, peanut, safflower, soybean, sunflower
Vegetable oil

Salad Dressing
Light or low-fat preferred (avoid fat-free or sweetened salad dressing), vinaigrette. Flavored vinegars are allowed.

Mayonnaise
Light or low-fat preferred

Olives

Avocado

Nuts and Snack Legumes
All nuts, including almonds, cashews, peanuts, macadamia nuts, pecans, pistachios, walnuts (Avoid coatings such as honey or cinnamon sugar, which contain carbohydrate.)

Seeds
Pumpkin seeds, sesame seeds, sunflower seeds, tahini paste (sesame seed paste)

NEUTRAL VEGETABLES (ARROW UP)

No need to check nutrition facts for net carb grams for the following foods:

Artichoke/hearts
Asparagus
Bean sprouts
Beans (green and wax)
Broccoli
Brussels sprouts
Cabbage
Cauliflower
Celery
Cucumber
Dill pickles
Eggplant
Onions/green onions

Greens (collards, kale,
mustard, turnip, spinach)
Jicama (max. 1 cup per
meal)
Kohlrabi
Leeks
Mushrooms
Okra
Peppers
Lettuces and salad greens
Radishes
Spaghetti squash
Sauerkraut
Tomatoes (max. 1 per
meal)

Cherry tomatoes (max.
10 per meal)
Crushed or canned
tomatoes (max. $\frac{1}{2}$ cup
per meal)
Tomato salsa (max.
$\frac{1}{2}$ cup per meal)
Tomato and vegetable
juices (max.
4 ounces per meal)
Turnips
Zucchini and summer
squash

FREEBIES DURING STEP ONE

During Step One you can eat these foods whenever you like, as they contain negligible carbohydrate grams.

All herbs and spices
Bouillon
Broth
Club soda
Coffee
Consommé
Diet soda
Dill pickles

Lemon and lime juice
Mustard
Salad dressing sprays
Selected fitness water,
flavored waters, and
flavored seltzers
Sugar-free chewing gum
Sugar-free gelatin

Sugar-free tonic water
Tea
Vinegar
White horseradish
Zero-carb jelly
Zero-carb syrup

Step One Foods Chart

THE
Arrow Sheet

YES
For all steps

PROTEIN ARROW
(Lean, lite, or low-fat preferred)

Meat
Poultry
Fish and shellfish
Cheese
Cottage cheese
Eggs
Egg substitutes

Natural nut butter
Natural seed butter
Tofu
Unsweetened soy milk
Edamame
*Select protein shakes

Although meats and cheeses are primarily protein, they vary tremendously in their fat content. The recommended protein sources in the Metabolism Miracle program will be heart healthy and lean. You can feel free to enjoy them liberally.

YES
For all steps

NEUTRAL VEGGIES ARROW

Artichokes and artichoke hearts
Asparagus
Green or wax beans
Bean sprouts
Broccoli
Brussels sprouts
Cabbage
Cauliflower
Celery
Cucumbers
Dill Pickles
Eggplant
Jicama (max 1 cup)
Onions and scallions
Greens (collards, kale, mustard, turnip, spinach)

Kohlrabi
Leeks
Mushrooms
Okra
Peppers (all varieties)
Lettuce and other salad greens
Radishes
Spaghetti squash
Sauerkraut
Tomatoes (maximum 1 fresh tomato per meal or 10 cherry tomatoes, ½ cup canned tomatoes, ½ cup tomato salsa, 4 oz. tomato/veggie juice)
Turnips
Zucchini and summer squash

YES
For all steps

FAT ARROW
(Lite or low-fat preferred)

Butter
Margarine
Sour cream
Mayonnaise
Cream
Half-and-half

Oil
Salad dressing
Olives
Avocados
Nuts
Seeds
Whipped Cream

CARBOHYDRATE ARROW
(Carbohydrate foods will require label check for **Step Two and Three**)

Bread
Wraps
Rolls
Buns
Bread Products
Pasta
Rice
Crackers, pretzels, chips
Cereal and granola bars
Cereal (hot or cold)
Other grains
Fruit
Fruit juice
Potatoes and sweet potatoes

Carrots
Parsnips
Beets
Winter squash
Acorn squash
Pumpkin
Milk
Yogurt
Sweetened beverages
Sweets and desserts
Carb-containing foods that fail the 5 gram "counter" test

NO
for Step One

YES for all Steps
* **5 GRAM "COUNTER" CARBS**
(Step One: optional at meals and bedtime snacks.
Steps Two and Three: can be added into carb total for a meal/snack on Steps Two and Three.)

* Low-carb juices
* Low-carb milk
* Low-carb protein drinks with 2–5 grams net carb
* Foods or recipes in the serving size that provide 5 or less grams net carb

* Low-carb bread
* Low-carb tortillas
* Low-carb wraps
* Low-carb crackers
* Low-carb ketchup
* Low-carb yogurts

* All of the starred foods must pass the net-carb test and fit the 5 gram "counter" carb rule (page 41).
Net carb grams ≤ 1 gram = neutral

STEP ONE CARBS TO AVOID (ARROW DOWN)

Breads
Regular bagels, bread, croissants,
    muffins, pancakes, pitas, rolls
    waffles, and wraps

Pasta
Semolina, white, and whole-grain

Rice
Basmati, brown, white, or wild rice

Chips, Crackers, and Pretzels

Protein Bars and Snack Bars
    (check carb grams)

Cereal and Grains
Barley, dry breakfast cereals, grits,
    and oatmeal

Fruit or Regular Fruit Juice

Sweetened Drinks
Regular sweetened punch, sodas,
    teas, and sweetened energy
    drinks

Certain Vegetables
Carrots or parsnips
Winter squash such as acorn or
    butternut squash
Pumpkin
Beets
Legumes such as cannellini beans,
    chickpeas (garbanzo beans),
    kidney beans, lentils, limas, and
    peas
Potatoes, including white potatoes
    and sweet potatoes

Sweets and Desserts

Milk
1%, 2%, buttermilk, lactose-free,
    nonfat, and skim

Yogurt
Low-calorie, regular, or sweetened
    yogurt

Foods that Fail the Net Carb Test
    (see page 41)

STEP ONE "COUNTER" CARBS

Note: Since I wrote the original *Metabolism Miracle*, I've made very few changes to the program. One change I did make was to rename 5×5 foods (carbohydrate foods with 5 grams of net carb or less). In this cookbook, I will refer to these 5×5 foods as "Counters."

In addition to liberal amounts of neutral foods (lean protein, healthy fat, neutral veggies), you have the *option* to add a 5-gram "Counter" at breakfast, lunch, dinner, bedtime, or the middle of the night. Keep in mind:

○ You can skip these treats, but you cannot save them up for later.
○ "Counters" cannot be used as snacks between your meals.
○ Snacks (except for bedtime and middle of the night) must be neutral foods only.
○ Try to keep your "Counters" four to five hours apart.

In Step One it is important to limit net carbs to a maximum of one "Counter" per meal. If you consume more than 5 grams of net carb at a meal, at bedtime, or the middle of the night, your blood sugar will spike and your insulin will retrigger.

"COUNTERS"

You *must* check Nutrition Facts for net carb grams for these foods.

(All must have no more than 5 grams net carb per serving)

Low-carb bread

Low-carb wraps

1 cup popcorn (light or hot-air popped without partially hydrogenated oils)

Crackers (in the quantity that nets 5 grams)

Low-carb milk

Low-carb yogurt

½ cup Greek yogurt

Low-carb protein shakes

Low-carb juice

Dark chocolate (in the quantity that nets 5 grams)

If you cannot find these foods in your local grocery store, try looking for online vendors that will deliver to your home.

These online sites will provide the Nutrition Facts for their products, and you can choose the items that fit into your net carb parameters by following the easy guidelines that follow.

All of these items must be run through the Net Carb Formula (see page 43) and must fit into the 5-gram "Counter" rule.

Low-carb breads   Low-carb tortillas

Low-carb wraps   Low-carb crackers

Low-carb bars   Low-carb ketchup

Low-carb bread crumbs   Select sugar-free puddings

Low-sugar juice   Carb-controlled milk

Carb-controlled protein drinks   Carb-controlled yogurt

Low-carb yogurt smoothies

IT'S ALL IN THE NUMBERS!

Fortunately, there is one very easy and accurate way to determine the true carbohydrate content (net carb grams) of any packaged food item. Focus on just three numbers on the label: (1) serving size, (2) total carbohydrate grams, and (3) dietary fiber grams. Never rely on the front of food packaging; always check the Nutrition Facts label on the package for yourself.

DECODING CARBS THE EASY WAY

It will take you less than thirty seconds to determine if the "Counter" you are considering fits our parameter of 5 grams of carb or less:

Look first at the serving size. Be careful, as serving sizes can be deceptive. For example, many bottle beverages have serving sizes of 8 ounces when the bottle contains 24 ounces. This means you would get three times the carb listed if you chose to drink the entire bottle. Companies sometimes do this to make their product appear healthier than it truly is.

Next, look at total carbohydrate grams. The phrase **Total Carbohydrate** is always in bold font. Underneath this term, slightly indented, will be unbolded entries for the carb breakdown, such as dietary fiber, sugar, sugar alcohol, and other carb grams. The total carbohydrate is the sum total of every carbohydrate gram in a serving of that particular food.

Last, look at dietary fiber grams. If the food choice contains dietary fiber, it will be listed right underneath total carbohydrate grams. You will need to subtract the dietary fiber grams from the total carbohydrate grams to find the net carbohydrate grams. Dietary fiber is the only part of the total carbohydrate grams that will *not* convert into blood sugar and affect insulin. The fiber will pass right through your body without converting to blood sugar. So, you get to subtract it away!

Total carb grams – dietary fiber grams = net carb grams

Lynn's Low-Carb Bread
Serving size 1 slice
Total carbohydrate 8 grams
Dietary fiber 4 grams
Sugar alcohol 1 gram
Other carbs 3 grams
Total carb – dietary fiber = net carb
8 grams – 4 grams – 4 grams net carb
One slice of this bread fits into the
    Counter zone at only 4 grams of net carb!

Remember that in Step One, if you are opting to add a 5-gram "Counter" at breakfast, lunch, dinner, bedtime, or the middle of the night, *one* slice of this bread would work at any of those allotted times, but *two* slices at once (a total of 8 grams net carb) would be excessive and would cause an insulin release.

BUYER BEWARE

The trick to keeping carbs under control when you eat is to know how to identify which of the "low-carb" products are legitimate and which are a marketing scheme. There are now genuinely low-carb breads, wraps, crackers, juices, milk, yogurt, and protein drinks that contain such a small amount of carb that they won't upset your carb control if used correctly. Unfortunately, many other products are marked *sugar-free*, *low-sugar*, *low-carb*, *low-sugar*, or *carb-controlled*, but are really nothing more than repackaged regular products.

Portion Sizes of Neutral Foods: How Much Is Right?

The Metabolism Miracle is not a calorie-counting program, so don't be anxious about *exactly* how much of the neutral foods you are eating. But you should use common sense when eating. Some examples of sensible versus excess:

> *Sensible:* A handful of almonds three to four times throughout the day
> *Excessive:* 3 pounds of almonds throughout the day
> *Inadequate:* 10 almonds throughout the day

> *Sensible:* A heaping spoon of natural peanut butter in midafternoon
> *Excessive:* 1/2 jar of natural peanut butter in a day
> *Inadequate:* 1 level teaspoon of peanut butter in midafternoon

> *Sensible:* 3 string cheeses spread throughout the day
> *Excessive:* A 1-pound bag of string cheeses (16 cheese sticks)
> *Inadequate:* 1/2 string cheese as your afternoon snack

People who "count out" ten almonds, break string cheese in half, or level off a teaspoon of natural almond butter err on the side of starvation. By undereating neutral foods, they may deprive their body of adequate energy, slow their metabolic rate, and slow weight loss.

On the other hand, grossly overeating neutral foods, such as snacking on an 8-ounce block of cheese, will provide excess fat, and your body will be forced to burn the cheese's fat content before it can move on to burning your fat stores.

It's all about moderation. Being overly conservative or overly liberal with neutral foods will work against you in terms of weight loss! The answer? When you are hungry during Step One . . . eat. Eat foods from the neutral arrows at any time. When you are full during Step One . . . stop. There is no reason to eat more than you normally would just because the food is neutral! Just eat normally, keep your carbs in check, and you will soon see and feel the wonderful benefits of this program.

SWEETENERS

As a registered dietitian who prefers to eat simply and naturally, I would not normally be inclined to choose an artificial sweetener over a natural sweetener. Simply put, if I did not have Met B, I would not choose to use sucralose or stevia. But the fact is, I do have Met B and using a fast-acting, high-glycemic sweetener such as sugar or honey could be harmful to my health.

Remember that a person with Metabolism B has a physiological condition that, when unmonitored, results in wide swings in blood sugar, fat deposits in and on the body, chronic health conditions, and low energy. Sugar, honey, syrup, and agave (likewise other sweeteners as molasses, brown rice syrup, or date sugar) are carbohydrates that exacerbate that condition by causing an immediate, sharp rise in blood sugar, which snaps the pancreas to attention and results in the overrelease of insulin.

Consider that one can of regular soda contains eleven to twelve teaspoons of sugar. Baked products, ice cream, sweets, and sweetened drinks are all sugar dense. Although honey and agave appeal because they are natural, they have the same effect on blood sugar and insulin as pure sugar does.

It is true that you can choose to use one level teaspoon (one standard packet) of sugar, honey, syrup, or agave nectar as your 5-gram "Counter" at meals, bedtime, or in the middle of the night, but keep in mind that these sweeteners add no benefit to the program. Low-carb wraps, low-carb bread, low-carb yogurt, and low-carb protein shakes, on the other hand, provide calcium, vitamins, fiber, and a sense of fullness.

I suggest replacing sugar, honey, syrup, or agave with sucralose or stevia. You needn't count the carb grams in either of these sweeteners because they are not absorbed like carbohydrate and don't significantly influence blood sugar or insulin release. Aspartame and saccharin are also approved by the FDA and can fit into the guidelines of the Metabolism Miracle, but they are not my personal favorites.

Just as I don't advocate excessive consumption of any neutral foods, I certainly don't recommend the excessive use of sucralose or stevia. FDA-approved sucralose is made from sugar that is put through a multistep process that substitutes 3 atoms of chlorine for 3 hydroxyl groups on the sugar molecule. It contains minimal calories and does not absorb like sugar, therefore it causes no significant rise in blood sugar or insulin release. It is very stable and can be used in cooking or baking.

To date, the FDA has not permitted the stevia plant itself to be used as a food additive, but only the rebaudioside A extracted from the plant. For the time being, the product is used primarily as a sweetener for coffee, tea, and beverages. It has a licorice-like taste and is not as stable as sucralose for cooking or baking.

ALCOHOL

Because wine is derived from grapes and most liquors and light beer are made from grains, people tend to believe that they must avoid alcohol completely. While it is true that grape juice, oats, and potatoes have carbs, fermentation and distillation change the chemical structure of these ingredients so they metabolize via the fat pathway rather than the carbohydrate pathway.

With the exception of sweetened drinks, dessert wines, port, and sangria, you will not count most wines or liquors such as gin, whiskey, vodka, and light beer as carbohydrates on the Metabolism Miracle plan.

There is one fact you'll want to keep in mind should you decide to drink alcohol during Step One. The liver is the detox factory of the body. In Step One, your liver is resting and works at a slower pace. During this step, you will feel "tipsy" sooner than usual when drinking alcohol and therefore you should pace your drinking. Also, always check with your physician regarding the use of alcohol. Many medical conditions and medications do not support the intake of alcohol.

The maximum servings of alcohol in any given day would be limited to two drinks (with physician's approval only). A drink is defined as:

5 ounces wine
$1\frac{1}{2}$ ounces alcohol
12 ounces light beer

Remember to check the carb content of the "mixers" you use in alcohol-containing drinks. Choose sugar-free tonic water, sugar-free soda, low-carb juice (may need to be a counter at that meal), seltzer, club soda, or sugar-free drink mixes.

Frequently Asked Questions for Step One

Do I have to have a 5-gram "Counter" at each meal, at bedtime, and in the middle of the night?

No. The 5-gram "Counters" are optional. Some people choose the purist approach and avoid these carbs completely, but I am not one of those people! Whether you include the 5-gram "Counters" or not, your progress will be the same throughout Step One.

Do I have to space the 5-gram "Counters" five hours or more apart?

There is no need to plot your 5-gram "Counters" by your clock. I suggest using these foods at breakfast, lunch, dinner, bedtime, and in the middle of the night (if you are awake). Don't use "Counters" as between-meal snacks. If you keep them as options at mealtimes and bedtime only, you will avoid piggy-backing carb grams, causing insulin release.

Remember, if you choose not to use a "Counter" at one meal, you can't save it for the next and add it to that meal's "Counter." This would stack the carb grams, trigger insulin release, and slow weight loss.

Note: In the original *Metabolism Miracle*, it was advised that these 5×5 choices be spaced at least five hours apart. Carbohydrate foods have a maximum life span of four to five hours and the idea was to space these optional foods so they would not "piggy-back" or stack and cause blood sugar to rise and insulin to flow. To make it easier, I now suggest using the "Counters" at breakfast, lunch, dinner, and bedtime, and in the middle of the night if you are awake. Don't use "Counters" as midmorning or midafternoon snacks; use neutral foods instead.

I hadn't weighed myself for eight weeks, as suggested. Everyone has been telling me that I look fantastic and I certainly feel fantastic. I thought I'd lost 20 pounds. But when I got on the scale, it showed I had only lost 10 pounds. How can this be?

On calorie-counting diet plans, people lose three body components—water weight, muscle tissue, and fat tissue. Water and muscle are very heavy in comparison to fat tissue. On the Metabolism Miracle, you lose only fat tissue, which is large and voluminous. A 10-pound loss of fat alone on the Metabolism Miracle looks and feels like a 20-pound loss on a typical diet.

I caved and had an ice-cream cone on Step One. Now what do I do?

For every "mistake" you make in a five-hour block during Step One, you need to add three days to the end of your eight-week stint. Unfortunately, you will have to go through three rough days with fatigue, irritability, and cravings. Your body needs to detox again, so be very mindful that you don't slip again during those next three days.

Sample Menus for Step One

Breakfast

Tex-Mex eggs (page 248) = neutral
1 slice low-carb toast ("Counter")
Whipped butter and zero-carb strawberry jelly = neutral
Coffee with half-and-half and sucralose = neutral

Low-fat cottage cheese = neutral
Tomato wedges = neutral
5 multigrain wheat crackers ("Counter")
Tea with stevia = neutral

Low-carb wrap ("Counter") filled with:
Thinly sliced ham and low-fat Cheddar (microwave
   to melt) = neutral
Green tea with stevia or sucralose = neutral

Low-carb chocolate shake ("Counter")
Handful of "Miracle Granola" (page 260) = neutral
Water with lemon = neutral

Chocolate–Peanut Butter Smoothie (page 100) ("Counter")
Handful of pecans = neutral

Breakfast (*continued*)

Low-carb yogurt/Greek yogurt ("Counter")
Celery sticks with natural peanut butter = neutral
Water with lime and stevia = neutral

Crustless Quiche (page 253) ("Counter")
Quartered tomato
Coffee with creamer and sucralose = neutral

Broccoli-Mushroom Frittata (page 251) = neutral
Low-carb toast ("Counter")
Coffee with nondairy creamer and stevia = neutral

Legal Pancakes (page 257) = neutral
Zero-carb syrup = neutral
Faux Breakfast Hash Browns (page 259) = neutral
Decaf with half-and-half and sucralose = neutral

Peanut Butter Hot "Cereal" with 1 cup low-carb
     milk (page 262) = ("Counter")
Green tea with lemon = neutral

Lunch

Low-carb wrap ("Counter")
Tuna, egg, shrimp, chicken, or ham salad (with light mayo or a
   light amount of regular mayo) = neutral
Lettuce and/or a tomato slice = neutral
Herbal iced tea with stevia and lemon = neutral

Turkey Salad with Pistachios and Grapes (page 140) ("Counter")
Sugar-free gelatin cup = neutral
Water with lemon wedge = neutral

Lunch *(continued)*

Chicken Marsala (page 163) = neutral
Low-carb wrap ("Counter")
Side salad with light ranch dressing = neutral
Diet soda = neutral

Take-out Chinese Meal
Hot and sour soup = neutral
Steamed chicken or shrimp = neutral
Steamed vegetables (broccoli, green onions, onions,
   water chestnuts) = neutral
Chicken broth (use as a "sauce" over the chicken and/
   or veggies) = neutral
Green tea = neutral

Your Own Chinese Meal
Egg Drop Soup (page 152) = neutral
Ginger Flank Steak (page 179) = neutral
Snow Peas and Water Chestnuts (page 244) = neutral
Green tea = neutral

Mushroom-Cheese "Burger" (page 202) = neutral
Lettuce leaf wrap with tomato, onion, and low-carb ketchup =
   neutral
1 cup popcorn ("Counter") (light or hot-air popped without partially hydrogenated oils)
Sparkling water with lemon = neutral

My Favorite Cobb Salad (page 141) = neutral
Low-carb wrap ("Counter")
Water with lime wedge = neutral

Lunch *(continued)*

Chicken Quesadilla (page 121) (5-gram "Counter")
Almond Meringue Kisses (page 287) = neutral
Decaf herbal tea with lemon = neutral

Pantry-Ready Tuna Niçoise (page 142) = neutral
Whole-grain crackers with <5 grams net carb ("Counter")
Sugar-free decaf soda = neutral

Dinner

5 ounces white wine = neutral
Basil Chicken with Vegetables (page 169) = neutral
Cauliflower "Rice" (page 245) = neutral
Peanut Butter Cookie (page 288) ("Counter")
Decaf coffee with creamer = neutral

Lemony Scallop and Shrimp Soup (page 157) = neutral
Crusted Salmon (page 215) ("Counter")
Tossed salad with light dressing = neutral
Sugar-free gelatin with light whipped topping = neutral
Sparkling water = neutral

5 ounces red wine = neutral
Steak with Sherry Sauce (page 178) = neutral
Mini Zucchini Pancakes with dollop of light sour cream (page
    237) = neutral
Butter-Rum Cupcake (page 274) ("Counter")
Flavored seltzer = neutral

Dinner (*continued*)

Vegetable Frittata (page 250) (neutral)
1 slice low-carb toast ("Counter")
Natural almond butter = neutral
Decaf tea with lemon = neutral

Eggplant Parmesan (page 197) = neutral
Italian Garden Salad (page 135) = neutral
1 slice low-carb garlic bread ("Counter")
Water with lemon = neutral

Sirloin burger on a Portobello "Bun" (page 203) = neutral
Above burger, plus Lorraine Swiss cheese = neutral
Above burger, plus lettuce, tomato, and/or onions = neutral
Above burger, plus low-fat mayo (or small amount of regular
    mayo) = neutral
Above burger, plus low-carb ketchup (small amount) = neutral
5 baked tortilla chips ("Counter")
Diet drink = neutral

Step One Snacks

These neutral snacks can be used on any step of the Metabolism Miracle.

Cheese cubes or sliced cheese (low-fat preferred)
Cottage cheese
String cheese
Olives
Celery with natural peanut butter
Nuts
Low-carb protein shakes with 1 gram or less net carb
Boiled egg

Step One Snacks *(continued)*

Seeds (e.g., sunflower or pumpkin)

Sugar-free gelatin with whipped topping

Spoonful of peanut or almond butter

Ham or turkey and cheese roll-ups

Allowed neutral veggies with dip (sour cream and herbs and/or
    seasonings, light or low-fat preferred)

Dry-roasted edamame

Dip of egg salad, tuna salad, or chicken salad (low-fat mayon-
    naise preferred)

Note: Low-carb protein shakes with 2–5 net carb grams are a
    "Counter."

STEP TWO: TRANSITIONS
FINDING YOUR HEALTHY WEIGHT

> **Time commitment:** 8 weeks or longer, until your lab work is normal on as little medication as possible, and you love the way your body looks and feels.
>
> **Why do it?** This step will transition and gently reawaken the pancreas–liver combination. Step Two will control insulin by smoothing blood sugar curves and preventing the liver from over-releasing glycogen. Because the carbohydrate is kept to a predetermined limit, you will continue to burn fat and lose weight at the same rate as in Step One.
>
> **How You'll Feel:** You will feel continued energy, be in a state of well-being and tranquility, and have no carb cravings. You will be amazed that even as you increase carbohydrate grams, you will continue to lose fat in and on your body until you reach a weight that feels right.

After eight weeks of Step One, it is time to reawaken the pancreas and liver and get them back to work. During Step Two, you will reintroduce mild, healthy carbohydrate—the preferred fuel for your body—and get your metabolism functioning normally once and for all.

If you like, you may stay longer in Step One, but there is no real benefit to remaining longer than eight weeks in the lowest carb phase. At the end of eight weeks, your pancreas and liver are rested and you have lowered lipids (cholesterol and triglycerides), decreased insulin resistance, improved energy, and lost weight.

To restart your metabolism the right way, you will need to keep three things in mind:

1. Consume the *right amount* of carbohydrate at each meal and snack.
2. Eat the *right type* of carbohydrate to allow the pancreas to adjust slowly.
3. Choose the *right timing* for the introduction of carbohydrate to maintain smooth blood sugar curves rather than spikes.

The beauty of Step Two is that it trains your pancreas and liver to work normally, allowing for normal blood sugar and insulin levels to let you to lose weight, reduce blood lipids such as cholesterol and triglycerides, and have energy!

Don't Be Scared—Carbs Are Your Allies

After Step One, many people are wary about reintroducing carbohydrate foods. They have come to regard carbs as the "bad guys" of the nutrient world. But in reality, it is your pancreas's reaction to blood sugar that was out of line. And believe it or not, the right amount of carbohydrate distributed throughout the entire day (and even into the night) will help to keep you in a weight-losing mode.

The amount of mild carb necessary for Step Two was not arbitrarily picked out of a hat. It is the amount that is low enough to keep the pancreas relaxed but just high enough to prevent the liver from engaging in the "self-feed" mode. After much research in my nutritional therapy practice, I found the magic number in Step Two is 11–20 grams of net carbohydrate. To determine carbohydrate grams, you will use the same formula that you used in Step One: total carbohydrate grams – dietary fiber = 11–20 grams net carb!

THE NEW CARB THRESHOLD: 11–20 GRAMS

When you begin gently reintroducing carbohydrates to your metabolism, your liver will systematically refill with its glycogen stores. After three to four days, your liver and muscles will be back to their normal state of affairs, storing glycogen and releasing sugar as needed.

When the liver is refilled with glycogen, it is capable of performing one of its main functions—self-feeding the body with sugar if blood sugar drops. The thing to keep in mind is not to wait more than five hours without eating carbohydrate. If you do, your liver can recover the equivalent of 45 to 65 grams of carbohydrate into the bloodstream to self-feed the body over the next five hours. Your blood sugar will automatically rise, causing your Met B pancreas to overrelease insulin. In response, excess fat cells will open and you will need to double-dip into your bloodstream to retrieve sugar to feed those excess cells. You will get fatter, your blood sugar will dip lower, and here come those cravings again!

You don't want to go down this road again, and the Metabolism Miracle can prevent you from taking that road. If you regulate your carb intake throughout the day and even into the night, keep the carb at each interval in an amount that is neither too much nor too little, and if the type of carbohydrate is low impact so that it won't overstimulate your relaxed pancreas, you will be in control of your weight . . . permanently.

Reminders for Step Two

You'll notice that all but a few of these rules remain the same as those for Step One:

1. All neutral foods in Step One remain neutral in Step Two.
2. Eat within one hour of awakening, within one hour of sleeping, and go no longer than five hours without eating.
3. Drink a daily minimum of 64 ounces of water and decaffeinated fluid.
4. You should continue to take vitamins, minerals, and other supplements (see page 19 for a list of supplements).
5. Exercise a minimum of thirty minutes, five times per week. Change it up for variety!
6. Drink at least two cups of green tea per day.
7. (Step Two) Add 11–20 gram carb choices as directed at your breakfast, lunch, dinner, bedtime, in the middle of the night (if you are awake), and in between any meals that exceed five hours. **The 11–20 gram carb choices are mandatory, not options.**
8. Use neutral foods to satisfy hunger once you've met your 11–20 gram carb choice at meals and snacks. You may always have neutral foods.
9. (Step Two) If you choose to exercise in the morning, before breakfast, take an 11–20 gram carb choice *before* your morning workout and also at your breakfast *after* exercise.

10. (Step Two) When you go more than five hours between meals, you'll need an **additional** 11–20 gram carb choice as a snack between the meals. Don't remove the 11–20 gram carb choice from the next meal.

HOW SHOULD YOU TIME THE 11–20 GRAM CARB CHOICES?

To keep your carbohydrates on the right track, you will have "mandatory" carb choices of 11–20 grams net carb *at breakfast, lunch, dinner, bedtime, and in the middle of the night if you are awake.* If any meals will occur more than five hours after the previous meal, eat an additional 11–20 gram carb "dam" between the meals to keep the liver suppressed.

Here's a sample Monday from a Day in the Life of Step Two:

7:00 AM	**Wake up**
8:00 AM	**Breakfast** (always requires an 11–20 g carb choice)
11:00 AM	**Snack** (Because the time between breakfast and lunch is greater than five hours, this snack will include an 11–20 g carb choice.)
1:30 PM	**Lunch** (always requires an 11–20 g carb choice)
4:30 PM	**Snack** (Because the time between lunch and dinner is greater than five hours, this snack will include an 11–20 g carb choice.)
7:00 PM	**Dinner** (always requires an 11–20 g carb choice)
11:00 PM	**Bedtime** (always requires an 11–20 g carb choice)
3:00 AM	**You're Awake** (so have an 11–20 g carb choice)

On this Monday, 11–20 gram carb choices make an appearance seven times, based on the day's events and timing of meals.

Here's a very different day, Wednesday, of the same week:

7:00 AM	**Wake up**
8:00 AM	**Breakfast** (always requires an 11–20 g carb choice)
11:00 AM	**Snack** (neutral foods like nuts, cheese if you're hungry, because breakfast and lunch occur within five hours today)
12:30 PM	**Lunch** (always requires an 11–20 g carb choice)

4:00 PM   **Snack** (neutral foods like nuts, cheese if you're hungry, because lunch and dinner occur within five hours today)

5:30 PM   **Dinner** (always requires an 11–20 g carb choice)

10:00 PM   **Bedtime**: (always requires an 11–20 g carb choice)

No middle-of-the-night snack because you didn't awaken.

On this Wednesday, 11–20 gram carb choices made an appearance four times, based on the day's events and timing of meals.

As you can see, your carb placement may change on a daily basis, just as life does. You don't have to modify your life to fit Step Two, you will modify Step Two to fit your life.

You know how to determine the carbohydrates from any foods with the same formula you used in Step One:

Total carb grams – dietary fiber grams = 11–20 grams net carb

And you know where to place the 11–20 gram carb choices throughout the day — *breakfast, lunch, dinner, bedtime, the middle of the night if you're awake, and between any meals more than five hours apart.* You must also make sure to take an 11–20 gram snack if you are going to exercise in the morning before breakfast.

Step Two Foods

LOW-IMPACT CARB CHOICES

In Step Two, it is important to choose your carbs wisely. Sure, you can get 16 grams of net carb from gumdrops, but the speed at which your blood sugar would respond to that pure sugar would rock your rested pancreas. The following lists provide low-impact carb choices that will allow your blood sugar to rise gently and your pancreas to release insulin in a more relaxed fashion. They all have a lower glycemic index, which means they will change into blood sugar slower than a high-impact carb such as a gumdrop.

Notice that low-impact carb choices are generally higher in fiber. The suggested breads are made of whole grain, rice should be brown or wild, pasta should be whole grain or whole wheat, potatoes should be sweet potatoes rather than white, and most fruits are fresh and unprocessed. These foods allow for gentle blood sugar fluctuation throughout the entire day, which will enable normal insulin flow throughout the day.

Note: Check the labels of bread, rolls, English muffins, wraps, cereal, crackers, bars, and other grain-based foods to make sure that the dietary fiber on the Nutrient Facts label is 2 grams or more.

The Perfect Gentle Carb Choice:

Light multigrain English muffin
Serving size 1 muffin
Total carbohydrate 22 grams
Dietary fiber 8 grams

22 grams total carbs – 8 grams dietary fiber = 14 net carb grams. With a net carb within the range of 11–20 grams and fiber well over 2 grams, this is a perfect choice!

Not a great English muffin choice:

Light white English muffin
Serving size 1 muffin
Total carbohydrate 20 grams
Dietary fiber 0 grams

20 grams total carbs – 0 grams dietary fiber = 20 net carb grams. Although it fits the 11–20 grams net carb, this English muffin has no fiber. It would not be a low-impact carb, but instead act as a wild carb and increase blood sugar at a fast rate! This fiber-free muffin is not a good choice for Step Two.

GENTLE CARB CHOICES

This following list includes excellent gentle, low-impact carb choices. Choose any food from the low-impact carbs list for your breakfast, lunch, dinner, bedtime snack, and in the middle of the night if you are awake. If the time between meals exceeds five hours, place an extra carb serving between them.

All portions shown are "ready to eat" and equal 11–20 grams carb.

Breads

Read the label for bread, cereal, bars, and crackers to make certain that dietary fiber is 2 grams or greater.

2 slices thin-sliced, light whole-grain bread (2 g fiber or more)

1 slice whole-grain bread (2 g fiber or more)

1 light whole-grain English muffin (2 g fiber or more)

½ whole-grain English muffin (2 g fiber or more)

1 light or lower-carb whole-grain pita (2 g fiber or more)

½ whole-grain pita (2 g fiber or more)

Cereals and Grains

½ cup cooked oatmeal

½ cup cooked barley

½ cup cooked brown or wild rice

½ cup cooked whole-grain pasta (cook al dente)

½ cup cooked bulgur

Dry cereal (11–20 g carb and 2 g fiber or more)

Chips, Crackers, Pretzels, and Popcorn

Whole-grain crackers (11–20 g carb and 2 g fiber or more)

3 cups popcorn (light or hot-air popped without partially hydrogenated oils)

Whole-grain pretzels (11–20 g carb and 2 g fiber or more)

Tortilla chips (11–20 g carb and 2 g fiber or more)

Protein Bars or Snack Bars

Protein bars (11–20 g net carb and 2 g fiber or more)

Legumes and Starchy Vegetables

½ cup corn

½ ear fresh corn

½ cup peas

½ cup legumes such as black beans, chickpeas (garbanzo beans),

kidney beans, lentils, lima beans, white beans, white kidney beans

⅓ cup hummus

½ whole or ½ cup mashed sweet potato or yam

Legumes and Starchy Vegetables (cont.)

1½ cups cooked carrots (½ cup or less of carrots is considered neutral in Step Two)

1 cup beets

1 cup mashed acorn, butternut, or other winter squash

1 cup canned pure pumpkin

¾ cup cooked, boiled parsnips

Soups

1 cup tomato soup (water-based; check label)

½ cup lentil soup or other bean soup (or check label)

½ cup split pea soup (or check label)

Other canned or prepared soups in a portion size that provides 11–20 grams carb and 2 grams fiber or more

Fruit

Whole fruit choices should be average in size.

1 apple

1 pear

1 peach

2 plums

1 nectarine

12 cherries

½ cup natural applesauce

6–8 whole strawberries

¾ cup blackberries

¾ cup blueberries

1 cup raspberries

½ grapefruit (not recommended if you are taking the medication Lipitor)

2 clementine oranges or small tangerines

1 orange

4 apricots or 8 dried apricot halves

12 grapes

¾ cup pineapple cubes

½ banana

1 cup melon (honeydew, watermelon, canteloupe)

Milk and Other Dairy

8 fluid ounces (1 cup) fat-free, nonfat, 1%, 2%, or Skim Plus milk

Plain or Greek yogurt (11–20 g carb)

8 fluid ounces (1 cup) buttermilk (11–20 g carb)

Fruit-flavored yogurt sweetened with non-nutritive sweetener (11–20 g net carb)

½ cup sugar-free/fat-free pudding (11–20 g net carb)

No-sugar-added ice-cream products (11–20 g net carb)

Frequently Asked Questions for Step Two

I'm desperate to lose weight! It makes the most sense to stick to net carbs closer to 11 grams than 20 grams, right?

There is no difference in terms of weight loss, blood sugar control, or insulin rise if, on average, you choose your gentle carbohydrates from anywhere within the 11–20 gram range (inclusive). The lower end of the 11–20 gram carb range offers no extra benefit.

I'm really not that hungry at breakfast, so I'd like to skip the 11–20 gram carb choice. Why take those extra calories if I'm not even hungry?

The 11–20 gram carb choices are not options, they are mandatory and necessary. In fact, they enable you to lose weight. If you skip the necessary carbs during Step Two or Three, your liver will step up to the plate and release 45 to 65 grams of carbohydrate. The resulting spiked insulin release will slow down your weight loss and allow your liver to take control. Be sure to follow the 11–20 gram carbo-hydrate schedule at meals, bedtime, and in the middle of the night if you are awake. If the time between meals exceeds five hours, you must have an 11–20 gram snack choice between the meals!

I really enjoy some of the 5-gram "Counters" I used in Step One. How can I incorporate them into Step Two?

If you are having a 5-gram "Counter" at one of your meals, bedtime, or in the middle of the night, make sure that the combined net carb of the "Counter" and your 11–20 gram carb choice doesn't exceed 20 grams.

For example, if you choose a 19-gram carb choice at lunch along with a 5-gram low-carb tortilla, you'd be over your 20-gram limit. But, if you choose a 12-gram carb choice at lunch along with a 5-gram low-carb tortilla, the combined 17 net carb grams would be within target range.

I moved on to Step Two yesterday and I feel bloated! Am I regaining weight?

Some people experience a feeling of bloating during the first three to four days of Step Two. As your liver refills with glycogen stores, it takes some water with it.

This is temporary, much like the fatigue and cravings when you began Step One. By day five of Step Two, you will be back to feeling like yourself.

What if I slip up on Step Two? I have a bridal shower next month and a week's vacation on a cruise ship this summer. What should I do?

There are two types of slip-ups: the one-meal slip-up and the extended slip-up.

They require different remedies.

1. The one meal slip-up often occurs when you attend a dinner with friends, celebration meal, or single holiday meal, or you find yourself in need of a "one-meal break" after being in the program for a period of time.

Unlike other diet plans that encourage you to "save up your points or calories" to use for a special meal, people with Metabolism B cannot save 11–20 gram carb targets. Each missed 11–20 gram carb choice would cause the liver to self-feed, the pancreas to release excess insulin, and your body to gain fat.

The beauty of the Metabolism Miracle is that if you find yourself "off program" for a meal, you can do nothing to make up for it. Take all your necessary 11–20 gram carb targets in the day leading up to the meal and remember to resume your 11–20 gram carb targets after the meal. That's it. Just be sure to get right back on course right afterward.

2. Extended slip-ups often occur during a vacation, long weekend, or holiday period. If you find yourself having more than two slip-ups in a one-week period, you *must* return to Step One for ten days to clean up the metabolic mess. If you are going on vacation, stay in Step Two as closely as possible, but if you slip up more than twice during that week, just resign yourself to clean up when you get back.

What makes a slip-up?
- More than 20 grams net carb at a meal or snack
- Less than 11 grams net carb at a meal or snack
- Skipping your 11–20 gram bedtime carb target
- Skipping your 11–20 gram target within an hour of waking up
- Going more than five hours without an 11–20 carb snack between meals
- Exercising before breakfast without first taking an 11–20 gram carb target

When more than two slip-ups occur in a week, think Big Eraser! Ten days of Step One!

Sample Menus for Step Two

Breakfast

Scrambled eggs or egg whites with ham and low-fat cheese, peppers, onions = neutral

Light multigrain English muffin (11–20 net carb and 2 or more grams fiber)

Whipped butter = neutral

Carb-free jelly = neutral

Coffee with half-and-half and sucralose or stevia = neutral

---

2 slices light whole-grain bread (11–20 g net carb and 2 g fiber or more)

Natural peanut butter = neutral

Carb-free jelly = neutral

Low-carb protein shake (with 2 g net carb—add to the carb grams from the 2 slices of bread.

Chocolate-Strawberry Smoothie (page 103) (11–20 g net carb)

Handful of almonds = neutral

Blueberry French Toast (page 258) (11–20 g net carb and 2 g fiber or more)

Coffee with creamer and stevia = neutral

Melon and Ricotta Salad (page 136) (11–20 g net carb)

Handful of walnuts = neutral

Green tea with lemon = neutral

Breakfast (*continued*)

Baked Ham Omelet Cups (page 261) = neutral
Tomato wedges = neutral
Low-carb whole-grain mini-bagel (11–20 g net carb and
    2 g fiber or more)
Whipped butter = neutral
Green tea with lemon = neutral

¾ cup cereal (containing 11–20 g net carb and 2 g fiber or more)
1 cup organic unsweetened soy milk = neutral
Coffee with cream and sucralose = neutral

Lunch

Pear and Goat Cheese Salad (page 128) ("Counter," add to the
    carb grams in the crackers)
Whole-grain crackers (11–20 g net carb, 2 g fiber or more)
Sparkling water with lemon slice = neutral

Turkey Melt (page 176) (11–20g net carb, 2 g fiber or more)
Celery sticks with peanut butter = neutral
Sugar-free drink = neutral

Roast beef and sliced low-fat American cheese = neutral
2 slices light whole-grain bread (11–20 g net carb, 2 g fiber or
    more)
Lettuce and tomato slices = neutral
Light mayo or a small amount of regular mayo = neutral
Herbal iced tea with stevia = neutral

Lunch *(continued)*

Shrimp Salad with Fruit (page 144) (11–20 g net carb)
Dip of low-fat cottage or ricotta cheese = neutral
Ice water with lemon wedge = neutral

Minestrone soup (page 149) (11–20 g net carb)
Baby Artichoke Salad (page 131) = neutral
String cheese = neutral
Sugar-free beverage = neutral

Roma Tofu Bake (page 198) = neutral
Whole-grain Italian bread (in quantity to provide 11–20 g net
    carb and 2 g fiber or more)
Side garden salad with light dressing = neutral
Cranberry Spritzer (page 105) = neutral

Low-carb protein bar (11–20 g net carb and 2 g fiber or more)
Bottle of water = neutral

Low-carb protein shake ("Counter"; add to the 15 g from the apple)
1 apple (contains 15 g carb)
Handful of almonds = neutral

Low-carb pita (11–20 g net carb and 2 g fiber or more)
Shredded lettuce, chopped tomatoes = neutral
Grilled Pork Kebabs (grapes omitted) (page 188) = neutral
Sugar-free beverage = neutral

Dinner

Tofu Marsala (page 200) ("Counter"; add to the 15 g of carb in
the ½ cup of natural applesauce)
Cauliflower "Rice" (page 245) = neutral
½ cup natural applesauce with a sprinkle of ground cinnamon
(15 g carb)
Sugar-free beverage = neutral

BBQ Chicken (page 166) = neutral
Broccoli Rabe Salad with Orzo (page 132) (11–20 g net carb)
Sugar-free gelatin with light whipped topping = neutral
Decaf with creamer and sucralose = neutral

Grilled Rosemary Salmon (page 216) = neutral
Tabbouleh with Artichokes (page 133) (11–20 g net carb)
Coconut Macaroons (page 289) = neutral
Tea with stevia = neutral

5 ounces red wine = neutral
Baked Beef Tenderloin with Brown Sauce (page 181) = neutral
Grilled Sweet Potato "Fries" (page 228) (11–20 g net carb)
Steamed broccoli with lemon = neutral

Creamy Vegetable Soup (page 146) (11–20 g net carb)
Spinach Feta Pie (page 194) = neutral
Sugar-free iced tea = neutral

5 ounces white wine = neutral
Broiled Flounder with Parmesan (page 218) = neutral
Herbed Mashed Parsnips (page 234) (11–20 g net carb)
Fresh and Crunchy Spring Vegetables (page 238) = neutral

Dinner *(continued)*

Japanese Pork and Spinach Soup (page 160) = neutral
Ginger Flank Steak (page 179) = neutral
Brown Rice Pilaf (page 240) (11–20 g net carb)
Green tea = neutral

Eggplant Parmesan (page 197) = neutral
½ cup cooked whole wheat pasta (11–20 g net carb and 2 g fiber
   or more)
Tossed salad with balsamic vinaigrette = neutral
Sugar-free beverage = neutral

Snacks (when an 11–20 gram snack is required)

Whole-grain crackers (11–20 g net carb serving with 2 g fiber or
   more)
Piece of fresh fruit from allowed list (page 62)
1 cup nonfat or low-fat milk
Yogurt (with 11–20 g net carb)
3 cups popcorn (light or hot-air popped without partially hydrogenated oils)
Baked tortilla chips (11–20 g net carb serving with 2 g fiber or
   more)
Baked soy crisps (11–20 g net carb serving with 2 g fiber or more)
½ cup natural applesauce (these come individually packaged,
   too)
Whole wheat pretzels (11–20 g net carb serving with 2 g fiber or
   more)
Sugar-free ice-cream (11–20 g net carb serving)
Sugar-free pudding (11–20 g net carb serving)
Protein or cereal bar (11–20 g net carb serving with 2 g fiber or
   more)

STEP THREE:
KEEPING WEIGHT OFF FOR A LIFETIME
EXCELLENT HEALTH AND ENERGY

Time Commitment: Step Three is a way of life, to be followed as a maintenance program. Once you have reached your desired weight and your lab work is normal on as little medication as possible, Step Three will keep you feeling terrific for life.

Why do it? Step Three will keep you healthy, energized, and at your desired weight. Steps One and Two got your metabolism in check and your weight under control. Step Three establishes the correct carbohydrate range for *you* to maintain your health and well-being with a greater amount and variety of carbohydrate foods.

How You'll Feel: You will feel great as you use Step Three to maintain the right weight, health, and energy. You may enjoy more carbohydrates and a greater variety of carbohydrate choices. Life is good!

Counting Carbs in Step Three

In Step Three you will have a certain number of carbohydrate "servings" that fit your body's needs. In Step Two, we used 11–20 grams net carb as a mandatory serving of carbohydrate at breakfast, lunch, dinner, bedtime, middle of the night (if you were awake), and between any meals that were more than five hours apart. In Step Three, we will call these 11–20 gram amounts "carb servings" and discover just how many servings your body needs.

Remember, 11–20 grams net carb equal one carb serving. To keep it simple, some people consider 15 grams of carbohydrate, the midpoint between 11 and 20, to be one carb serving. Using 15 grams of net carb makes reading food labels convenient for Step Three.

You will use the same net carb formula that you used in Steps One and Two to determine a carb serving: total carbohydrate grams – dietary fiber = net carb grams. The twist? If you divide your net carb grams by 15, you can find the number of "carb servings" in any food. For example:

Chicky's Hearty Chicken Soup
Total carbohydrate 48 grams
Dietary fiber 3 grams

$48 - 3 = 45$ grams total net carbs
$45 \div 15 =$ **3 carb servings**

Cluncky's Hearty Chicken Soup
Total carbohydrate 33 grams
Dietary fiber 2 grams

$33 - 2 = 31$ grams total net carbs
$31 \div 15 =$ **2 carb servings**

If you'd rather skip the math, this handy chart automatically converts your net carb grams into carb servings:

If your net carb grams are . . .	Your carb servings are . . .
5.5–10 gram range	$\frac{1}{2}$ carb serving
11–20 gram range	1 carb serving
21–25 gram range	$1\frac{1}{2}$ carb servings
26–35 gram range	2 carb servings
36–40 gram range	$2\frac{1}{2}$ carb servings
41–50 gram range	3 carb servings
51–55 gram range	$3\frac{1}{2}$ carb servings
56–65 gram range	4 carb servings

HOW MANY CARB SERVINGS CAN *YOU* HAVE?

Now that you've reached your desired weight and the health and energy level you desire, it's time to configure the right amount of carbohydrate to keep you at this healthy place. Your carb range will vary based on your sex, age, and activity level. Use these guidelines to assess your activity level:

> *Sedentary*: 30 minutes or less of physical activity, 4–5 times per week
> *Moderate*: 40–60 minutes of moderate physical activity, 4–5 times per week
> *High*: more than 1 hour of strenuous physical activity, 4–5 times per week

Based on your sex, age, and activity level, the following carb charts will help you ascertain the maximum number of carbohydrate servings you can use per day.

WOMEN

CARB CHART

Female 5'0" to 5'3" with a maintenance weight of 100–130 pounds

Age	Activity	Maximum carb servings/day
Teens–age 20	Sedentary	8.5
	Moderate	9
	High	9.5
20s and 30s	Sedentary	8
	Moderate	8.5
	High	9
40s and 50s	Sedentary	7.5
	Moderate	8
	High	8.5
60s and 70s	Sedentary	7
	Moderate	7.5
	High	8
Over 80	Sedentary	6.5
	Moderate	7
	High	7.5

Age	Activity	Maximum carb servings/day
Female 5'4" to 5'7" with a maintenance weight of 120–150 pounds		
Teens–age 20	Sedentary	9.5
	Moderate	10
	High	10.5
20s and 30s	Sedentary	9
	Moderate	9.5
	High	10
40s and 50s	Sedentary	8.5
	Moderate	9
	High	9.5
60s and 70s	Sedentary	8
	Moderate	8.5
	High	9
Over 80	Sedentary	7.5
	Moderate	8
	High	8.5
Female 5'8" to 5'11" with a maintenance weight of 140–170 pounds		
Teens–age 20	Sedentary	10
	Moderate	11
	High	12
20s and 30s	Sedentary	9.5
	Moderate	10.5
	High	11.5
40s and 50s	Sedentary	9
	Moderate	10
	High	11
60s and 70s	Sedentary	8.5
	Moderate	9.5
	High	10.5
Over 80	Sedentary	8
	Moderate	9
	High	10

Age	Activity	Maximum carb servings/day
Female 6'0" to 6'3" with a maintenance weight of 155–185 pounds		
Teens–age 20	Sedentary	11
	Moderate	12
	High	13
20s and 30s	Sedentary	10.5
	Moderate	11.5
	High	12.5
40s and 50s	Sedentary	10
	Moderate	11
	High	12
60s and 70s	Sedentary	9.5
	Moderate	10.5
	High	11.5
Over 80	Sedentary	9
	Moderate	10
	High	11

MEN

CARB CHART

Age	Activity	Maximum carb servings/day
Male 5'0" to 5'3" with a desired maintenance weight of 106–136 pounds		
Teens–age 20	Sedentary	9
	Moderate	10
	High	11
20s and 30s	Sedentary	8.5
	Moderate	9.5
	High	10.5
40s and 50s	Sedentary	8
	Moderate	9
	High	10

Age	Activity	Maximum carb servings/day
60s and 70s	Sedentary	7.5
	Moderate	8.5
	High	9.5
Over 80	Sedentary	7
	Moderate	8
	High	9

Male 5'4" to 5'7" with a desired maintenance weight of 130–160 pounds

Teens–age 20	Sedentary	10
	Moderate	11
	High	12
20s and 30s	Sedentary	9.5
	Moderate	10.5
	High	11.5
40s and 50s	Sedentary	9
	Moderate	10
	High	11
60s and 70s	Sedentary	8.5
	Moderate	9.5
	High	10.5
Over 80	Sedentary	8
	Moderate	9
	High	10

Male 5'8" to 5'11" with a desired maintenance weight of 154–185 pounds

Teens–age 20	Sedentary	11
	Moderate	12
	High	13
20s and 30s	Sedentary	10.5
	Moderate	11.5
	High	12.5

Age	Activity	Maximum carb servings/day
40s and 50s	Sedentary	10
	Moderate	11
	High	12
60s and 70s	Sedentary	9.5
	Moderate	10.5
	High	11.5
Over 80	Sedentary	9
	Moderate	10
	High	11

Male 6'0" to 6'3" with a desired maintenance weight of 178–210 pounds

Teens–age 20	Sedentary	12
	Moderate	13
	High	14
20s and 30s	Sedentary	11.5
	Moderate	12.5
	High	13.5
40s and 50s	Sedentary	11
	Moderate	12
	High	13
60s and 70s	Sedentary	10.5
	Moderate	11.5
	High	12.5
Over 80	Sedentary	10
	Moderate	11
	High	12

Male 6'3" to 6'6" with a desired maintenance weight of 196–235 pounds

Teens–age 20	Sedentary	13
	Moderate	14
	High	15

Age	Activity	Maximum carb servings/day
20s and 30s	Sedentary	12.5
	Moderate	13.5
	High	14.5
40s and 50s	Sedentary	12
	Moderate	13
	High	14
60s and 70s	Sedentary	11.5
	Moderate	12.5
	High	13.5
Over 80	Sedentary	11
	Moderate	12
	High	13

Male over 6'6" with a desired maintenance weight of 226–250 pounds

Age	Activity	Maximum carb servings/day
Teens–age 20	Sedentary	14
	Moderate	15
	High	16
20s and 30s	Sedentary	13.5
	Moderate	14.5
	High	15.5
40s and 50s	Sedentary	13
	Moderate	14
	High	15
60s and 70s	Sedentary	12.5
	Moderate	13.5
	High	14.5
Over 80	Sedentary	12
	Moderate	13
	High	14

SPREAD THE CARBS

The key to Step Three is to spread your personalized number of carb servings throughout the day so they work to your advantage. Too much will overengage the pancreas but too little will stimulate the liver to release glycogen. The rules are similar to those in Step Two, with a few additions.

1. You must start your day with a minimum of 1 carb serving (11–20 grams)
2. You must end your day with a minimum of 1 carb serving (11–20 grams)
3. You must put an additional carb serving (11–20 grams) between your meals if they are separated by more than five hours.
4. If you are awake in the middle of the night, you should have a carb serving snack.
5. If you exercise first thing in the morning before breakfast, you must eat at least 1 carb serving (11–20 grams).
6. (Step Three) Remember that you cannot exceed 4 carb servings (56–65 grams of carb) at any one time (assuming your carb allotment allows it— see chart on page 73).
7. (Step Three) You must use a minimum of 1 carb serving (11–20 grams) as a meal or necessary snack.

A DAY IN THE LIFE OF STEP THREE

A five-foot-six, forty-five-year-old woman with moderate physical activity has a maximum amount of 9 carb servings per day.

6:00 AM	**Wake up**
6:30 AM	**Breakfast:** 2 carb servings
9:30 AM	**Snack:** 1 carb serving
1:00 PM	**Lunch:** 2 carb servings
4:30 PM	**Snack:** 1 carb serving
7:00 PM	**Dinner:** 2 carb servings
11:00 PM	**Bedtime:** 1 carb serving
Maximum/day	**9 carb servings**

A five-foot-nine, fifty-five-year-old man with sedentary physical activity has a maximum amount of 10 carb servings in a day.

8:00 AM   **Wake up**
8:30 AM   **Breakfast:** 2 carb servings
11:00 AM   **Snack:** neutral foods (breakfast and lunch fall within five hours of each other)
12:30 PM   **Lunch:** 2 carb servings
4:00 PM   **Snack:** 1 carb serving
6:00 PM   **Dinner:** 3 carb servings
11:00 PM   **Bedtime:** 2 carb servings
Maximum/day   10 carb servings

LOOK FOR FIBER

As during Step Two, the more fiber your carb choices have, the lower the impact they will have on your pancreas and liver. Consult the following chart for an idea of which Step Three carbohydrates fall into the low-impact zone (good) and which fall into the high-impact zone (use occasionally).

Step Three Foods

STEP THREE CARBOHYDRATES

All portions = 1 carb serving

BREADS—LOWER IMPACT

2 slices light, thin sliced whole grain bread (2 g fiber or more)

1 slice whole-grain bread (2 g fiber or more)

1 light whole-grain English muffin (2 g fiber or more)

½ whole-grain English muffin (2 g fiber or more)

1 light or lower-carb whole-grain pita (2 g fiber or more)

½ whole-grain pita (2 g fiber or more)

BREADS—HIGHER IMPACT

1-ounce slice white, rye,
    pumpernickel bread
1 hot dog roll
1/2 burger bun
1/2 pita bread
3/4 ounce matzoh
1 ounce chapati (use food scale)
1 ounce mini-bagel or mini-
    muffin
1 fajita shell

1 soft taco shell
2 hard taco shells
1 frozen waffle
2 (4-inch) pancakes
Breading
1 (2-inch) cube corn bread
1 ounce bakery bread (use a
    food scale)
3/4 cup croutons

CEREALS AND GRAINS—LOWER IMPACT

1/2 cup cooked oatmeal
1/2 cup cooked barley

1/2 cup cooked brown or wild rice
1/2 cup cooked whole-grain pasta
1/2 cup cooked bulgur

CEREALS AND GRAINS—HIGHER IMPACT

1/2 cup cooked cream of wheat
1/2 cup cooked farina
1/2 cup cookcd grits
1/3 cup cooked white rice
1/2 cup basmati rice

1/3 cup cooked white pasta
1/2 cup pasta salad
1/2 cup macaroni and cheese
1/2 cup casserole dish made with
    pasta

Bagels and Breading

- Big isn't always better. A mini-bagel contains just one carb serving but the standard 4-ounce bagel most Americans eat packs four!
- Don't forget to count the breading on fish or chicken. The breading on most items counts as one carb serving.

A Kitchen Scale

You may want to purchase a simple food scale for bakery bread, homemade bread, rolls, and bagels. Every ounce of bread is equal to one carb serving.

CRACKERS AND STARCHY SNACKS—LOWER IMPACT

Crackers (in a serving with 11–20 g net carb, 2 g fiber or more, and no trans fats)

3 cups popcorn (light or hot-air popped without partially hydrogenated oils)

Whole-grain pretzels (in a serving with 11–20 g carb and 2 g fiber or more)

Corn tortilla chips (in a serving with 11–20 g carb and 2 g fiber or more)

Cereal bar (11–20 g carb and 2 g fiber or more)

CRACKERS AND STARCHY SNACKS—HIGHER IMPACT

Crackers (in a serving with 11–20 g carb)

Chips (in a serving with 11–20 g)

Pretzels (in a serving with 11–20 g carb)

1½ oblong graham crackers (3 squares)

4 slices melba toast

2 large rice cakes

8 small rice cakes

6 saltines

½ cup chow mein noodles

3 sandwich crackers with cheese or peanut butter filling

STARCHY LEGUMES AND VEGETABLES—LOWER IMPACT

½ cup or ½ ear corn

½ cup legumes such as black beans, chickpeas, kidney beans, lentils, lima beans, peas, white beans, or white kidney beans

⅓ cup hummus

½ cup mashed sweet potato or yam

½ sweet potato

1 cup pumpkin

1½ cups cooked carrots

1 cup beets

¾ cup parsnips

1 cup acorn, butternut, or other winter squash

STARCHY LEGUMES AND VEGETABLES—HIGHER IMPACT

$\frac{1}{2}$ cup mashed potatoes

$\frac{1}{2}$ baked white potato

3 ounces boiled potato

$\frac{1}{2}$ small order of French fries

$\frac{1}{3}$ cup baked beans

$\frac{1}{2}$ cup potato salad

$\frac{1}{2}$ cup mashed plantain

SOUPS—LOWER IMPACT

1 cup tomato soup (water-based)

$\frac{1}{2}$ cup lentil soup

$\frac{1}{2}$ cup split pea soup

SOUPS—HIGHER IMPACT

1 cup broth-based soup with noodles, potatoes, rice, or barley

1 cup creamed soup (high in fat)

$\frac{1}{2}$ cup pasta e fagioli

1 cup "greens and beans"

$\frac{1}{2}$ cup minestrone soup

1 cup chili with beans

PROTEIN BARS—LOWER IMPACT

Must contain 11–20 g of net carb and have 2 g fiber or more

PROTEIN BARS—HIGHER IMPACT

Any that contain 11–20 g net carb containing less than 2 g fiber

FRUIT—LOWER IMPACT

All portions represent 11–20 g carb. Fruit choices should be average in size.

1 apple

1 pear

1 peach

2 plums

1 nectarine

12 cherries

$\frac{1}{2}$ cup natural applesauce

6–8 whole strawberries

$\frac{3}{4}$ cup blackberries

$\frac{3}{4}$ cup blueberries

1 cup raspberries

$\frac{1}{2}$ grapefruit (avoid if you take Lipitor)

2 clementine oranges or small tangerines

4 apricots or 8 dried apricot halves

12 grapes

1 orange

$\frac{3}{4}$ cup pineapple cubes

$\frac{1}{2}$ banana

1 cup honeydew, watermelon, canteloupe

FRUIT—HIGHER IMPACT

4 rings dried apples

3 dates

2 figs

1 kiwi

¾ cup mandarin oranges

½ small or ½ cup mango

½ papaya or 1 cup papaya cubes

2 prunes

2 tablespoons raisins

Other dried fruit (in a serving
with 11–20 g net carb)

MILK AND OTHER DAIRY—LOWER IMPACT

All portions represent 11–20 grams net carb.

1 cup (8 fluid ounces) of fat-free,
1%, or 2% milk

1 cup (8 fluid ounces) Skim Plus
milk

Plain or Greek yogurt (11–20 g
net carb)

Fruit-flavored yogurt sweetened
with sucralose (11–20 g net
carb)

½ cup sugar-free/fat-free
pudding (11–20 g net carb)

No-sugar-added ice cream
products (11–20 g net carb)

MILK AND OTHER DAIRY—HIGHER IMPACT

½ cup light, low-fat, or regular
ice cream

½ cup light or regular frozen
yogurt

OCCASIONAL TREATS

Many of these high-impact carbs are often high in fat and have little nutritional benefit. Still, they can be a wonderful treat from time to time. They are shown in a typical serving size along with the carb servings.

Brownie, 4-inch square, unfrosted: 2 carb servings

Brownie, 4-inch square, frosted: 4 carb servings

Cake, 4-inch square, unfrosted: 2 carb servings

Cake, 4-inch square, frosted: 4 carb servings

2 sandwich-type cookies with filling in the middle: 1 carb serving

2 cookies, average size, homemade, such as chocolate chip: 1 carb serving

Frosted cupcake (small): 2 carb servings

Plain cake doughnut: 2 carb servings

Glazed-type doughnut: 2 carb servings

$\frac{1}{8}$ fruit pie with double crust: 3 carb servings

$\frac{1}{8}$ fruit pie with single crust: 2 carb servings

$\frac{1}{8}$ pumpkin or custard pie: 2 carb servings

$\frac{1}{8}$ large pizza: 3 carb servings

$\frac{1}{8}$ large pizza, thick outer edge of crust removed: 2 carb servings

Bagel: 4 carb servings

$\frac{1}{2}$ bagel: 2 carb servings

"Hollowed" bagel with insides scooped out: 2 carb servings

Hard roll, kaiser roll, or 6-inch sub roll: 3 carb servings

"Hollowed" hard roll, kaiser roll, or sub roll: 2 carb servings

Wrap: 3 carb servings

1 cup pasta-based casserole dishes such as lasagne, mac and cheese, or tuna casserole: 2 carb servings

Small fries: 2 carb servings

Medium fries: 3 carb servings

Large fries: 4 carb servings

Breaded fish sandwich on a bun: 3 carb servings

Breaded chicken on a bun: 3 carb servings

Bun for large burgers or fast-food sandwiches: 3 carb servings

Chicken nuggets, 6 pieces: 1 carb serving

Sushi, 6 pieces (1 sushi roll cut in 6): 1 carb serving

Chinese food such as beef and broccoli, shrimp and veggies with sauce, 1 cup: 1 carb serving

Chinese rice, white or fried, 1 cup: 3 carb servings

Wontons, two: 1 carb serving

Sauce or breading on any food: 1 carb serving

The Slip-Up Remedy

You can live in Step Three for most of the year, finding that it is less common to slip up because of a broader carb range and variety. If you find that you have more than two dietary slips in a week, return to Step One for ten days followed by ten days in Step Two, and then resume Step Three.

Certain times of the year almost require a ten-day cleanup in Step One. After vacation, holidays, or a long weekend in which you went off your Step Three maintenance plan more than twice, you should return to ten days of Step One and ten days of Step Two. Always follow a detox in Step One by an equal or greater amount of time in Step Two before resuming Step Three.

Remember that high levels of stress, both emotional and physical, may also upset your balance. During very high-stress times, including over-the-top emotional stress, pre- or postsurgery, or illness or pain that lasts more than three days, it is always safest to revert to Step One. When things settle down, return to a stint in Step One followed by an equal amount of time in Step Two before resuming Step Three.

Frequently Asked Questions for Step Three

If I don't want to increase my carbohydrate targets to the recommended amount for Step Three, what do I have to do to succeed?

Step Three shows you the maximum carbohydrate servings to be used throughout the day. You may absolutely take the lower end of the range of carbohydrate for your body (see chart, page 73) but realize that going to the maximum will not trigger weight gain.

I spent eight weeks on Step One, 24 weeks in Step Two, and have maintained my desired weight for more than a year on Step Three. I've cured my Met B, right?

You can't cure your genetic makeup! You have learned to keep Metabolism B under control. Your body looks great and feels great because you are in hormonal balance. If you veer off course and go back to your old way of eating and living, you will most certainly cause your liver and pancreas to go right back to square one! Step Three is a way of life designed for the health and well-being of anyone with Met B. It gives you great freedom in carb amount and variety. Don't consider yourself cured of Metabolism B, consider yourself in control of your Metabolism B. Congratulations!

I'm in Step Three. I look and feel great. But in the past month, I've noticed that my jeans are becoming a little tighter in the waist. What do you recommend?

It's time to reassess. Keep a three-day food log, noting the time you wake up and the time of all your meals and snacks. Jot down all foods eaten, approximate portion sizes, and the carb grams in your carb foods. Keep track of your fluid intake, vitamins and minerals, and exercise. Make note if you are under high stress, are ill, or have significant pain.

After the third complete day, carefully review the log and answer these questions:

- Am I eating the appropriate amount of carbohydrate within one hour of waking up?
- Am I taking a night snack with the appropriate amount of carb grams at bedtime?
- Do I take an appropriate carb snack if I awaken in the middle of the night?
- Am I taking the right amount of carb before early morning exercise?
- If the time between my meals exceeds five hours, do I take the correct amount of carb as my between-meals snack?
- Am I taking carb at each meal and appropriate snack?
- Am I exercising a minimum of thirty minutes, five times per week? Is it time to change up my exercise routine?
- Am I drinking adequate water/decaf fluid?

If you answered yes to the above questions, it means you are following the program correctly. Now look at the stressors that might be wreaking havoc. Answer these questions:

- Am I under very high stress?
- Am I ill?

❍ Am I in significant pain?

❍ Am I taking a new medication that causes an increase in blood sugar, such as Prednisone?

❍ Am I taking thyroid hormone replacement? (The dosage might need a tweak.)

If you answered no to the above questions, it means your life is fairly stable. Since you are eating your carbs properly and your life is fairly calm, you may be overconsuming protein and fat. Take a look at portion sizes of salad dressing, butter, meats, and nuts to see if you might be overdoing the neutral foods in your life.

If you are not overeating neutral foods, ask your physician to consider checking your thyroid panel, cortisol level, and serum insulin. It is rare, but another metabolic issue may occur in the life of someone with Metabolism B.

During Step Three I can occasionally have some "nutrient-empty" carb choices such as cookies, candy, jelly, and marshmallows. How often can I choose these questionable treats, even though they fit into the guidelines' net carb amount?

You are wise to consider that not only does the amount of carbohydrate impact insulin release, but also the type of carb. The 30 grams of carb (2 carb servings) in the marshmallows you ate at the end of a carb-free dinner of broiled fish, veggies, and salad will make your blood sugar spike hard and quick. The pancreas, as a result, gets jarred by the responding quick need for insulin. If that same 30 grams of carb came from an ear of corn, your blood sugar would rise to a reasonable height at an easy pace, keeping the pancreas relaxed.

Try to limit the use of empty calorie carbs to no more than twice a week and not on the same day. Treat your body very well and use these foods the way they were intended—as occasional treats, not daily staples.

My husband and I both have Metabolism B. It is a good bet that our children, ages six and nine, will manifest this metabolism's symptoms in their future. Children should not be on a diet because it could interrupt their growth, so what can we do to prevent their Met B symptoms?

You can make changes right now in your children's lives to promote excellent health and weight in their future. A few ideas that are easy to implement in your home:

1. Make sure your children get a minimum of sixty minutes of physical activity (over and above their normal activity) five days per week.

2. To quench thirst, offer water rather than juice, sports drinks, or soda.

3. Ask their pediatrician for advice regarding a daily multivitamin and mineral supplement.

4. Stock your pantry with snacks that fit the Step Two guidelines, keeping portion sizes within the 11–20 gram range. Buy the individual bags of multigrain pretzels rather than family-size, or repackage the family-size bag into 11–20 gram portions.

5. Purchase grain products with more than 2 grams of fiber per serving.

6. Focus on lean protein, heart-healthy fats, and neutral veggies at mealtime, using carbohydrate foods as side dishes, not main courses.

7. Consider buying organic (especially eggs, milk, poultry, and meats). Organic proteins should be free of hormones and chemical additives.

8. Encourage your children to eat within one hour of wake-up and have a snack right before bed. Try to make sure your kids don't go longer than five hours without eating during the day.

9. Make "empty calorie" junk foods an occasional choice, not a daily "treat." Moderation is key. If you never allow empty calorie sweets, they will become revered as the Holy Grail for the rest of your children's life. Allowing these foods on an occasional basis will make junk food less of a mystery and help your children prioritize it properly in their future.

Sample Menus for Step Three

All of the following menus represent 2 carb servings.

Breakfast

Broccoli-Mushroom Frittata (page 251) = neutral

1 light multigrain English muffin (1 carb serving)

Whipped butter and zero-carb jelly = neutral

1 cup cubed cantaloupe (1 carb serving)

Coffee with creamer and sucralose = neutral

Legal Pancakes (page 257) = neutral

Carb-free syrup = neutral

½ sliced banana (1 carb serving)

6 strawberries, sliced (1 carb serving)

Light whipped cream = neutral

Coffee with creamer and sucralose = neutral

Crustless Quiche (page 253) = ("Counter")

Light turkey sausage = neutral

1 regular multigrain English muffin (2 carb servings)

Whipped cream cheese = neutral

Green tea with stevia = neutral

---

1 cup Greek yogurt (1 carb serving)

¾ cup fresh blueberries (1 carb serving)

Flavored water = neutral

Oat-Nut Muffin (page 255) (1 carb serving)

1 cup 1% milk (1 carb serving)

½ cup cooked oatmeal (1 carb serving)

Dash of low-carb milk or unsweetened soy milk = neutral

½ banana sliced (1 carb serving)

Breakfast *(continued)*

1 slice multigrain toast (1 carb serving)
Whipped butter = neutral
Dip of ricotta cheese = neutral
6 strawberries, sliced (1 carb serving)

Lunch

2 slices light whole wheat bread (1 carb serving)
Turkey and low-fat cheese = neutral
Lettuce and tomato slices = neutral
Light mayonnaise = neutral
1 medium peach (1 carb serving)
Diet drink = neutral

Split Pea Soup in a Hurry (page 150) (1 carb serving)
Crackers (a serving with 11–20 grams net carb = 1 carb serving)
My Favorite Cobb Salad (page 141) = neutral
Sparkling water = neutral

Chicken and Wild Rice Soup (page 154) (1 carb serving)
Turkey Waldorf Salad (page 139) (1 carb serving)
Sugar-free iced tea with a lemon wedge = neutral

Chicken Fajitas (page 173) = neutral
Wrap (one with 11–20 grams net carb = 1 carb serving)
Caribbean Corn on the Cob (page 226) (1 carb serving)
Water with lemon = neutral

Manhattan-Style Clam Chowder (page 156) (1 carb serving)
Turkey Melt (page 176) (1 carb serving)
Sugar-free drink = neutral

Lunch (*continued*)

Crab-Stuffed Tomato (page 114) = neutral
2 ounces multigrain bakery bread (2 carb servings)
Flavored water = neutral

Burger bun (2 carb servings)
Grilled sirloin burger = neutral
Side garden salad with low-fat dressing = neutral
Miracle Mojito (page 107) = neutral

Crustless Quiche (page 253) = ("Counter")
1 slice whole-grain toast with natural peanut butter
    (1 carb serving)
Mixed Berry Smoothie (page 102) (1 carb serving)

Light yogurt (1 carb serving)
Banana Muffin (page 256) (1 carb serving)
Decaf iced coffee with creamer and stevia = neutral

Dinner

Crunchy Oven-fried Fish (page 214) (1 carb serving)
Carrot-Parsnip Latkes (page 232) (1 carb serving)
Sweet-and-Sour Coleslaw (page 230) = neutral

5 ounces red wine = neutral
Broken Noodles (page 185) (1 carb serving)
Garden salad with dressing = neutral
1 ounce garlic bread (1 carb serving)

Dinner *(continued)*

Vegetarian Pot Luck (page 196) (1 carb serving)
1 ounce multigrain bakery bread (1 carb serving)
Ginger Chai Refresher (page 106) = neutral

Lemon-Garlic Chicken (page 162) = neutral
Baked potato (2 carb servings)
Whipped butter and light sour cream = neutral
Sautéed Brussels Sprouts (page 235) = neutral

Smoked Sausage Gumbo (page 175) (1 carb serving)
1 ounce crusty multigrain bread (1 carb serving)
Garlic butter = neutral
Decaf coffee with creamer and Splenda = neutral

Glazed Ham (page 186) = neutral
Roasted Sweet Potato "Fries" (page 229) (1 carb serving)
Steamed cauliflower = neutral
Watermelon Sorbet (page 278) (1 carb serving)
Sugar-free beverage – neutral

Grilled Lime Chicken (page 171) = neutral
Mesclun and Sweet Potato Salad (page 137) (1 carb serving)
Caribbean Corn on the Cob (page 226) (1 carb serving)
Sugar-free iced tea = neutral

Sausage and Egg Casserole (page 252) = neutral
Light multigrain English muffin (1 carb serving)
Whipped butter = neutral
1 cup cantaloupe (1 carb serving)
Decaf coffee with creamer and sucralose = neutral

PART III
Metabolism Miracle Recipes

7

BEVERAGES

○ Ginger-Lemon Green Tea   98
○ Icy Melon Tea   99
○ Frozen Cranberry-Apple Slushies   100
○ Chocolate–Peanut Butter Smoothie   100
○ Pineapple Smoothie   101
○ Orange Dreamsicle Smoothie   102
○ Mixed Berry Smoothie   102
○ Chocolate-Strawberry Smoothie   103
○ Instant Espresso Chiller   104
○ Dark Chocolate Dreamer   104
○ Cranberry Spritzer   105
○ Berry Dreamer   106
○ Ginger Chai Refresher   106
○ Miracle Mojito   107

GINGER-LEMON GREEN TEA

Steps One, Two, and Three
Start to finish: 15 minutes
Serves: 6 (8 ounces/serving)

Steeping green tea releases an antioxidant that has been linked to tremendous health benefits, including lowered LDL cholesterol, decreased cancer risk, and even antiaging properties. Green tea has a unique flavor. You can add lemon, sucralose, or stevia to this version, which also sports the zing of ginger.

6 cups water
2 tablespoons sucralose or stevia
1 piece fresh ginger, peeled and very thinly sliced
8 strips lemon zest (use a potato peeler to zest the lemon)
6 green tea bags
Lemon slices

1. In a large saucepan, combine the water, sweetener, ginger, and lemon zest strips. Bring to a boil. Lower the heat and simmer uncovered for 5 minutes. Remove the ginger and lemon strips with a slotted spoon and discard.
2. Place the tea bags in a teapot. Immediately add the simmering liquid. Cover and let stand for 3 to 5 minutes.
3. Remove and discard the tea bags. Serve immediately in mugs garnished with lemon slices or let cool, refrigerate, and serve later as iced tea.

Step One = Yes (neutral)
Step Two = Yes (neutral)
Step Three = Yes (neutral)

Icy Melon Tea

Steps Two and Three
Start to finish: 5 minutes
Serves: 2

The fresh taste of melon in lemon tea will wow you. This is a great refresher on a hot summer day.

1¾ **cups ice**
¾ **cup coarsely chopped seedless watermelon, cantaloupe, or honeydew**
1 **cup brewed lemon-flavored herbal tea, at room temperature**

1. Combine all the ingredients in a blender. Cover and blend on high speed until smooth, pulsing as necessary to break up the ice.
2. Pour into two tall glasses. Serve immediately.

Step One = No
Step Two = Yes (5 grams net carb)
Step Three = Yes (5 grams net carb)

FROZEN CRANBERRY-APPLE SLUSHIES

Steps Two and Three
Start to finish: 10 minutes
Serves: 4

A flavor combination of apples and cranberries with a hint of cinnamon. Serve with a cinnamon stick stirrer for an extra kick!

1½ cups (12 ounces) diet cranberry juice (containing 2 grams or less net carb in 8 ounces)

1 large Red Delicious apple, peeled, cored, and cut into chunks

⅛ teaspoon ground cinnamon

4 cups ice cubes

1. Place the cranberry juice, apple, and cinnamon in a blender. Blend until smooth.
2. Add the ice cubes, 1 cup at a time. Cover and blend until smooth and icy. Serve immediately.

Step One = No
Step Two = Yes (5 grams net carb)
Step Three = Yes (5 grams net carb)

CHOCOLATE-PEANUT BUTTER SMOOTHIE

Steps One, Two, and Three
Start to finish: 2 minutes
Serves: 1

The taste of peanut butter cups in a high-protein beverage. You'll get lots of staying power from this smooth and satisfying drink.

CHOCOLATE–PEANUT BUTTER SMOOTHIE (CONTINUED)

8 ounces cold water

4 ice cubes

1 tablespoon whipping cream

1 tablespoon natural smooth peanut butter

2 heaping tablespoons low-carb chocolate protein powder

1. Place all the ingredients in a blender and blend to your preferred consistency.

Step One = Yes (5-gram net carb "Counter")
Step Two = Yes (5 grams net carb)
Step Three = Yes (5 grams net carb)

PINEAPPLE SMOOTHIE

Steps Two and Three

Start to finish: 2 minutes

Serves: 1

The protein powder recommended for MM smoothies can be found in your supermarket, chain discount store, pharmacy, vitamin shop, or health food store. Make sure that the net carb grams per scoop are less than 5 grams!

8 ounces cold water

4 ice cubes

2 heaping tablespoons low-carb vanilla protein powder

¾ cup pineapple chunks

1. Place all the ingredients in a blender and blend to your preferred consistency.

Step One = No
Step Two = Yes (18 grams net carb, or one 11–20 gram carb serving)
Step Three = Yes (18 grams net carb, or one 11–20 gram carb serving)

ORANGE DREAMSICLE SMOOTHIE

Steps Two and Three
Start to finish: 2 minutes
Serves: 1

This citrus-based shake can be used as your first-thing-in-the-morning "pre-exercise fueler" or even in place of a large breakfast. It provides a refreshing wake-up on a warm summer morning!

8 ounces cold water
4 ice cubes
2 heaping tablespoons low-carb vanilla protein powder
1 peeled orange, membrane and seeds removed

1. Place all the ingredients in a blender and blend to your preferred consistency.

Step One = No
Step Two = Yes (18 grams net carb, or one 11–20 gram carb serving)
Step Three = Yes (18 grams net carb, or one 11–20 gram carb serving)

MIXED BERRY SMOOTHIE

Steps Two and Three
Start to finish: 2 minutes
Serves: 1

With two different berries, creamy vanilla, and the refreshing icy texture, this shake tastes almost too good to contain just 18 grams net carb! It will leave you feeling healthy, happy, and oh so cool.

MIXED BERRY SMOOTHIE (CONTINUED)

8 ounces cold water

4 ice cubes

2 heaping tablespoons low-carb vanilla protein powder

⅓ cup blueberries

3 strawberries, hulled

1. Place all the ingredients in a blender and blend to your preferred consistency.

Step One = No
Step Two = Yes (18 grams net carb, or one 11–20 gram carb serving)
Step Three = Yes (18 grams net carb, or one 11–20 gram carb serving)

CHOCOLATE-STRAWBERRY SMOOTHIE

Steps Two and Three

Start to finish: 2 minutes

Serves: 1

It doesn't get better than chocolate and strawberries! Either fresh or frozen berries will do the trick.

8 ounces cold water

4 ice cubes

2 heaping tablespoons low-carb chocolate protein powder

6 strawberries, hulled

1. Place all the ingredients in a blender and blend to your preferred consistency.

Step One = No
Step Two = Yes (18 grams net carb, or one 11–20 gram carb serving)
Step Three = Yes (18 grams net carb, or one 11–20 gram carb serving)

INSTANT ESPRESSO CHILLER

Steps One, Two, and Three
Start to finish: 2 minutes
Serves: 1

Iced coffee was popular long before trendy coffee bars began to dot our cities. Try this pick-me-up at midday or anytime you can use a little lift.

1 tablespoon instant coffee
   powder
½ cup cold water
½ cup ice cubes
2 individual serving packets
   sucralose or stevia

1. Combine all the ingredients in a blender and blend until smooth.

   Step One = Yes (neutral)
   Step Two = Yes (neutral)
   Step Three = Yes (neutral)

DARK CHOCOLATE DREAMER

Steps One, Two, and Three
Start to finish: 2 minutes
Serves: 1

Similar to hot cocoa, this hot coffee drink is a delicious treat on a cold winter day, even when you haven't come off the ski slopes.

6 ounces hot brewed coffee
⅓ cup half-and-half or
   unsweetened soymilk
½ ounce dark chocolate,
   chopped
Dollop of light whipped cream
   (chocolate-flavored, if
   preferred)

1. Pour the hot coffee into a mug and set aside.
2. Heat the half-and-half and dark chocolate together in a saucepan over low heat until melted and smooth, stirring constantly.
3. Pour into the coffee and serve topped with whipped cream.

Step One = Yes (5-gram net carb "Counter")
Step Two = Yes (5 grams net carb)
Step Three = Yes (5 grams net carb)

CRANBERRY SPRITZER

Steps One, Two, and Three
Start to finish: 1 minute
Serves: 1

This drink will wake you up and cool you down on a summertime afternoon. To dress it up, you can replace the ice cubes with a few frozen cranberries and serve in a frosted martini glass.

Ice cubes (optional)
4 ounces diet cranberry juice cocktail (2 grams net carb in 8 ounces)
Juice of ½ lemon
8 ounces lemon-lime-flavored seltzer
Sucralose or stevia

1. Fill a 20-ounce tumbler with your desired quantity of ice, or frost a martini glass.
2. Pour in the cranberry juice and lemon juice. Add the seltzer. Stir, taste, and add sweetener as desired.

Step One = Yes (neutral)
Step Two = Yes (neutral)
Step Three = Yes (neutral)

BERRY DREAMER

Steps Two and Three
Start to finish: 2 minutes
Serves: 1

Not quite a smoothie and not quite a spritzer, this drink is reminiscent of an old-fashioned ice-cream soda. Consider it the best of both worlds.

1 cup ice
2 ounces light cream or half-and-half
¼ cup berries of choice
4 ounces berry-flavored seltzer
1 sprig fresh mint, for garnish (optional)

1. In a blender, mix together the ice, cream, and berries until smooth and creamy.
2. Pour into a tall tumbler or martini glass and stir in the seltzer.
3. Garnish with a sprig of mint, if desired.

Step One = No
Step Two = Yes (5 grams net carb)
Step Three = Yes (5 grams net carb)

GINGER CHAI REFRESHER

Steps One, Two, and Three
Start to finish: 30 minutes
Serves: 4

Traditional to India, the spiced tea called chai, with its cardamom, cloves, cinnamon, and pepper, is now sold in most American coffee and tea shops. This is a cold, dairy-free version of the exotic original.

GINGER CHAI REFRESHER (CONTINUED)

4 chai tea bags

3 cups boiling water

Ice

1 liter diet ginger ale

4 cinnamon sticks, for garnish
(optional)

1. Place the tea bags in a teapot. Pour the boiling water over the tea bags and brew for 10 minutes. Remove and discard the tea bags and let cool completely.
2. Add your desired quantity of ice to four beverage glasses. Pour ¾ cup of cooled tea into each glass. Top with the ginger ale and garnish each glass with a cinnamon stick.

Step One = Yes (neutral)
Step Two = Yes (neutral)
Step Three = Yes (neutral)

MIRACLE MOJITO

Steps One, Two, and Three
Start to finish: 3 minutes
Serves: 1

This mojito recipe includes the option of adding an ounce of vodka. Liquors such as vodka, gin, scotch, and whiskey do not significantly increase a recipe's carb content. (Check with your physician regarding the use of alcohol in regard to any medications or medical conditions.)

2 sprigs fresh mint

1 tablespoon lime juice

1 ounce vodka (optional)

Ice

2 ounces diet cranberry-
raspberry cocktail (2 grams
net carb in 8 ounces)

4 ounces seltzer

Lime slice, for garnish

1. Remove the mint leaves from one sprig and place in the bottom of a glass with lime juice and vodka (if using).
2. Muddle the mint leaves slightly to infuse the mint flavor.

(CONTINUES)

MIRACLE MOJITO (CONTINUED)

3. Fill a glass halfway with ice and pour in the cranberry-raspberry cocktail. Top with the seltzer.

4. Garnish with the rest of the mint and the slice of lime.

Step One = Yes (neutral)
Step Two = Yes (neutral)
Step Three = Yes (neutral)

APPEECTIZERS

○ Stuffed Jalapeños   110
○ Mushrooms Stuffed with Three Cheeses   111
○ Grilled Portobellos   112
○ Pesto Cherry Tomatoes   113
○ Crab-Stuffed Tomatoes   114
○ Avocado Tomatoes   115
○ Miracle Guacamole   116
○ Edamame-Feta Spread   117
○ Spinach Party Dip   118
○ Dijon Deviled Eggs   119
○ Smoked Salmon with Herb Sauce   120
○ Chicken Quesadillas   121
○ Ham and Pickle Spirals   122
○ Mini Meat Loaves   123
○ Savory Lettuce Bowls   124
○ Cocktail Sauce   125

STUFFED JALAPEÑOS

Steps One, Two, and Three
Prep: 15 minutes
Start to finish: 60 minutes
Serves: 8 (3 jalapeños/serving)

The intense "heat" from the seeds in jalapeños can irritate a cook's fingers. Consider wearing latex gloves during preparation and be sure to avoid touching your eyes afterward. These little packages are well worth the extra caution!

24 large jalapeños
Cooking oil spray
1 pound 85–93% lean ground beef
Salt and pepper
16 ounces light cream cheese, at room temperature
1 cup shredded light Cheddar cheese

1. Preheat the oven to 350°F.
2. Cut the stems off the jalapeños and slice down one side to remove the seeds and veins. Set aside.
3. Coat a large skillet with cooking oil spray. Cook the ground beef over medium-high heat, breaking it apart and stirring frequently until browned, 7 to 8 minutes. Drain any excess fat, season with salt and pepper to taste, and let cool.
4. Combine the cream cheese, Cheddar cheese, and beef in a large bowl.
5. Coat a cookie sheet with cooking oil spray. Stuff the mixture into the peppers, using a small spoon, and arrange the peppers on the cookie sheet.
6. Bake for 40 to 45 minutes, until the peppers are soft. Serve immediately.

Step One = Yes (neutral)
Step Two = Yes (neutral)
Step Three = Yes (neutral)

MUSHROOMS STUFFED WITH THREE CHEESES

Steps One, Two, and Three
Start to finish: 28 minutes
Serves: 8 (3 mushrooms/serving)

A yummy version of the classic stuffed mushroom, this appetizer dresses up any party. Fresh basil and sun-dried tomatoes add pizzazz and color to the mushroom caps.

24 large mushrooms
¼ cup olive oil
8 sun-dried tomatoes (not oil-packed)
1 cup part-skim ricotta cheese
½ cup shredded Monterey Jack cheese
¾ cup well washed and finely chopped fresh spinach
1 tablespoon chopped fresh basil
¼ teaspoon salt
¼ teaspoon black pepper
2 cloves garlic, minced
¼ cup grated Parmesan cheese

1. Preheat the oven to 350°F.
2. Wipe the mushrooms clean with a paper towel and discard the stems. Brush the mushroom caps with olive oil and arrange, cap side up, in a shallow baking pan. Bake for 10 minutes.
3. Remove the mushrooms from the oven and drain off the liquid. Place the caps on a plate to cool, cap side down.
4. Increase the oven temperature to 450°F.
5. Cover the sun-dried tomatoes with boiling water and let stand for 10 minutes. Then, drain and chop the tomatoes.
6. Combine the tomatoes, ricotta and Monterey Jack cheeses, spinach, basil, salt, pepper, and garlic in a medium bowl.
7. Fill the caps with the tomato mixture and sprinkle with the grated Parmesan. Bake the mushrooms for 8 to 10 minutes, until lightly browned. Serve hot.

Step One = Yes (neutral)
Step Two = Yes (neutral)
Step Three = Yes (neutral)

GRILLED PORTOBELLOS

Steps One, Two, and Three
Start to finish: 30 minutes
Serves: 4 (as an appetizer)

When you grill portobello mushrooms, develop a hearty, earthy flavor that some say is similar to that of grilled steak—without the meat! This is a great appetizer for vegetarians and meat eaters alike.

4 portobello mushroom caps, wiped off with a paper towel
Olive oil
1 green bell pepper, seeded and chopped
1 red bell pepper, seeded and chopped
½ medium onion, chopped
1 clove garlic, minced
½ cup light Italian dressing or balsamic vinaigrette
½ teaspoon salt (if desired)
½ teaspoon black pepper
¼ cup grated Parmesan cheese

1. Brush the mushroom caps with the olive oil and set aside.
2. In a mixing bowl, mix together all the remaining ingredients
3. Place one-quarter of the spread over the gill side of each mushroom cap.
4. Heat your grill. Lightly oil the grill grate. Place the mushrooms over indirect medium heat, cover, and cook for 15 to 20 minutes.

Step One = Yes (neutral)
Step Two = Yes (neutral)
Step Three = Yes (neutral)

PESTO CHERRY TOMATOES

Steps One, Two, and Three
Prep: 45 minutes
Start to finish: 45 minutes
Serves: 6 (5 tomatoes/serving)

Each of these tasty "cherry bombs" is packed with the rich flavor of fresh herbs infused into soft cheese. Serve them at room temperature for the creamiest texture and fullest flavor.

30 large cherry tomatoes
¾ cup firmly packed fresh basil leaves
¾ cup firmly packed fresh flat-leaf parsley leaves
½ cup pine nuts, toasted
1 large clove garlic, quartered
⅛ teaspoon black pepper
2 tablespoons olive oil
4 ounces soft or mild goat cheese or feta cheese, crumbled (about 1 cup)

1. Slice the top off each tomato (about one-quarter of each tomato). Cut a thin slice off the bottom of each tomato so it stands level. Using a melon baller, scoop and discard the tomato pulp. Place the tomatoes upside down on a paper towel to drain.
2. To make the pesto, combine the basil, parsley, pine nuts, garlic, and pepper in a blender or food processor and blend until creamy. Add the oil and pulse until well mixed.
3. Transfer to a small bowl and gently stir in the cheese.
4. Spoon the pesto mixture into a small zippered plastic bag. Seal the bag, snip a small hole in one corner, and squeeze the pesto into the scooped-out tomatoes. Arrange the tomatoes on a serving plate. Can be served chilled or at room temperature.

Step One = Yes (neutral)
Step Two = Yes (neutral)
Step Three = Yes (neutral)

CRAB-STUFFED TOMATOES

Steps One, Two, and Three
Prep: 15 minutes
Start to finish: 15 minutes
Serves: 4

These tomatoes make an excellent lunch entrée as well as a substantial appetizer. The delicate flavor of crabmeat combined with the light sweetness of bell peppers make this pretty dish a real taste treat.

4 large tomatoes
¾ pound crabmeat
½ yellow bell pepper, seeded and chopped
½ red bell pepper, seeded and chopped
½ green bell pepper, seeded and chopped
½ cup light mayonnaise
¼ cup finely chopped red onion
2 tablespoons light sour cream
Juice of 1 lemon
¼ teaspoon salt
¼ teaspoon black pepper
4 lemon wedges, to serve

1. Slice the top off each tomato (about one-quarter of each tomato). Scoop out the pulp with a melon baller, reserving about 1 cup of seedless pulp. Set aside. Place the tomatoes upside down on a paper towel to drain.
2. Chop the reserved tomato pulp. Mix with the crabmeat, peppers, mayonnaise, onion, sour cream, lemon juice, salt, and pepper in a medium bowl.
3. Fill each tomato with about ⅔ cup of the crab mixture. Chill until ready to serve. Serve each with a lemon wedge.

Step One = Yes (neutral)
Step Two = Yes (neutral)
Step Three = Yes (neutral)

AVOCADO TOMATOES

Steps One, Two, and Three
Start to finish: 20 minutes
Serves: 4

At the height of summer, when tomatoes are at their most succulent and flavorful, this combination is sublime. The avocado adds a rich creaminess to the bright flavors of the tomato, and sunflower seeds add a little crunch.

4 large ripe tomatoes
2 large ripe avocados, peeled, pitted, and diced
1 cup diced celery
1 grated sweet onion (such as Vidalia)
3 tablespoons olive oil
1 tablespoon lemon juice
2 tablespoons hulled sunflower seeds
½ teaspoon salt, or to taste
⅛ teaspoon black pepper
1 tablespoon light mayonnaise
1 tablespoon minced fresh parsley
Sour cream, preferably light

1. Slice the top off each tomato (about one-quarter of each tomato). Scoop out the pulp with a melon baller, reserving about 1 cup of seedless pulp. Place the tomatoes upside down on a paper towel to drain. Meanwhile, drain the pulp through a sieve.
2. Combine the avocado, celery, onion, and olive oil. Toss to coat. Add the lemon juice and toss again. Add the remaining ingredients, including the reserved tomato pulp.
3. Spoon the avocado mixture lightly into the tomato cups. Top each with a dollop of sour cream.

Step One = Yes (neutral)
Step Two = Yes (neutral)
Step Three = Yes (neutral)

MIRACLE GUACAMOLE

Steps One, Two, and Three

Prep: 5 minutes

Start to finish: 1 hour 5 minutes (including chilling time)

Makes: 1 cup guacamole (½ cup/serving)

A perfectly ripe avocado yields slightly to pressure but isn't so soft that it leaves an imprint. An excellent source of monounsaturated fats, the avocado has a delicate flavor and smooth texture that make guacamole a perfect accompaniment to Chicken Fajitas (page 173).

1 ripe avocado, halved and pitted

½ small onion, grated

1 medium ripe tomato, chopped

2 teaspoons lemon juice

1 tablespoon fresh cilantro, chopped

Hot chili sauce (optional)

1. Use a spoon to scoop the avocado flesh into a small bowl.
2. Mash until soft but still a little lumpy.
3. Stir in the onion, tomato, lemon juice, and cilantro, plus hot sauce to taste.
4. Chill for 1 hour to allow the flavors to blend.

Step One = Yes (neutral)
Step Two = Yes (neutral)
Step Three = Yes (neutral)

EDAMAME-FETA SPREAD

Steps One, Two, and Three
Prep: 20 minutes
Start to finish: 1 hour
Makes: 1³/₄ cups (4 servings)

In their green state, edamame soybeans are plump, firm, and delicious. You can often find them fresh in the produce section, but the frozen version is just as good.

2 cups frozen shelled edamame
2 cloves garlic, peeled
½ cup crumbled feta cheese
2½ tablespoons lemon juice
2 tablespoons olive oil
¼ teaspoon onion powder
¼ teaspoon salt
¼ teaspoon black pepper

1. Bring a large saucepan of lightly salted water to a boil.
2. Add the edamame and garlic and return to a boil. Lower the heat to medium-low and simmer until the edamame are tender, about 7 minutes. Drain, reserving ½ cup of the cooking liquid.
3. Place the cooked edamame, the remaining ingredients, and ¼ cup of the reserved cooking liquid in a food processor or blender. Mix until completely smooth. Transfer to a medium serving bowl.
4. Cover the bowl with plastic wrap and leave at room temperature for 30 minutes to allow the flavors to blend.
5. Stir the dip before serving and add the remaining ¼ cup of reserved cooking liquid to thin, if needed. Serve at room temperature with a variety of cut-up raw, crunchy vegetables such as celery, broccoli, cauliflower, and peppers.

Step One = Yes (neutral)
Step Two = Yes (neutral)
Step Three = Yes (neutral)

SPINACH PARTY DIP

Steps One, Two, and Three
Start to finish: 2 hours 10 minutes (including chilling time)
Makes: about 3 cups dip (1/2 cup/serving)

This reliable standby is a crowd pleaser at parties. Serve it with raw veggies such as celery sticks, broccoli, and cauliflower florets, or red, orange, and green bell pepper strips for a colorful yet "neutral" appetizer.

12 ounces 1% low-fat cottage cheese

1 (10-ounce) package frozen chopped spinach, thawed

1 (8-ounce) can water chestnuts, drained and chopped

1/2 cup light sour cream

1/4 cup dried vegetable soup mix

2 teaspoons grated onion

1/4 teaspoon salt

1. In hand mixer or food processor, blend the cottage cheese until smooth and creamy. Transfer to a large mixing bowl.
2. Drain the thawed spinach in a colander, pressing it to free its excess liquid. Wrap the spinach in paper towels and press to remove all excess liquid.
3. Add the spinach, water chestnuts, sour cream, soup mix, onion, and salt to the cheese; stir well.
4. Cover and chill for at least 2 hours. Serve with a platter of neutral veggies.

Step One = Yes (neutral)
Step Two = Yes (neutral)
Step Three = Yes (neutral)

DIJON DEVILED EGGS

Steps One, Two, and Three
Start to finish: 35 minutes
Makes: 2 dozen egg halves (2 halves/serving)

Think of an egg as nature's perfect little nutrition package, full of high-quality protein, vitamin B$_{12}$, selenium, and iron. Recent research has helped loosen restrictions on eggs and even heart associations have okayed 5 yokes per week.

1 dozen hard-boiled eggs
2 tablespoons Dijon mustard
6 tablespoons light mayonnaise
1 tablespoon minced onion
¼ teaspoon celery seeds
¼ teaspoon Tabasco sauce
¼ teaspoon salt
⅛ teaspoon black pepper
1 teaspoon paprika

1. Peel the eggs and rinse under water, removing any pieces of shell. Dry with a paper towel.
2. Using a sharp knife, slice the eggs in half lengthwise. Gently remove the yolk halves and place in a small mixing bowl. Arrange the egg whites, cut side up, on a serving platter.
3. With a fork, mash the yolks until crumbly. Add the mustard, mayonnaise, onion, celery seeds, Tabasco, salt, and pepper, and mix well.
4. Spoon the yolk mixture into the egg white halves. Sprinkle with paprika.

Step One = Yes (neutral)
Step Two = Yes (neutral)
Step Three = Yes (neutral)

Tip: To hard-boil eggs, in a medium saucepan, cover the eggs with cold water to a depth of 1 inch above the eggs. Add 1 teaspoon of white vinegar and a pinch of salt. Bring the water to a boil over high heat. Cover, remove from the heat, and let sit for 15 minutes. Drain the hot water from the pan and run cold water over the eggs.

SMOKED SALMON WITH HERB SAUCE

Steps One, Two, and Three
Prep: 10 minutes
Start to finish: 2 hours
Serves: 4 (2 pieces/serving)

The contrast of smoky salmon with the fresh lemony flavor of the white sauce makes for a great appetizer. Serve chilled with fancy toothpicks on the side.

½ **cup light mayonnaise**
¼ **cup light sour cream**
2 **teaspoons lemon juice**
1 **teaspoon snipped fresh thyme**
1 **teaspoon chopped fresh dill**
8 **ounces smoked salmon, cut into 8 pieces**
1 **lemon, cut into 8 slices**
1 **tablespoon finely chopped red onion**
1 **tablespoon finely chopped flat-leaf parsley**

1. To make the dipping sauce, in a small bowl, stir together the mayonnaise, sour cream, lemon juice, thyme, and dill. Cover and chill for at least 1 hour.
2. To serve, arrange salmon and lemon alternately on a platter.
3. Sprinkle with the red onion and parsley. Serve with the dipping sauce in a bowl on the side.

Step One = Yes (neutral)
Step Two = Yes (neutral)
Step Three = Yes (neutral)

CHICKEN QUESADILLAS

Steps One, Two, and Three
Prep: 15 minutes
Start to finish: 18 minutes
Serves: 6 as an appetizer (1 tortilla/serving)

Packed with protein, monounsaturated "good" fat, and flavor, these fun little triangles make great party food. They keep a team of hungry kids happy as well.

Cooking oil spray
6 low-carb tortillas (with 5 grams or less net carb per tortilla)
1½ cups shredded light Cheddar cheese
1½ cups grilled chicken breast, cut into cubes
2 avocados, peeled, pitted, and chopped
¾ cup prepared salsa
½ cup light sour cream

1. Preheat the oven to 200°F.
2. Coat a heavy skillet with nonstick cooking oil spray and place over medium heat.
3. Lightly coat one side of a tortilla with cooking oil spray and place, oil side down, in the skillet.
4. Sprinkle ¼ cup of cheese evenly over one-half of the surface of the tortilla.
5. Top with ¼ cup of chicken, ¼ cup of avocado, and a heaping tablespoon of salsa.
6. Fold the other half of the tortilla over the ingredients and cook for 1 to 2 minutes per side, or until the cheese melts and the tortilla is browned. Place the cooked quesadilla on a baking tray in a warm oven. Repeat with the five remaining tortillas.
7. Cut each tortilla into three small wedges. Serve warm with a dollop of sour cream and the remaining salsa.

Step One = Yes (5-gram net carb "Counter")
Step Two = Yes (5 grams net carb)
Step Three = Yes (5 grams net carb)

HAM AND PICKLE SPIRALS

Steps One, Two, and Three
Start to finish: 15 minutes
Makes: a 9-inch party tray of appetizers

This "old school" hors d'oeuvre that's been around since the '50s is as easy to make now as it was then! The spirals make a festive platter arranged with curly parsley, olives, and cherry tomatoes.

1 (1-quart) jar whole kosher dill pickles
2 (8-ounce) packages light cream cheese, at room temperature
¾ pound thinly sliced deli ham

1. Drain the pickles, pat dry with paper towels, and set aside on paper towels.
2. Gently spread the cream cheese on two slices of ham, being careful not to tear the ham.
3. Roll up a pickle in one cheese-spread ham slice, place atop the other cheese-spread ham slice, and roll up again.
4. With a sharp knife, slice the pickle log into 1-inch pieces. Repeat until you reach your desired quantity of roll-ups.
5. Arrange on a serving tray, cover, and refrigerate for at least 2 hours before serving.

Step One = Yes (neutral food)
Step Two = Yes (neutral food)
Step Three = Yes (neutral food)

MINI MEAT LOAVES

Steps One, Two, and Three
Start to finish: 40 minutes
Serves: 8 (1 mini meat loaf/serving)

The secret to these meat loaves is the use of three kinds of ground meat. Baking the loaves in a muffin tin keeps them uniform in shape and size.

Cooking oil spray
8 ounces 85–93% lean ground beef
8 ounces lean ground pork
8 ounces lean ground turkey breast
1 large egg, beaten lightly
½ cup quick-cooking oats
¼ cup chopped fresh parsley
½ cup low-sugar ketchup
¼ cup half-and-half
1 medium onion, finely chopped
1 medium green bell pepper, seeded and finely chopped
¾ teaspoon salt
¼ teaspoon black pepper
2 tablespoons water
2 teaspoons Worcestershire sauce

1. Preheat the oven to 375°F. Coat the cups of an eight-muffin tin with cooking oil spray.
2. In a large bowl, mix the beef, pork, turkey, egg, oats, parsley, ¼ cup of the ketchup, and the half-and-half, onion, bell pepper, salt, and black pepper. Form the mixture into eight balls and press each meatball down to fill the bottom of each muffin cup.
3. In a small bowl, whisk together the remaining ketchup, the water, and the Worcestershire sauce. Spoon 1 teaspoon of this sauce over the top of each meat loaf. Fill any empty muffin tin cups halfway with water.
4. Place the muffin pan on a baking sheet and bake until the loaves' internal temperature reaches 160°F, 25 to 30 minutes. Pour off the fat before serving.

Step One = Yes (5-gram net carb "Counter")
Step Two = Yes (5 grams net carb)
Step Three = Yes (5 grams net carb)

SAVORY LETTUCE BOWLS

Steps One, Two, and Three

Start to finish: 45 minutes

Serves: 8 as an appetizer (2 lettuce cups/serving)

Curved lettuce leaves make these pretty packages easy-to-eat finger foods and keeps them neutral, too! They are a great start to a meal of Asian flavors.

Stir-fry sauce:
- **2 tablespoons cornstarch**
- **2 tablespoons soy sauce (low-sodium, if desired)**
- **1 tablespoon sesame or peanut oil**
- **1 cup water**

- **1 head Boston lettuce**
- **1 tablespoon peanut oil**
- **2 cloves garlic, minced**
- **2 teaspoons minced fresh ginger**
- **3 bell peppers (combine red, yellow, and/or green for color), seeded and chopped**
- **1 pound 85–93% lean beef or lean ground turkey**

1. To prepare the sauce, in a small bowl whisk together the cornstarch, soy sauce, oil, and water until smooth. Set aside.
2. Remove eight small bowl-shaped leaves from the lettuce; rinse, dry with towels, and set aside.
3. Heat the peanut oil in a large nonstick skillet over medium-high heat. Cook the garlic and ginger for 1 minute, stirring constantly. Stir in the peppers and cook for 3 minutes. Remove the peppers and set aside. In the same skillet, brown the ground beef for 8 to 10 minutes, breaking the meat apart with a fork to create a smooth consistency. Drain the fat.
4. Add the peppers to the browned meat. Stir in the stir-fry sauce and cook for 1 minute, or until thickened.
5. Spoon $1/3$ cup of the beef mixture into each lettuce cup and serve.

> **Step One** = Yes (neutral)
> **Step Two** = Yes (neutral)
> **Step Three** = Yes (neutral)

COCKTAIL SAUCE

Steps One, Two, and Three

Start to finish: 2 minutes

Makes: 1/2 cup (four 2-tablespoon servings)

Chilled, cooked shrimp get a kick from a dollop of cocktail sauce. Two tablespoons of regular cocktail sauce, made with regular ketchup, is too high in carbohydrate. Enjoy this lower-carb version as a spicy dip for a favorite appetizer.

½ cup low-sugar ketchup
(containing 5 grams or less
net carb)

2 teaspoons prepared
horseradish

2 drops Tabasco sauce

½ teaspoon lemon juice

1. Whisk together all the ingredients. Store in the refrigerator in a container with a tight-fitting lid.

   Step One = Yes (neutral in a 2-tablespoon serving)
   Step Two = Yes (neutral in a 2-tablespoon serving)
   Step Three = Yes (neutral in a 2-tablespoon serving)

SALADS

O Pear and Goat Cheese Salad   128

O Snap Pea Salad   129

O Cauliflower Salad   130

O Baby Artichoke Salad   131

O Broccoli Rabe Salad with Orzo   132

O Tabbouleh with Artichokes   133

O Caribbean Watermelon Salad   134

O Italian Garden Salad   135

O Melon and Ricotta Salad   136

O Mesclun and Sweet Potato Salad   137

O Turkey Waldorf Salad   139

O Turkey Salad with Pistachios and Grapes 140

O My Favorite Cobb Salad   141

O Pantry-Ready Tuna Niçoise   142

O Asian Shrimp Salad   143

O Shrimp Salad with Fruit   144

PEAR AND GOAT CHEESE SALAD

Steps Two and Three
Start to finish: 20 minutes
Serves: 4

Sometimes less is more. This very simple yet elegant salad adds a unique touch to the start of any meal. Roasting the walnuts intensifies their flavor.

½ cup walnuts
⅓ cup olive oil
2 tablespoons lemon juice
6 cups romaine lettuce
1 pear, preferably Bosc, cored and thinly sliced
4 ounces goat cheese
Salt and pepper

1. Preheat the oven to 300°F.
2. Spread the walnuts on a baking tray and bake until fragrant and lightly browned, 8 to 10 minutes. Cool, chop coarsely, and set aside.
3. In a small bowl, whisk together the oil and lemon juice.
4. Place the lettuce and pear slices in a salad bowl. Season with salt and pepper, add the dressing, and toss.
5. Divide among four plates, sprinkle the cheese and walnuts on top, and serve.

Step One = No
Step Two = Yes (5 grams net carb)
Step Three = Yes (5 grams net carb)

SNAP PEA SALAD

Steps One, Two, and Three
Start to finish: 10 minutes
Serves: 6 (1$\frac{1}{3}$ cups/serving)

Snap peas have an irresistible crunch and pair beautifully with the Asian-inspired dressing. Hoisin sauce is Chinese "barbecue sauce." A fragrant, pungent, and very distinctive addition, it can be found in the Asian foods section of your supermarket.

6 cups torn romaine lettuce

2 cups fresh snap peas, trimmed and halved crosswise

¼ cup sesame seeds

½ cup light Italian dressing

1 tablespoon hoisin sauce

1. In a large salad bowl, toss together the romaine and snap peas.
2. In a small pan over medium heat, stir the sesame seeds until toasted.
3. In a small bowl, whisk together the Italian dressing and hoisin sauce. Pour over the romaine mixture and toss to coat. Sprinkle the salad with the toasted sesame seeds.

Step One = Yes (neutral)
Step Two = Yes (neutral)
Step Three = Yes (neutral)

CAULIFLOWER SALAD

Steps Two and Three
Start to finish: 10 minutes
Serves: 4 (1 cup/serving)

Cauliflower is one of the unsung heroes of the nutrition world. Like broccoli and Brussels sprouts, this crucifer may help prevent certain cancers. The high fiber in this dish keeps you feeling full longer.

1 cup homemade (page 151) or canned chicken or vegetable broth (low-sodium, if desired)
10 ounces frozen cauliflower
10 ounces frozen peas
¼ cup light ranch dressing
¼ cup light sour cream
¼ teaspoon salt
½ teaspoon dried dill
1 cup peeled, diced cucumber

1. In a saucepan, bring the broth to a boil over medium-high heat. Add the cauliflower and peas, and return to a boil. Cover and cook for 5 to 7 minutes, until tender. Drain in a colander and let cool.
2. Whisk together the ranch dressing, sour cream, salt, and dill in a small bowl.
3. Combine the cauliflower mixture with the cucumber and dressing in a small bowl and toss until combined. Serve chilled.

Step One = No
Step Two = Yes (11 grams net carb, or one 11–20 gram carb serving)
Step Three = Yes (11 grams net carb, or one 11–20 gram carb serving)

BABY ARTICHOKE SALAD

Steps One, Two, and Three
Prep: 30 minutes
Start to finish: 2$^1/_2$ hours
Serves: 6

Baby artichokes lack the fuzzy choke in their center, so you can eat them with less mess. Look for them in the produce section of supermarkets in late spring when they are in high season.

12 baby artichokes
3 tablespoons lemon juice
3 tablespoons olive oil
¼ teaspoon salt
¼ teaspoon black pepper
2 large cloves garlic, minced
1 small bulb fennel, halved, cored, and thinly sliced
½ small red onion, finely chopped
1 cup halved cherry tomatoes

1. To prepare the artichokes, trim the stems and cut off the top quarter of each artichoke. Remove the outer leaves until you expose the lighter interior green parts. Cut the artichokes in half lengthwise. Brush the cut edges with some of the lemon juice.

2. In a large saucepan, boil enough water to cover the artichokes. Add the artichoke halves to the boiling water and cook for 12 to 15 minutes, or until tender. Drain in a colander and rinse with cold water. Drain again and place in a medium mixing bowl.

3. In a small bowl, whisk together the remaining lemon juice, olive oil, salt, pepper, and garlic to make the dressing.

4. Add the fennel, red onion, and cherry tomatoes, and to the artichokes. Pour the dressing over the vegetables and toss to coat.

5. Cover and chill at least 2 hours.

   Step One = Yes (neutral)
   Step Two = Yes (neutral)
   Step Three = Yes (neutral)

Broccoli Rabe Salad with Orzo

Steps Two and Three
Start to finish: 40 minutes
Serves: 4 ($3/4$ cup/serving)

Broccoli rabe has a pungent bite that brings flair to a meal. Often used in Italian recipes, it adds B vitamins and color to this healthful whole-grain dish.

¾ **cup whole wheat orzo**
1 **bunch broccoli rabe (about**
    1 **pound), rinsed, trimmed,**
    and chopped
2 **tablespoons extra-virgin olive**
    oil
2 **cloves garlic, minced**
2 **teaspoons chopped fresh**
    oregano
¼ **teaspoon salt**
¼ **teaspoon black pepper**
½ **cup crumbled blue cheese**
Lemon juice (optional)

1. Bring a large pot of salted water to a boil. Add the orzo and cook for 3 minutes.
2. Add the broccoli rabe to the pot and cook for 3 more minutes. Drain the mixture in a colander and gently press out as much water as possible.
3. Dry the pot, pour in the oil, and return to medium heat. Add the garlic and cook until golden brown, about 2 minutes.
4. Add the oregano, salt, pepper, broccoli rabe, and orzo. Cook, stirring, until heated through, about 3 minutes. Remove from the heat.
5. Stir in the blue cheese and lemon juice, if using. Serve warm or chilled.

Step One = No
Step Two = Yes (20 grams net carb, or one 11–20 gram carb serving)
Step Three = Yes (20 grams net carb, or one 11–20 gram carb serving)

TABBOULEH WITH ARTICHOKES

Steps Two and Three
Start to finish: 30 minutes
Serves: 6 (1 cup/serving)

The key to good tabbouleh (ta-BOO-lay) is to include more vegetables and herbs than bulgur. In Syria, where tabbouleh is king, they would double the parsley in this dish.

1 cup homemade (page 151) or canned chicken or vegetable broth (low-sodium, if desired)

1 cup uncooked bulgur

1 (6½-ounce) jar marinated artichoke hearts

3 medium tomatoes, chopped

2 green onions, chopped

⅓ cup chopped fresh parsley

3 tablespoons finely chopped fresh mint leaves

2 tablespoons lemon juice

⅛ teaspoon black pepper

1. In a medium saucepan, bring the broth to a boil. Add the bulgur, stir, cover tightly with a lid, and let stand for 15 to 20 minutes, or until the bulgur has doubled in size and the broth is absorbed.

2. Meanwhile, drain the artichoke hearts, reserving the liquid in a small bowl, and cut the artichokes in half.

3. Add the halved artichokes, tomatoes, green onions, parsley, and mint to the cooked bulgur.

4. Mix the lemon juice and pepper with the reserved artichoke liquid. Add to the bulgur mixture and toss to coat.

5. Serve immediately or cover and refrigerate until serving time.

Step One = No
Step Two = Yes (18 grams net carb, or one 11–20 gram carb serving)
Step Three = Yes (18 grams net carb or one 11–20 gram carb serving)

CARIBBEAN WATERMELON SALAD

Steps Two and Three

Start to finish: 10 minutes

Serves: 4 (1 cup/serving)

When you're tired of salads consisting of greens and the "same old, same old," try this extraordinary combination. The coconut in this island salad adds an element of surprise and the cilantro contrasts beautifully with the sweet watermelon.

2 tablespoons lemon juice

1 tablespoon sucralose or stevia

1½ cups diced, seeded watermelon

2½ cups diced cucumber

1 cup shredded fresh coconut

½ cup very finely chopped fresh cilantro

1. In a medium bowl, stir together the lemon juice and sweetener until it dissolves.
2. Add the watermelon, cucumber, coconut, and cilantro. Toss gently to combine.

Step One = No
Step Two = Yes (5 grams net carb)
Step Three = Yes (5 grams net carb)

ITALIAN GARDEN SALAD

Steps One, Two, and Three
Start to finish: 15 minutes
Serves: 8 (1 cup/serving)

Do your vegetable chopping on a Monday and you can use this salad for several meals during the week. Just remember to add the lettuce right before serving. The combination is full of great vitamins and antioxidants to boost your health and brain power.

1 cup fresh broccoli florets
1 cup fresh cauliflower florets
½ cup chopped celery
½ cup sliced red onion
¼ cup seeded and chopped
   green bell pepper
¼ cup seeded and chopped red
   bell pepper
½ cup bottled light Italian
   salad dressing
2 medium tomatoes, chopped
4 cups shredded romaine
   lettuce
¼ cup grated Parmesan cheese
¼ cup sliced black olives

1. In a large salad bowl, combine the broccoli, cauliflower, celery, onion, and peppers. Add the salad dressing and toss to coat. Cover and chill.
2. Just before serving, add the tomatoes and lettuce and toss to coat. Sprinkle the grated Parmesan cheese over all and garnish with the black olives.

Step One = Yes (neutral)
Step Two = Yes (neutral)
Step Three = Yes (neutral)

MELON AND RICOTTA SALAD

Steps Two and Three

Start to finish: 20 minutes

Serves: 4

Three kinds of melons and strawberries make this summer fruit salad a nice complement to grilled chicken or fish. You might also enjoy it as a light lunch.

1 (6-ounce) bag mixed baby greens, rinsed and dried

1 cup cubed and seeded watermelon

1 cup cubed honeydew

1 cup cubed cantaloupe

7 medium strawberries, hulled

2 cups low-fat cottage or ricotta cheese

1 teaspoon vanilla extract

1 individual serving packet sucralose or stevia (optional)

1. In a large mixing bowl, combine the greens, melons, strawberries.

2. In a small bowl, mix the cheese, vanilla, and sweetener.

3. Spoon the fruit and greens onto four salad plates. Top each with $\frac{1}{2}$ cup of the cheese mixture. Serve chilled.

Step One = No

Step Two = Yes (17 grams net carb, or one 11–20 gram carb serving)

Step Three = Yes (17 grams net carb, or one 11–20 gram carb serving)

MESCLUN AND SWEET POTATO SALAD

Steps One, Two, and Three
Start to finish: 40 minutes
Serves: 4

This unique salad can be a creative way to incorporate leftover ham from your holiday meal. The sweet potatoes and smoky ham complement each other and the goat cheese makes for a creamy, tangy contrast.

Cooking oil spray
1 medium sweet onion, chopped
1 medium sweet potato, peeled and cut into ½-inch slices
½ cup olive oil
½ teaspoon dried rosemary
¾ teaspoon salt
½ teaspoon black pepper
¾ pound ham steak, cut into cubes
2 tablespoons carb-free maple-flavored pancake syrup
3 tablespoons balsamic vinegar
5 ounces mesclun salad mix
4 ounces fresh goat cheese, crumbled

1. Preheat the oven to 450°F. Coat a rimmed cookie sheet with cooking oil spray.
2. Place the onion and sweet potato on the cookie sheet and toss with 2 tablespoons of the olive oil, all of the rosemary, ½ teaspoon of the salt, and ¼ teaspoon of the pepper. Shake the pan to spread the vegetables evenly. Roast until the vegetables start to become tender, about 20 minutes.
3. In a small bowl, toss the ham with the maple syrup. Push the vegetables on the baking sheet aside to make room for the ham and bake until the ham and onions are browned in places, about 10 minutes.
4. To make the vinaigrette, in a small bowl, whisk the remaining olive oil with the balsamic vinegar and the remaining ¼ teaspoon each of salt and pepper.
5. In a large bowl, toss the mesclun with ¼ cup of vinaigrette. Taste and correct the seasonings if you desire.

(CONTINUES)

6. Divide the mesclun among four plates. Top with the roasted vegetables and ham. Sprinkle with the goat cheese, drizzle with the remaining vinaigrette, and serve.

Step One = Yes (5-gram net carb "Counter")
Step Two = Yes (5 grams net carb)
Step Three = Yes (5 grams net carb)

TURKEY WALDORF SALAD

Steps Two and Three
Prep: 10 minutes
Start to finish: 70 minutes
Serves: 6

Adding turkey to a Waldorf salad provides a dose of heart-healthy protein for satiety, while the cabbage, apple, and walnuts pack lots of crunch!

¾ cup light ranch dressing

3 tablespoons apple cider vinegar

2 level tablespoons sucralose or stevia

½ teaspoon black pepper

1 (16-ounce) bag coleslaw mix

1 (1-ounce) bag shredded carrots

1 (9-ounce) package precooked carved turkey pieces, cut into ½-inch chunks, or 9 ounces turkey breast

1 apple, cored and cut into ½-inch chunks

¾ cup chopped walnuts

1. In a small bowl, whisk together the ranch dressing, vinegar, sweetener, and pepper; set aside.
2. Combine the coleslaw mix, carrots, turkey, apple, and walnuts in a large bowl. Drizzle the salad dressing over the top and toss well to combine. Refrigerate for at least 1 hour before serving.

Step One = No
Step Two = Yes (13 grams net carb, or one 11–20 gram carb serving)
Step Three = Yes (13 grams net carb, or one 11–20 gram carb serving)

TURKEY SALAD WITH PISTACHIOS AND GRAPES

Steps Two and Three
Start to finish: 15 minutes
Serves: 4 (1 cup/serving)

The contrast of salted nuts and sweet grapes adds a unique taste sensation to this hearty salad meal.

1 pound roast turkey, cut into ½-inch cubes

3 stalks celery, chopped

12 seedless red grapes, sliced in half

1 small sweet onion, minced

½ cup shelled salted pistachios, chopped

⅓ cup light mayonnaise

⅓ cup light sour cream

¼ teaspoon salt

¼ teaspoon black pepper

1. Combine the turkey, celery, grapes, onion, and pistachios in a large mixing bowl.
2. Whisk the mayonnaise, sour cream, salt, and pepper in small bowl until creamy. Add the dressing to the turkey mixture, stir to coat, and refrigerate until ready to serve.

Step One = No
Step Two = Yes (5 grams net carb)
Step Three = Yes (5 grams net carb)

My Favorite Cobb Salad

Steps One, Two, and Three
Start to finish: 45 minutes
Serves: 4

Cobb salad originated in 1939 by the owner of Hollywood's Brown Derby restaurant, Bob Cobb. The uniqueness comes from chopping two varieties of lettuce and topping it with rows of cubed turkey, eggs, bacon, and avocado.

1 head romaine lettuce, rinsed, dried, and coarsely chopped

½ head Boston lettuce, rinsed, dried, and coarsely chopped

6 slices cooked turkey bacon, crumbled

1 pound boneless, skinless chicken breast, cooked and cubed

4 hard-boiled eggs, peeled and chopped

2 tomatoes, seeded and chopped

2 ripe avocados, peeled, pitted, and cut into ½-inch cubes

2 tablespoons chopped fresh chives

⅓ cup red wine vinegar

1 tablespoon Dijon mustard

Salt and pepper

⅔ cup olive oil

1 to 2 teaspoons sucralose or stevia

½ cup blue cheese crumbles

1. In a large salad bowl, toss together the lettuces.
2. In a small skillet, cook the turkey bacon until well browned. Drain on paper towels. Crumble the cooked bacon and set aside.
3. In a shallow serving bowl, arrange the salad, placing the lettuce in the bottom, and the chicken, bacon, eggs, tomato, and avocado in side-by-side rows over the greens. Garnish the salad with the chives.
4. In a small bowl, whisk together the vinegar, mustard, salt, pepper, and olive oil. Whisk until completely mixed. Stir in the blue cheese. Add the sweetener to taste, ½ teaspoon at a time. Serve the dressing separately or drizzle it over the entire salad.

Step One = Yes (neutral)
Step Two = Yes (neutral)
Step Three = Yes (neutral)

PANTRY-READY TUNA NIÇOISE

Steps One, Two, and Three
Start to finish: 15 minutes
Serves: 4

This recipe has been reconfigured to use pantry-ready canned tuna in place of traditional fresh tuna. Removing the potatoes from the original allows this delicious salad to remain a neutral food for all steps of the Metabolism Miracle program.

3 tablespoons red wine vinegar
2 tablespoons red wine
2 teaspoons Dijon mustard
¼ teaspoon sucralose or stevia
⅛ teaspoon salt
⅛ teaspoon black pepper
¼ cup olive oil
8 leaves Boston lettuce, rinsed and dried
2 (6-ounce) cans white tuna packed in oil
½ pound green beans, trimmed and steamed
1 bunch radishes, washed, trimmed, and sliced
4 hard-boiled eggs, peeled and quartered
16 pitted black olives

1. In a small bowl, whisk together the vinegar, wine, mustard, sweetener, salt, and pepper. Slowly drizzle in the olive oil, whisking continuously, until the mixture is evenly blended. Set aside.
2. On each of four salad plates, overlap two lettuce leaves side by side. For each serving, break up one-quarter of the tuna and place it in the center of the lettuce leaves. Arrange the green beans, radishes, egg quarters, and olives around the tuna in a decorative fashion.
3. To serve, drizzle the dressing over the salad arrangement.

Step One = Yes (neutral)
Step Two = Yes (neutral)
Step Three = Yes (neutral)

ASIAN SHRIMP SALAD

Steps Two and Three
Start to finish: 30 minutes
Serves: 8

The unique flavors and textures in this Asian-inspired salad make it as delicious as it is healthy. It's a nice change from typical mayonnaise-intense shrimp salad!

8 ounces frozen shelled edamame

2 navel oranges

8 ounces cooked medium shrimp

6 cups bagged coleslaw mix

2 green onions, trimmed and thinly sliced

⅓ cup rice vinegar

1 tablespoon hoisin sauce

2 teaspoons sucralose or stevia

1 tablespoon sesame oil

1 teaspoon soy sauce

Salt (optional)

½ cup olive oil

1. Cook the edamame per the package instructions. Drain, let cool, and set aside.
2. With a sharp knife, cut apart the orange sections, remove and discard the membranes, and place in a large bowl.
3. Add the cooked edamame, shrimp, coleslaw mix, and green onions.
4. In a small bowl, whisk together the rice vinegar, hoisin sauce, sweetener, sesame oil, soy sauce, and salt, if using. While whisking, add the olive oil.
5. Pour the dressing over the contents of large bowl and toss lightly to mix thoroughly. Serve chilled.

Step One = No
Step Two = Yes (5 grams net carb)
Step Three = Yes (5 grams net carb)

SHRIMP SALAD WITH FRUIT

Steps Two and Three
Start to finish: 15 minutes
Serves: 4

You can't find a prettier salad than this combination of bright fruit and tender shrimp. It reminds me of the salads offered at spas and resorts. Packed with healthful antioxidants and omega-3 fats, it will help to keep your cardiovascular system young.

1 (5-ounce) package spring mix
   salad greens
½ pound cooked medium
   shrimp, peeled and cleaned
1 cup canned mandarin
   oranges, drained
1 ripe medium avocado, peeled,
   pitted, and sliced
1 cup sliced fresh strawberries
12 red seedless grapes, halved
¼ cup finely chopped Vidalia
   onion
Bottled balsamic vinaigrette, as
   desired

1. On each of four plates, arrange a small bed of chilled salad greens, shrimp, orange segments, avocado, strawberries, grapes, and onion.
2. Drizzle with the vinaigrette and serve chilled.

   Step One = No
   Step Two = Yes (17 grams net carb,
      or one 11–20 gram carb serving)
   Step Three = Yes (17 grams net carb,
      or one 11–20 gram carb serving)

SOUPS

○ Creamy Vegetable Soup   146

○ Easy French Onion Soup   147

○ Vegetable-Lentil Soup   148

○ Minestrone   149

○ Split Pea Soup in a Hurry   150

○ Chicken Stock   151

○ Egg Drop Soup   152

○ Hot and Sour Soup with Chicken   153

○ Chicken and Wild Rice Soup   154

○ Postholiday Turkey Soup   155

○ Manhattan-Style Clam Chowder   156

○ Lemony Scallop and Shrimp Soup   157

○ Creamy Shrimp Chowder   158

○ Mini Meatball Soup   159

○ Japanese Pork and Spinach Soup   160

CREAMY VEGETABLE SOUP

Steps Two and Three
Start to finish: 60 minutes
Serves: 6 (1 cup/serving)

Roasting the root vegetables before adding them to this soup brings out a caramelized sweetness that you can't get by simply simmering them. You'll taste the robust flavor in each cup of this hearty, healthy soup.

Cooking oil spray
2 medium carrots, peeled and chopped
1 medium sweet potato, peeled and cubed
1 medium parsnip, peeled and cubed
1 medium red onion, chopped
1 stalk celery, chopped
2 cloves garlic, thinly sliced
2 tablespoons olive oil
1 teaspoon dried dill
¼ teaspoon black pepper
2½ cups nonfat or low-fat milk
½ cup half-and-half
1 cup homemade (page 151) or canned chicken broth (low-sodium, if desired)
¼ cup whole wheat flour

Step One = No
Step Two = Yes (20 grams net carb, or one 11–20 gram carb serving)
Step Three = Yes (20 grams net carb, or one 11–20 gram carb serving)

1. Preheat the oven to 425°F. Coat the bottom of a 9- by 13-inch baking pan or a cookie sheet with cooking oil spray.

2. Place the carrots, sweet potato, parsnip, red onion, celery, and garlic in the baking pan and drizzle with 1 tablespoon of the olive oil. Sprinkle the vegetables with ½ teaspoon of the dill and ⅛ teaspoon of the black pepper. Toss to coat.

3. Cover with foil and bake for 20 minutes. Remove the foil, stir the vegetables, drizzle with the remaining tablespoon of olive oil. Bake uncovered for 20 minutes more, until the vegetables are tender. Remove from the oven and set aside.

4. Meanwhile, in a large saucepan, whisk together the milk, half-and-half, chicken broth, flour, and the remaining ½ teaspoon of dill and ⅛ teaspoon of pepper, until smooth without lumps. Stir continuously over medium heat until thickened and bubbly.

5. Add the roasted vegetables. Cook, stirring, for about 10 minutes more, until heated through.

EASY FRENCH ONION SOUP

Steps One, Two, and Three
Prep: 30 minutes
Start to finish: 30 minutes
Serves: 4 (1$\frac{1}{2}$ cups/serving)

It's the simplicity of this bistro fare that allows you to taste the sweet Vidalia onions and cheese in every spoonful of this popular soup with a low-carb spin.

2 teaspoons olive oil

1 teaspoon butter

2 large sweet Vidalia onions, quartered and finely chopped

3 (14½-ounce) cans beef broth (low-sodium, if desired)

⅛ teaspoon black pepper

4 slices lightly buttered low-carb toast (with 5 grams or less net carb per slice)

4 ounces shredded Swiss cheese

2 teaspoons grated Parmesan cheese

1. Heat the oil and butter in a Dutch oven or large saucepan over medium heat, until hot. Add the onions and cook for 15 to 20 minutes, stirring occasionally, until tender and browned. Stir in the broth and pepper. Bring to a boil, lower the heat to low, and simmer for 10 minutes.

2. Top each slice of buttered bread with 1 ounce of shredded Swiss cheese and sprinkle with ½ teaspoon of Parmesan cheese.

3. Microwave for 15 seconds, or until the Swiss cheese is melted.

4. Place the cheese toast on the bottom of each soup bowl, ladle the onion soup over the toast, and serve immediately.

Step One = Yes (5-gram net carb "Counter")
Step Two = Yes (5 grams net carb)
Step Three = Yes (5 grams net carb)

VEGETABLE-LENTIL SOUP

Steps Two and Three
Prep: 15 minutes
Start to finish: 4 hours 45 minutes (including slow-cook time)
Serves: 10 (1 cup/serving)

Lentils are the legume of choice in this classic soup. High in protein, fiber, iron, and potassium, lentils provide great nutrition on a tight budget. Slow-cooked to perfection, this soup is perfect to feed a larger group on a weekend night.

5 cups homemade or canned vegetable broth (low-sodium, if desired)
1 cup water
3 cups peeled, seeded, and cubed butternut squash
1 cup dried lentils, rinsed well
1 cup chopped fresh carrots
1 cup chopped onion
2 teaspoons minced garlic
1 teaspoon dried basil
1 (14½-ounce) can Italian diced tomatoes, undrained
1 (9-ounce) package frozen cut green beans (do not thaw)

1. In a 5-quart slow cooker, combine the broth, water, squash, lentils, carrots, onion, garlic, and basil. Cover and cook on LOW for 4 hours, or until the lentils are tender.
2. Stir in the tomatoes and frozen beans. Cover and cook on HIGH for 30 minutes, or until the beans are heated through.

Step One = No
Step Two = Yes (19 grams net carb, or one 11–20 gram carb serving)
Step Three = Yes (19 grams net carb, or one 11–20 gram carb serving)

Chocolate Cupcakes (page 275)

Vegetable Frittata (page 250)

Grilled Pork Kebabs (page 188)

Shrimp Salad with Fruit (page 144)

Ginger Flank Steak (page 179)

Roasted Sweet Potato "Fries" (page 229)

Vegetarian Pot Luck (page 196)

Chicken and Wild Rice Soup (page 154)

MINESTRONE

Steps Two and Three
Prep: 10 minutes
Start to finish: 55 minutes
Serves: 6 ($3/4$ cup/serving)

The bulgur in this minestrone adds fiber and flavor to a traditional Italian favorite. If you don't have these exact vegetables on hand, improvise with what you find in the refrigerator. Any and all neutral vegetables make welcome additions.

1 (14½-ounce) can vegetable broth (low-sodium, if desired)

1 cup water

¾ cup uncooked bulgur

1 (14½-ounce) can stewed tomatoes, undrained

½ medium onion, chopped

2 cloves garlic, minced

2 medium zucchini, halved and finely chopped

8 ounces frozen whole-kernel corn

1 cup canned navy beans, drained and rinsed

1 teaspoon dried oregano

1 teaspoon dried basil

1. In a nonstick Dutch oven over medium-high heat, bring the broth and water to a boil. Stir in the bulgur and tomatoes, and return to a boil. Lower the heat to medium, cover, and cook for 20 minutes.

2. Add the onion, garlic, zucchini, corn, beans, oregano, and basil. Mix well. Cover and cook over medium-low heat for 20 minutes, or until the bulgur and zucchini are tender.

Step One = No
Step Two = Yes (20 grams net carb, or one 11–20 gram carb serving)
Step Three = Yes (20 grams net carb, or one 11–20 gram carb serving)

SPLIT PEA SOUP IN A HURRY

Steps Two and Three
Prep: 20 minutes
Start to finish: 1 hour
Serves: 8 (1 cup/serving)

Turkey bacon adds a rich, smoky flavor to this hearty soup. It's a great meal for a cold winter's evening.

1 tablespoon olive oil

2 carrots, sliced

1 medium onion, finely chopped

2 cloves garlic, minced

6 cups homemade (page 151) or canned chicken or vegetable broth (low-sodium, if desired)

1 cup dried green split peas, rinsed

Ground pepper

4 slices turkey bacon, cooked and crumbled (optional)

1. Heat the oil in a Dutch oven or large pot over medium-high heat. Add the carrots, onion, and garlic. Cook, stirring, until softened, 8 to 10 minutes. Add the broth and split peas and bring to a boil. Lower the heat to low and simmer, partially covered, until the vegetables are tender and the split peas have broken down, 50 to 60 minutes. Season with pepper.

2. Meanwhile, cook the bacon in a small skillet over medium heat, stirring, until crisp, 3 to 5 minutes. Drain on paper towels and crumble into small pieces.

3. Ladle the soup into bowls and garnish with the bacon bits.

> **Step One** = No
> **Step Two** = Yes (19 grams net carb, or one 11–20 gram carb serving)
> **Step Three** = Yes (19 grams net carb, or one 11–20 gram carb serving)

CHICKEN STOCK

Steps One, Two, and Three
Prep: 1 hour
Start to finish: 5 hours
Serves: 8 (1 cup/serving)

You can never have enough chicken stock on hand. Making your own means you get the benefit of the succulent chicken meat for salads and sandwiches, along with the broth that makes a great base for so many soups and other recipes. I often freeze the stock to use in recipes I'll make in the next few weeks.

1 (5-pound) roasting chicken, halved or cut into serving portions

1 large yellow onion, quartered

3 carrots, peeled and halved

3 stalks celery with leaves, cut into thirds

4 sprigs fresh flat-leaf parsley

4 sprigs fresh thyme

4 sprigs fresh dill

3 peeled cloves garlic, cut in half crosswise

½ teaspoon black pepper

7 chicken bouillon cubes (low-sodium, if desired)

10 cups water

1. In a 5- to 6-quart stockpot, combine the chicken, onion, carrots, celery stalks, parsley, thyme, dill, garlic, pepper, and bouillon cubes. Add the 10 cups of water. Simmer uncovered for 4 hours.

2. Lift out the chicken and let cool on a plate, then refrigerate. (The chicken can be used on salads, in chicken salad, as sandwich meat, or in soup.)

3. Strain the remaining contents of the pot through a colander and discard the solids. Put the broth in 2-quart containers and chill overnight. Remove the fat that has hardened and risen to the top of the broth.

4. Refrigerate or freeze for future use.

Step One = Yes (neutral)
Step Two = Yes (neutral)
Step Three = Yes (neutral)

EGG DROP SOUP

Steps One, Two, and Three

Start to finish: 10 minutes

Serves: 4 (1 cup/serving)

With just four ingredients, this soup is a snap to make and very satisfying. Use homemade chicken stock (page 151) for the best flavor.

4 cups homemade (page 151) or canned chicken broth (low-sodium, if desired)

1 tablespoon low-sodium soy sauce

¼ cup chopped green onion

2 eggs, lightly beaten

1. Combine the broth, soy sauce, and green onion in a medium saucepan and bring to a boil.
2. Slowly pour the beaten eggs into the boiling broth. Stir while cooking for about 1 minute. Serve immediately.

Step One = Yes (neutral)
Step Two = Yes (neutral)
Step Three = Yes (neutral)

HOT AND SOUR SOUP WITH CHICKEN

Steps One, Two, and Three
Start to finish: 40 minutes
Serves: 4 (1¹/₂ cups/serving)

Use this soup as an accompaniment to the Shrimp Lo Mein (page 210) for a "take-in" night. Make the chicken stock on the weekend and you've got both the broth and the cooked chicken for this recipe early in the week. Convenience foods such as bagged coleslaw mix can save you a lot of time that would otherwise be spent chopping.

2 teaspoons peanut oil

8 ounces fresh mushrooms, stems removed, caps thinly sliced

2 cloves garlic, minced

28 ounces homemade (page 151) or canned chicken broth (low-sodium, if desired)

2 tablespoons rice vinegar

2 tablespoons soy sauce

½ teaspoon black pepper

8 ounces shredded cooked chicken

2 cups bagged coleslaw mix

1 tablespoon cornstarch

1 green onion, thinly sliced

1. Pour the peanut oil into a large saucepan. Cook the mushrooms and garlic over medium heat for about 5 minutes, stirring occasionally.

2. Add the broth, rice vinegar, soy sauce, and pepper. Bring to a boil. Stir in the chicken and coleslaw mix. Return to a boil. Lower the heat and simmer uncovered for 20 minutes.

3. Add the cornstarch to the soup mixture and gently whisk until smooth. Simmer for 5 minutes, or until slightly thickened. Remove from the heat and stir in the sesame oil.

4. Sprinkle with the green onion slices and serve.

Step One = Yes (neutral)
Step Two = Yes (neutral)
Step Three = Yes (neutral)

CHICKEN AND WILD RICE SOUP

Steps Two and Three
Start to finish: 60 minutes
Serves: 6

Using wild rice lowers the glycemic index and adds fiber and texture to this classic soup. Serve a satisfying bowlful to warm a chilly autumn night.

1 cup uncooked wild rice

4 cups homemade (page 151) or canned chicken broth (low-sodium, if desired)

1 tablespoon chopped fresh thyme, or 1 teaspoon dried, crushed

1 tablespoon chopped fresh dill, or 1 teaspoon dried

2 cloves garlic, minced

4 cups seeded and chopped tomatoes

12 ounces boneless skinless chicken breast, cooked and cubed

1 cup chopped zucchini

2 stalks celery, chopped

2 medium carrots, peeled and chopped

1 medium onion, chopped

½ teaspoon black pepper

1. Prepare the wild rice according to package directions and set aside.
2. Meanwhile, in a Dutch oven, combine the chicken broth, thyme, dill, and garlic. Bring to a boil.
3. Stir in the tomatoes, chicken, zucchini, onion, celery, carrots, and pepper, and return to a boil.
4. Lower the heat and simmer uncovered for 45 minutes, until the vegetables are soft.
5. Place ½ cup of cooked wild rice in each soup bowl.
6. Ladle the soup over the rice.

Step One = No
Step Two = Yes (17 grams net carb, or one 11–20 gram carb serving)
Step Three = Yes (17 grams net carb, or one 11–20 gram carb serving)

POSTHOLIDAY TURKEY SOUP

Steps One, Two, and Three
Start to finish: 2 hours (including simmering time)
Serves: 6 to 8

Thanksgiving leftovers don't stop with turkey salad or a turkey sandwich. This soup sports a trio of Thanksgiving herbs — thyme, rosemary, and sage. Feel free to substitute a green pepper for the red.

Turkey carcass
1 onion, peeled and left whole
2 cloves garlic, peeled and left whole
¼ teaspoon dried thyme
¼ teaspoon dried rosemary
¼ teaspoon dried sage
2 teaspoons poultry seasoning
½ cup white wine
2 tablespoons olive oil
2 carrots, peeled and chopped
2 stalks celery, chopped
1 onion, chopped
1 red bell pepper, seeded and chopped
Salt and pepper
2 to 3 cups turkey meat, cut into bite-size pieces
14 ounces homemade (page 151) or canned chicken broth (low-sodium, if desired)
2 tablespoons chopped fresh parsley

1. Put the turkey carcass and any leftover turkey bones in a large stockpot and cover with water. Add the onion, garlic, thyme, rosemary, sage, poultry seasoning, and white wine. Bring to a boil, lower the heat, and simmer uncovered for 1½ hours. Strain the broth into a bowl and set aside, reserving the turkey meat.

2. Meanwhile, in the empty stockpot, sauté the carrots, celery, onion, and red pepper in the olive oil until onions are translucent, 5 to 7 minutes. Season with salt and pepper. Add the strained broth and the chicken broth.

3. Add the turkey meat and parsley. Taste and adjust the seasonings. Simmer for 30 minutes and serve.

Step One = Yes (neutral, eliminate carrots for Step One)
Step Two = Yes (neutral)
Step Three = Yes (neutral)

MANHATTAN-STYLE CLAM CHOWDER

Steps Two and Three
Start to finish: 50 minutes
Serves: 4

My friends are divided over which is better, Manhattan-style clam chowder or its creamy New England cousin. I'm partial to Manhattan with its tangy tomato base and lower fat content. The health benefits of tomatoes include lycopene's antioxidant, anticancer properties.

2 (6½-ounce cans) minced or chopped clams

8 ounces bottled clam juice, or 1 cup homemade (page 151) or canned chicken broth

1 medium onion, chopped

2 stalks celery, chopped

1 medium carrot, chopped

2 tablespoons olive oil

¼ cup white wine

½ pound parsnips, peeled and cubed

1 teaspoon dried thyme, crushed

¼ teaspoon dried dill

¼ teaspoon black pepper

1 (14½-ounce) can diced tomatoes, undrained

1. Drain the clams, reserving their juice in a medium bowl. Set the clams aside.

2. Add the bottled clam juice (or broth, if using) to the reserved clam juice. Stir until blended and set aside.

3. In a large saucepan, sauté the onion, celery, and carrots in the olive oil until tender. Stir in the clam juice mixture. Add the parsnips, thyme, dill, and pepper. Bring to a boil. Lower the heat and simmer covered for 25 minutes. Stir in the tomatoes and clams. Return to a boil. Lower the heat and simmer uncovered for 10 minutes.

4. Ladle the chowder into four soup bowls and serve steaming hot.

Step One = No
Step Two = Yes (17 grams net carb, or one 11–20 gram carb serving)
Step Three = Yes (17 grams net carb, or one 11–20 gram carb serving)

LEMONY SCALLOP AND SHRIMP SOUP

Steps One, Two, and Three
Start to finish: 30 minutes
Serves: 4 (about 2 cups/serving)

A lovely combination of fresh flavors and bright ingredients. Be careful not to overcook this delicate soup as the shellfish should be tender, sweet, and succulent.

5 cups homemade (page 151) or canned chicken broth (low-sodium, if desired)

½ cup dry white wine

2 teaspoons finely grated lemon zest

¼ teaspoon black pepper

8 ounces fresh or frozen bay scallops, thawed, rinsed, and drained

8 ounces frozen cooked and cleaned small shrimp, thawed, rinsed, and drained

1 pound fresh asparagus spears, trimmed and cut into bite-size pieces

1 cup sliced fresh mushrooms

4 green onions, sliced

1 tablespoon lemon juice

1. In a large saucepan, combine the broth, wine, lemon zest, and pepper. Bring to a boil.
2. Add the scallops, shrimp, asparagus, mushrooms, and green onions. Return to a boil. Lower the heat and simmer uncovered for 20 minutes, or until the asparagus is tender and the shrimp and scallops are opaque.
3. Remove from the heat. Stir in the lemon juice and serve immediately.

Step One = Yes (neutral)
Step Two = Yes (natural)
Step Three = Yes (natural)

CREAMY SHRIMP CHOWDER

Steps One, Two, and Three
Start to finish: 30 minutes
Serves: 6

The use of cooked shrimp in this soup makes it a quick weeknight meal. You can serve this chowder over a base of warm soy noodles and you'll have a chowder with a "neutral" price tag.

1 tablespoon olive oil

2 stalks celery, chopped

1 medium onion, chopped

1 medium green pepper, seeded and chopped

2 (14½-ounce) cans diced tomatoes with basil, garlic, and oregano, undrained

8 ounces peeled and cooked small shrimp

½ cup light cream

1 cup homemade (page 151) or canned chicken or vegetable broth (low-sodium, if desired)

2 tablespoons chopped fresh dill

Salt and pepper

1. In a large saucepan over medium heat, heat the olive oil until hot. Add the celery, onion, and green pepper and cook until tender, about 7 minutes. Stir in the tomatoes and cook until warmed through, about 5 minutes.

2. Add the shrimp, cream, broth, and dill. Cook over medium heat for 5 to 7 minutes. Season with salt and pepper.

Step One = Yes (neutral)
Step Two = Yes (neutral)
Step Three = Yes (neutral)

MINI MEATBALL SOUP

Steps One, Two, and Three

Start to finish: at least 2 hours (minimum 1 hour to "set" meatball mixture [can be done day before]; 60 minutes cooking time)

Serves: 8 (1½ cups/serving)

Also known as "wedding" soup, a bowl of this hearty, flavorful concoction will keep you satisfied all evening. The spinach keeps its bright green color to make the soup particularly appealing.

1 pound 85–93% lean ground beef

½ pound ground pork

1 medium onion, finely chopped

2 cloves garlic, finely chopped

3 tablespoons Italian-style bread crumbs

1 teaspoon salt

½ teaspoon black pepper

1 large egg, beaten

3 tablespoons olive oil

6 cups canned beef broth (low-sodium, if desired)

3 cups water

1 cup fresh spinach, washed well and chopped

¾ teaspoon dried oregano

½ teaspoon dried basil

¾ teaspoon dried parsley

1. In a large bowl, mix the meats, ¼ cup of the chopped onion, half of the chopped garlic, and the bread crumbs, salt, pepper, and beaten egg. Cover and refrigerate for 1 hour (can be made the day before).

2. Heat 1 tablespoon of the olive oil in a medium stockpot over low heat. Add the remaining onion and garlic and cook, stirring frequently, for 5 to 7 minutes, until the onions are softened and golden in color.

3. Add the broth, water, spinach, dried oregano, basil, and parsley. Bring to a boil. Lower the heat to low and simmer for 20 minutes. Strain and keep warm.

4. Transfer the meat mixture to a food processor and blend until smooth, about 30 seconds. Shape into 1-inch meatballs and set aside.

5. Heat the remaining 2 tablespoons of olive oil in a large saucepan over medium-high heat. Cook the meatballs, turning frequently on

(CONTINUES)

all sides, until browned. Bring the broth to a simmer over medium heat. Add the meatballs and continue to simmer about 30 minutes.

Step One = Yes (neutral)
Step Two = Yes (neutral)
Step Three = Yes (neutral)

JAPANESE PORK AND SPINACH SOUP

Steps One, Two, and Three
Start to finish: 20 minutes
Serves: 4

Just five ingredients make this soup easy to whip up on a weeknight. All you need is twenty minutes.

5 cups homemade (page 151) or canned chicken or beef broth (low-sodium, if desired)

4 ounces lean pork, cut into very thin strips

2 green onions, minced

1 cup fresh spinach leaves, washed well

1 teaspoon soy sauce, or to taste

1. Bring the broth to a boil in a medium saucepan.
2. Add the pork strips to the boiling broth. Lower the heat and simmer for 8 minutes.
3. Add the green onions, spinach, and soy sauce, and continue to simmer for 5 minutes.

Step One = Yes (neutral)
Step Two = Yes (neutral)
Step Three = Yes (neutral)

POULTRY

○ Lemon-Garlic Chicken   162

○ Chicken Marsala   163

○ Easy Pesto Chicken   165

○ BBQ Chicken   166

○ Chicken Strata   167

○ Parmesan Bread Crumbs   168

○ Basil Chicken with Vegetables   169

○ Chicken with Mozzarella   170

○ Grilled Lime Chicken   171

○ Fresh Herb Marinade   172

○ Chicken Fajitas   173

○ Fajita Seasoning Mix   174

○ Smoked Sausage Gumbo   175

○ Turkey Melts   176

LEMON-GARLIC CHICKEN

Steps One, Two, and Three
Start to finish: 2 hours (including 1½ hours marinating time)
Serves: 4

This simple recipe is a snap to make. Consider doing the easy prep work in the morning, leaving the chicken to marinate in the refrigerator all day, and then popping it into the oven just before dinner.

4 skinless, boneless chicken breast halves (1 to 1¼ pounds total)

1 teaspoon finely grated lemon zest

3 tablespoons lemon juice

1 tablespoon olive oil

2 cloves garlic, finely minced

½ cup white wine

½ cup homemade (page 151) or canned chicken broth (low-sodium, if desired)

¼ teaspoon black pepper

½ teaspoon salt

1 tablespoon finely chopped fresh parsley

Cooking oil spray

1 ounce Parmesan cheese, grated

Step One = Yes (neutral)
Step Two = Yes (neutral)
Step Three = Yes (neutral)

1. Place the chicken breasts between two pieces of plastic wrap or waxed paper. Using the flat side of a meat mallet, pound each to an even thickness (about ¼ inch thick). Remove the plastic wrap and set the chicken aside.

2. In a large zippered plastic bag, combine the lemon zest and juice, oil, garlic, wine, broth, salt, pepper, and parsley. Add the chicken, seal the bag, and turn the bag to coat the chicken with the marinade. Place the sealed bag in a large bowl to prevent leaks. Marinate in the refrigerator for 1 to 2 hours, turning the bag once.

3. Preheat the broiler. Lightly coat the rack of broiler pan with cooking oil spray. Place the chicken on the rack of a broiler pan. Discard the marinade. Broil 4 to 5 inches from heat for 10 to 12 minutes, until a meat thermometer reads 170°F. Turn the chicken halfway through (at about the 5- to 6-minute point) and sprinkle with the cheese for the last minute of broiling.

CHICKEN MARSALA

Steps One, Two, and Three
Start to finish: 45 minutes
Serves: 4

In this traditional Italian dish, a rich sauce of mushrooms and Marsala wine smothers the chicken. It will become a family favorite. When you advance to Steps Two or Three, place the savory chicken atop the appropriate amount of whole wheat pasta or serve with Broccoli Rabe Salad with Orzo (page 132).

**4 skinless chicken breast
halves (about 1 pound)**
2 tablespoons olive oil
3 cups sliced fresh mushrooms
2 cloves garlic, finely minced
¼ teaspoon salt, plus a pinch
¼ teaspoon black pepper
1 cup dry Marsala wine
2 green onions, thinly sliced
1 tablespoon cold water
1 teaspoon cornstarch

1. Place the chicken breasts between two pieces of plastic wrap or waxed paper. Using the flat side of a meat mallet, pound each to an even thickness (about ¼ inch thick). Remove the plastic wrap and set the chicken aside.

2. Pour 1 tablespoon of the olive oil into a large skillet over medium heat. When the oil is warm, add the mushrooms and garlic and cook for about 5 minutes, until tender. Remove the cooked mushrooms from the skillet and place in a medium bowl.

3. Without wiping the skillet clean, add the remaining tablespoon of oil and heat over medium heat until hot. Place two chicken breast halves in the skillet and sprinkle with ⅛ teaspoon each of the salt and pepper. Cook over medium heat for 4 to 5 minutes per side, turning only once. Transfer the cooked chicken to dinner plates. Repeat for the remaining two chicken breast halves.

(CONTINUES)

CHICKEN MARSALA (CONTINUED)

Cover each plate with aluminum foil to retain warmth.

4. Add the wine to the drippings left in the skillet. Boil the mixture for 1 minute, scraping up the browned bits and mixing them through the sauce.

5. Return the mushrooms to the skillet and add the green onions. In a cup, stir together the cold water, cornstarch, and a pinch of salt. Add this to the skillet and cook until slightly thickened and bubbly. Cook, stirring, for 1 minute more.

6. Spoon the mushroom mixture over the chicken. Serve immediately.

Step One = Yes (neutral)
Step Two = Yes (neutral)
Step Three = Yes (neutral)

Easy Pesto Chicken

Steps One, Two, and Three
Start to finish: 50 minutes
Serves: 4

Some cooks prefer to make their own pesto from basil, garlic, pine nuts, olive oil, and Parmesan cheese. But there are high-quality prepared pestos at the supermarket. When time is tight and you're stressed, it's awfully nice to know you can grab a jar from the pantry.

1½ pounds boneless, skinless chicken breast
Salt and pepper
1 tablespoon olive oil
Cooking oil spray
1 cup jarred pesto
½ cup homemade (page 151) or canned chicken broth (low-sodium, if desired)
1 cup jarred sun-dried tomatoes, drained and chopped
1 cup shredded part-skim mozzarella

Step One = Yes (neutral)
Step Two = Yes (neutral)
Step Three = Yes (neutral)

1. Preheat the oven to 375°F.
2. Using kitchen shears, cut each chicken breast into cutlet-size pieces. Sprinkle with salt and pepper.
3. Heat the olive oil in a large skillet over medium-high heat, then add the chicken. Lightly brown on each side, about 3 minutes per side.
4. Coat a 9 by 13-inch baking pan with cooking oil spray.
5. In a small bowl, whisk together the pesto and broth. Pour ¾ cups of pesto mixture in the bottom of the baking pan. Place the chicken in a single layer on top of the sauce and cover with the remaining pesto mixture. Sprinkle with the sun-dried tomatoes.
6. Cover the baking dish with foil and bake the chicken until cooked through, about 25 minutes. Uncover and top with the cheese. Bake until the cheese is melted, about 10 minutes.

BBQ CHICKEN

Steps One, Two, and Three
Start to finish: 45 minutes
Serves: 4

Most barbecued chicken dishes rely on the grill or oven, but this stove-top version uses just one pan and produces tender chicken every time. Note that the barbecue sauce is "zero carb," allowing this dish to remain "neutral" and oh so good!

1½ **pounds boneless, skinless chicken breasts**
Salt and pepper
1 **tablespoon olive oil**
1 **cup zero-carb barbecue sauce**
½ **cup water**

1. Season the chicken on both sides with salt and pepper.
2. Heat the oil in a large nonstick skillet over medium-high heat. Add the chicken and cook until browned, 3 minutes per side.
3. Meanwhile, whisk together the barbecue sauce and the water.
4. Pour the barbecue sauce over the chicken, lower the heat to medium-low, and let simmer, covered for 35 to 40 minutes or until tender.

Step One = Yes (neutral)
Step Two = Yes (neutral)
Step Three = Yes (neutral)

CHICKEN STRATA

Steps Two and Three
Prep: 15 minutes
Start to finish: 2 hours 55 minutes (including 2 hours chilling time)
Serves: 6

This luscious chicken dish is elegant and indulgent. Broccoli, mushrooms, and peppers add fiber and flavor to this "comfort food" main dish.

1 tablespoon olive oil

2 cups trimmed and chopped fresh broccoli

2 cups sliced fresh mushrooms

½ red bell pepper, seeded and chopped

½ yellow bell pepper, seeded and chopped

Cooking oil spray

3 light multigrain English muffins, torn or cut into bite-size pieces

12 ounces cooked chicken breast, shredded

1 cup shredded Swiss cheese

4 eggs, beaten lightly

1 cup nonfat or low-fat milk

¼ teaspoon black pepper

¼ teaspoon salt

Step One = No
Step Two = Yes (11 grams net carb, or one 11–20 gram carb serving)
Step Three = Yes (11 grams net carb, or one 11–20 gram carb serving)

1. In a large nonstick skillet, heat the oil over medium-high heat. Add the broccoli, mushrooms, and bell peppers and cook for about 8 minutes, or just until the vegetables are crisp-tender.

2. Lightly coat six individual 12-ounce casserole dishes with cooking oil spray. Divide half of the English muffin pieces among the dishes. Top with the chicken, then the broccoli mixture, and sprinkle with ½ cup of the Swiss cheese. Top with the remaining English muffin pieces.

3. In a medium bowl, whisk together the eggs, milk, salt, and pepper. Pour the egg mixture evenly over each casserole. Using the back of a spoon, press the muffin pieces down. Sprinkle with the remaining ½ cup of Swiss cheese. Cover the dishes with plastic wrap and chill for a minimum of 2 hours.

4. Preheat the oven to 325°F.

5. Bake the casseroles for 30 minutes, or until a knife inserted in centers comes out clean. Let stand for 10 minutes before serving.

PARMESAN BREAD CRUMBS

Steps One, Two, and Three
Start to finish: 10 minutes
Serves: 8 ($^1/_4$ cup/serving)

I decided to place this "breading" recipe with the chicken entrées, but you can also use it to bread seafood, pork, or veal. Just dip your protein food of choice in beaten egg white and coat with this low-carb version in place of your regular bread crumbs. Costs just 5 grams of net carb!

8 slices low-carb bread (with 5 grams or less net carb per slice), left out overnight until hardened
4 tablespoons (¼ cup) butter
¼ teaspoon black pepper
¼ teaspoon salt
¼ teaspoon garlic powder
½ cup grated Parmesan cheese
2 tablespoons dried parsley

1. Break up the dried bread slices and place in a food processor. Process to fine crumb consistency.
2. In a large skillet over medium heat, melt the butter. Mix in the pepper, salt, and garlic powder. Add the bread crumbs and cook until the crumbs become toasted, about 5 minutes.
3. Remove from the heat and place the crumbs in a large mixing bowl. Stir the Parmesan cheese and parsley into the bread-crumb mixture and mix well.
4. Let the mixture cool. Toss to fluff.

Step One = Yes (5-gram net carb "Counter")
Step Two = Yes (5 grams net carb)
Step Three = Yes (5 grams net carb)

BASIL CHICKEN WITH VEGETABLES

Steps One, Two, and Three
Start to finish: 40 minutes
Serves: 4

This chicken dish is bursting with color and flavor. Serve over Cauliflower "Rice" (page 245) for a delicious one-bowl meal!

- 3 tablespoons olive oil, plus a dash
- 1½ pounds boneless chicken meat, cut into bite-size pieces
- Salt and pepper
- 2 cloves garlic, minced or pressed
- 1 small bunch fresh basil, finely chopped
- 1 red bell pepper, seeded and chopped
- 1 onion, chopped
- 8 ounces mushrooms, sliced
- 2 cups sliced zucchini or other summer squash
- ½ cup homemade (page 151) or canned chicken broth (low-sodium, if desired)

1. In a large skillet, heat the 3 tablespoons of olive oil over medium heat until hot.
2. Place the chicken in the pan and sprinkle with salt and pepper. Cook until golden brown, about 15 minutes, stirring occasionally.
3. Push the chicken to one side of the pan and add a dash of olive oil to the other side, along with the garlic and basil. Cook for about 1 minute, until the garlic is golden brown.
4. Add the red pepper, onion, mushrooms, zucchini, and broth, and stir. When the mixture is nearly cooked (another 15 minutes), the vegetables will be al dente.

Step One = Yes (neutral)
Step Two = Yes (neutral)
Step Three = Yes (neutral)

CHICKEN WITH MOZZARELLA

Steps One, Two, and Three
Start to finish: 45 minutes
Serves: 4

Simple, simple, simple. That's the way I like my weeknight meals, and this recipe fits the bill.

2 tablespoons olive oil

2 tablespoons butter

2 cloves fresh garlic, minced

1½ pounds boneless, skinless chicken breast

14 ounces homemade (page 151) or canned chicken broth (low-sodium, if desired)

¼ cup white wine

8 ounces shredded part-skim mozzarella cheese

1. In a large skillet over medium heat, heat the olive oil, butter, and garlic.
2. When the oil is hot, brown the chicken on both sides, about 10 minutes per side.
3. Lower the heat and add the broth and wine. Simmer for about 20 minutes, turning occasionally.
4. Sprinkle the chicken with the mozzarella and heat until melted. Serve immediately.

Step One = Yes (neutral)
Step Two = Yes (neutral)
Step Three = Yes (neutral)

GRILLED LIME CHICKEN

Steps One, Two, and Three
Start to finish: 60 minutes (minimum 30 minutes marinating time)
Serves: 4

Crank up the reggae music, close your eyes, and savor the taste sensations of the islands that come through in this flavorful dish. Although it is neutral on its own, it can be paired with Brown Rice Pilaf (page 240) or whole wheat couscous as your carb allotment for Step Two or Three.

1 tablespoon olive oil
1 tablespoon lime juice
1 jalapeño, seeded and diced
1 teaspoon ground cumin
1 teaspoon grated lime zest
2 cloves garlic, minced
⅓ teaspoon salt
1 pound boneless, skinless chicken breasts
Black olives, sliced (optional)

1. Combine the olive oil, lime juice, jalapeño, cumin, lime zest, garlic, and salt in a small bowl.
2. Rub or brush the seasoning mixture on both sides of the chicken and place in a medium container with a lid (or cover with plastic wrap).
3. Chill in the refrigerator for 30 minutes or up to 8 hours to infuse the flavors into the chicken meat.
4. Preheat the grill to medium-high (or until the coals are red hot). Grill the chicken for 7 to 8 minutes per side, until no longer pink in the center.
5. Garnish with black olives, if desired.

Step One = Yes (neutral)
Step Two = Yes (neutral)
Step Three = Yes (neutral)

FRESH HERB MARINADE

Steps One, Two, and Three
Start to finish: 5 minutes
Makes: enough marinade for 1 to 1¹/₂ pounds of chicken or fish

When you chop the fresh herbs for this marinade, your kitchen will smell heavenly. It does a great job adding a delicate flavor to both chicken and fish.

2 cloves garlic, sliced
¹/₂ cup dry white wine
2 tablespoons olive oil
1 tablespoon finely chopped fresh basil
1 tablespoon finely chopped fresh oregano
1 tablespoon finely chopped fresh mint
Salt and pepper

1. In a large bowl, combine the garlic, wine, olive oil, herbs, salt, and pepper.
2. Add your preferred chicken or fish, turn, and cover with plastic wrap. Refrigerate for at least 2 hours, turning occasionally.
3. Discard the marinade and cook or grill as desired.

Step One = Yes (neutral)
Step Two = Yes (neutral)
Step Three = Yes (neutral)

CHICKEN FAJITAS

Steps One, Two, and Three
Start to finish: 40 minutes
Serves: 6 (1 fajita/serving)

This is a great meal for a family returning from a Saturday soccer game, a single person who wants to make enough of a dish to last a few days, or for a quick and casual dinner out on the deck with friends!

- **4 boneless, skinless chicken breasts**
- **2 tablespoons olive oil**
- **3 tablespoons Fajita Seasoning Mix (recipe follows)**
- **⅓ cup water**
- **1 green bell pepper, seeded and cut into strips**
- **1 medium onion, chopped**
- **6 low-carb tortillas (with 5 grams or less net carb per tortilla)**
- **1 cup mild salsa**
- **1 cup shredded lettuce**
- **1 cup grated or shredded low-fat Cheddar cheese**
- **½ cup light sour cream**

1. With kitchen scissors or a sharp knife, cut the chicken into thin strips and set aside.
2. In a large skillet over medium heat, heat the olive oil until hot. Add the chicken and cook until the strips are cooked through, 8 to 10 minutes.
3. Add the fajita seasoning mix, water, peppers, and onion, and mix well. Simmer uncovered for about 20 minutes, until the vegetables are tender.
4. Serve by spooning about ½ cup of the chicken mixture onto a tortilla and topping with the salsa, shredded lettuce, shredded Cheddar, and a dollop of sour cream.

Step One = Yes (5-gram net carb "Counter")
Step Two = Yes (5 grams net carb)
Step Three = Yes (5 grams net carb)

FAJITA SEASONING MIX

Steps One, Two, and Three

Start to finish: 5 minutes

Makes: 3/4 cup seasoning mix (enough for 3 uses)

Mix up your own fajita seasoning mix and store the extra in a sealed container, for future use, with your other spices.

3 tablespoons cornstarch

2 tablespoons chili powder

1 tablespoon salt

1 tablespoon paprika

1 tablespoon sucralose or stevia

3 chicken bouillon cubes, crushed (low-sodium, if desired)

2 teaspoons onion powder

1 teaspoon garlic powder

½ teaspoon cayenne

¼ teaspoon crushed red pepper flakes

1. In a small bowl, mix together all the ingredients.
2. Place the mixture in a glass or plastic container. Seal tightly and store with your other spices in a cool, dry place.

Step One = Yes (neutral)

Step Two = Yes (neutral)

Step Three = Yes (neutral)

SMOKED SAUSAGE GUMBO

Steps One, Two, and Three
Start to finish: 2 to 2¹/₂ hours
Serves: 4

Cajun in origin, gumbo is a unique, rich stew of vegetables and smoky meats that proves especially satisfying when the weather outside is blustery. When on Step Two or Three, you can pair it with crusty whole-grain bread in an amount to match your carb allotment!

2 tablespoons olive oil

2 stalks celery, chopped

1 medium onion, chopped

1 medium green bell pepper, seeded and chopped

1 clove garlic, minced

1 medium carrot, chopped (not in Step One)

¼ cup all-purpose flour

1 cup homemade (page 151) or canned chicken broth (low-sodium, if desired)

1 pound smoked turkey sausage, cut into ½-inch pieces

1 (14 ½-ounce) can diced tomatoes, undrained

½ cup dry white wine

2 teaspoons dried oregano

2 teaspoons dried thyme

⅛ teaspoon cayenne

1. In a large skillet over medium heat, sauté the celery, onion, green bell pepper, garlic, and carrot in olive oil until tender, 10 to 12 minutes.

2. Stir in the flour until blended; gradually adding the broth. Bring to a boil. Cook, stirring, for 3 minutes, or until thickened.

3. Transfer to a 3-quart saucepot. Stir in the sausage, tomatoes, white wine, oregano, thyme, and cayenne. Cover and cook over low heat for 1½ to 2 hours to let the flavors meld.

Step One = Yes (5-gram net carb "Counter"; eliminate carrots in Step One)
Step Two = Yes (5 grams net carb)
Step Three = Yes (5 grams net carb)

TURKEY MELTS

Steps Two and Three
Start to finish: 20 minutes
Serves: 4

When you'd rather not fuss in the kitchen, consider making these quick sandwiches for dinner. They're tasty and will leave you with the energy for your "second job"—everything you need to do at home in the evening.

Cooking oil spray
4 light multigrain English muffins, split
1 pound oven-baked turkey breast (from deli, thinly sliced)
4 slices Canadian bacon
4 thick slices fresh tomato
1 cup light Alfredo sauce (jarred variety)
1 cup shredded Swiss cheese

1. Preheat the oven to 350°F. Lightly coat a baking sheet with cooking oil spray.
2. Place the English muffin tops and bottoms on the prepared baking sheet.
3. Divide the turkey among the four muffin bottoms. Stack with the Canadian bacon and tomato slices.
4. Top each muffin half with 2 tablespoons of Alfredo sauce and sprinkle with ¼ cup of the Swiss cheese.
5. Bake for 10 minutes, until the stacked bottoms are heated through, the cheese is bubbly, and tops are toasted. Place the muffin tops on the bottoms and serve warm.

Step One = No
Step Two = Yes (20 grams net carb, or one 11–20 gram carb serving)
Step Three = Yes (20 grams net carb, or one 11–20 gram carb serving)

BEEF, PORK, AND LAMB

○ Steak with Sherry Sauce 178
○ Ginger Flank Steak 179
○ Baked Beef Tenderloin with Brown Sauce 181
○ Mediterranean Meat Loaf 182
○ Veal or Beef Stroganoff 183
○ Sloppy Joes 184
○ Broken Noodles 185
○ Glazed Ham 186
○ Old Country Stew 187
○ Grilled Pork Kebabs 188
○ Bacon-Wrapped Pork Loin 189
○ Lamb Chops with Herbed Mushrooms 191
○ Red Wine Marinade 192

STEAK WITH SHERRY SAUCE

Steps One, Two, and Three
Prep: 10 minutes
Start to finish: 30 minutes
Serves: 4

Cube steaks are pounded thin by the butcher, so they cook quickly and are usually quite tender. A lovely sherry cream sauce adds an elegant richness to the dish. Pair it with steamed broccoli sprinkled with lemon juice for a fantastic meal.

4 cube steaks (4 to 6 ounces each)
½ teaspoon black pepper
½ teaspoon salt
¼ cup extra-virgin olive oil
2 cups sliced mushrooms
1 medium sweet onion, finely chopped
2 cloves garlic, minced
1 tablespoon all-purpose flour
¼ teaspoon dried thyme
¼ teaspoon dried rosemary
¼ teaspoon dried parsley
½ cup dry sherry
½ cup canned beef broth (low-sodium, if desired)
¼ cup light sour cream

Step One = Yes (neutral)
Step Two = Yes (neutral)
Step Three = Yes (neutral)

1. Sprinkle the steaks with salt and pepper. Heat 2 tablespoons of the oil over medium heat in a large nonstick skillet. Add the steaks and cook, turning once, until browned and cooked through (2 to 4 minutes per side).
2. Transfer the steaks to a plate and cover to keep warm.
3. Add the remaining oil to the pan. Add the mushrooms, onion, and garlic, and cook, stirring, until golden brown, about 5 minutes.
4. Sprinkle the vegetables with the flour. Continue cooking for 1 minute, stirring often.
5. Add the thyme, rosemary, parsley, sherry, and broth. Bring to a boil and cook, stirring, until the sauce begins to thicken, 2 to 3 minutes.
6. Remove from the heat and stir in the sour cream.
7. Return the steaks to the pan. Turn them over a few times to warm and coat with the sauce. Serve the steaks with the sauce.

GINGER FLANK STEAK

Steps One, Two, and Three
Prep: 15 minutes
Start to finish: 4¹/₂ hours (including marinating time)
Serves: 4

This beef dish has a distinctly Asian appeal with its ginger-soy marinade. Flank steak, a favorite in the East, is a particularly lean cut of meat. Take care not to overcook it, by keeping a little pink in the center. Some cooks score the steak before cooking to tenderize it even further.

1½ pounds flank steak, trimmed of excess fat
1 cup canned beef broth (low-sodium, if desired)
¼ cup hoisin sauce
3 tablespoons soy sauce (low-sodium, if desired)
2 green onions, sliced
¼ cup white wine
1 tablespoon sucralose or stevia
1 teaspoon grated fresh ginger
3 cloves garlic, minced
Cooking oil spray

1. Place the steak in a zippered plastic bag and set in a shallow dish.
2. To make the marinade, whisk together the broth, hoisin sauce, soy sauce, green onions, wine, sweetener, ginger, and garlic in a small bowl.
3. Pour the marinade over the steak in the bag and seal it. Refrigerate for at least 4 hours, turning the bag occasionally. The marinated steak can then be broiled or grilled.

To broil:
1. Preheat the broiler.
2. Drain the steak and discard the marinade.
3. Lightly coat the unheated rack of a broiler pan with cooking oil spray. Position the rack 5 inches from the heat source.
4. Place the steak on the prepared rack and broil for 15 to 18 minutes, turning once, until medium done (160°F).
5. To serve, thinly slice the steak across the grain.

(CONTINUES)

To grill:

1. Coat the grill rack with cooking oil spray before lighting it. Ignite the grill. When the coals are medium hot, place the steak directly on the rack and grill uncovered for 17 to 20 minutes, turning once, until medium done (160°F).

2. To serve, thinly slice the steak across the grain.

> **Step One** = Yes (neutral)
> **Step Two** = Yes (neutral)
> **Step Three** = Yes (neutral)

BAKED BEEF TENDERLOIN WITH BROWN SAUCE

Steps One, Two, and Three
Start to finish: 1 hour 10 minutes
Serves: 6

Tender and delicious, beef tenderloin is a great choice for entertaining. I like to use the leftovers, thinly sliced, on salad later in the week.

1½ pounds beef tenderloin
1 cup canned beef broth
   (low-sodium, if desired)
½ cup light sour cream
2 teaspoons cornstarch
1 tablespoon olive oil
2 green onions, chopped
½ cup fresh chopped parsley
½ teaspoon black pepper
1 tablespoon Dijon mustard

1. Preheat the oven to 400°F. Place a large sheet of aluminum foil on a baking pan or cookie sheet.
2. Place the beef tenderloin in the middle of the foil with the narrow end tucked under. Fold up the foil edges around the tenderloin to form a lip in which to catch the juices.
3. Bake the tenderloin for 40 to 45 minutes, until medium done (160°F).
4. Meanwhile, whisk together the broth, sour cream, and cornstarch in a small bowl. Set aside.
5. Heat the oil in a small nonstick skillet. Add the green onions and cook about 3 minutes, until soft.
6. Add the parsley, pepper, and mustard, and stir.
7. Slowly add the cornstarch liquid. Cook, stirring, over medium heat for 7 to 8 minutes, until the sauce is bubbly and thickened.
8. Slice the tenderloin into ½-inch pieces. Serve with the sauce poured over each slice.

Step One = Yes (neutral)
Step Two = Yes (neutral)
Step Three = Yes (neutral)

MEDITERRANEAN MEAT LOAF

Steps One, Two, and Three
Prep: 15 minutes
Start to finish: 2 hours 15 minutes
Serves: 8 (two ½-inch slices/serving)

A traditional comfort food made with a twist by adding roasted peppers, fresh herbs, and marinara sauce.

1 (12-ounce) jar roasted red peppers, drained and chopped

4 slices low-carb bread (with 5 grams or less net carb per slice), torn into small pieces

2 eggs, slightly beaten

1 cup marinara sauce (no-sugar-added variety)

¼ cup chopped fresh basil

¼ cup chopped fresh parsley

½ teaspoon salt

½ teaspoon black pepper

½ teaspoon garlic powder

2 pounds lean ground beef

1. Preheat the oven to 350°F.
2. Combine the peppers, bread, eggs, ¾ cup of the marinara sauce, basil, parsley, salt, pepper, and garlic powder in a large bowl. Mix well.
3. Add the ground beef and knead well until thoroughly blended. (Wear plastic gloves, if desired.)
4. Lightly pat the beef mixture into a 9 by 5-inch loaf pan. Spoon the remaining ¼ cup of marinara sauce over the meat loaf.
5. Bake uncovered for 1¼ to 1½ hours, or until a meat thermometer inserted in the center registers 160°F.
6. Remove from the oven and let the pan stand on a wire rack for 15 minutes.
7. Drain the fat from the pan. Loosen the meat loaf from the sides of the pan. Carefully remove the meat loaf and slice to serve.

Step One = Yes (5-gram net carb "Counter")
Step Two = Yes (5 grams net carb)
Step Three = Yes (5 grams net carb)

VEAL OR BEEF STROGANOFF

Steps One, Two, and Three
Start to finish: 50 minutes
Serves: 4

From its origins in nineteenth-century Russia, Stroganoff has become popular in much of Europe, North America, Australia, South Africa, Lebanon, Portugal, and Brazil with variations in the actual recipe. This recipe calls for veal, but Stroganoff is best known as Beef Stroganoff . . . and you can feel free to substitute thinly sliced sirloin steak in place of the veal.

Cooking oil spray
1½ pounds veal, cubed, or sirloin steak, sliced
2 tablespoons olive oil
2 green bell peppers, seeded and chopped
1 large onion, chopped
Salt
1 tablespoon finely chopped fresh basil
1 pint light sour cream
1 tablespoon whole wheat flour
Black pepper

Step One = Yes (neutral)
Step Two = Yes (neutral)
Step Three = Yes (neutral)

1. Spray a nonstick skillet with cooking oil spray. Add the veal cubes or steak and brown for 10 to 12 minutes. Remove from the skillet and set aside.
2. Pour the olive oil into the skillet. Add the bell peppers and onion. Sauté over medium heat until tender, stirring constantly, 7 to 9 minutes.
3. Add the browned veal or steak to the skillet. Add enough water to cover the veal, along with salt to taste and the basil. Simmer over medium heat until tender, 20 to 30 minutes.
4. Add the sour cream, black pepper, and flour. Stir well. Keep simmering until the sour cream sauce thickens.
5. Remove from the heat. Serve over steamed green beans or soy noodles to keep it neutral or over the appropriate amount of whole wheat noodles for Step Two or Three.

SLOPPY JOES

Steps One, Two, and Three
Start to finish: 25 minutes
Serves: 8

In northeast Pennsylvania, people call this dish Wimpies, but in the rest of the country it's Sloppy Joes. Whatever you call it, it makes a great weeknight meal. During Steps Two and Three, serve on buns that bring your total carb allotment into the appropriate range.

- 1½ pounds 85–93% lean ground beef
- 1 medium onion, chopped
- 1 medium green bell pepper, seeded and chopped
- 1 (10¾-ounce) can condensed tomato soup (low-sodium, if desired)
- 1 tablespoon Worcestershire sauce
- 1 tablespoon prepared mustard
- ½ teaspoon chili powder

1. Cook the ground beef, onion, and green pepper in a large skillet over medium-high heat until the beef is browned. Break the beef apart with a fork while cooking to remove any lumps.
2. Drain off the fat, keeping the meat mixture in the skillet.
3. Stir in the tomato soup, Worcestershire sauce, mustard, and chili powder.
4. Bring the mixture to a boil.
5. Lower the heat and simmer, partially covered, for 10 minutes.

Step One = Yes (5-gram net carb "Counter"; no bun)
Step Two = Yes (Sloppy Joe mixture contains 5 grams net carb; add the carb grams from the bun to hit the 11–20 gram net carb target for one serving)
Step Three = Yes (Sloppy Joe mixture contains 5 grams net carb; add the carb grams from the bun to hit the desired 11–20 gram net carb target for one serving)

BROKEN NOODLES

Steps Two and Three
Start to finish: 50 minutes
Serves: 6

Think of this recipe as really easy lasagne. You don't have to precook the noodles because they will cook in the same sauce. One less step + one less pot = more time to relax.

8 ounces ground turkey sausage

8 ounces 85–93% lean ground beef

1 medium onion, chopped

2 cloves garlic, minced

2 cups marinara sauce (no-sugar-added variety)

1 cup water

8 ounces whole-grain lasagna-type noodles, broken into pieces

2 cups chopped zucchini

1 cup part-skim ricotta cheese

¼ cup grated Parmesan cheese

1 tablespoon chopped fresh parsley

½ teaspoon salt

¼ teaspoon black pepper

1 cup shredded part-skim mozzarella cheese

Step One = No
Step Two = Yes (20 grams net carb, or one 11–20 gram carb serving)
Step Three = Yes (20 grams net carb, or one 11–20 gram carb serving)

1. Brown the sausage, ground beef, onion, and garlic in a large skillet over medium heat. Break the beef apart with a fork while cooking to remove any lumps.

2. Drain off the fat, keeping the meat mixture in the skillet.

3. Add the marinara sauce and water. Mix well. Bring the mixture to a boil, stirring occasionally.

4. Add the broken noodles and zucchini. Return to a boil.

5. Lower the heat and simmer, partially covered, for 12 to 14 minutes, or until the noodles are tender, stirring occasionally.

6. Meanwhile, combine the ricotta, Parmesan, parsley, salt, and pepper in a small bowl.

7. Using a spoon, drop the cheese mixture into six mounds over the mixture in the skillet. Sprinkle the shredded mozzarella over the top.

8. Cover and cook over low heat for 5 minutes, or until the cheese mixture is heated through.

9. Let stand, uncovered, for 5 minutes before serving so that the cheese can set.

GLAZED HAM

Steps One, Two, and Three

Start to finish: Using large oven bag, 12 minutes/pound

Makes: about 2¹/₂ servings per pound of ham

Using an oven bag to bake a ham cuts the cooking time, produces juicier meat, and makes for an easy cleanup. Serve first as a main entrée and afterward the leftovers can be used for sandwiches, salads, and soups.

1 tablespoon all-purpose flour
Precooked ham (shank portion)
Whole cloves
Dijon mustard
¹/₂ cup Splenda brown sugar

1. Preheat the oven to 325°F.
2. Place the flour in large (14 by 20-inch or 19 by 23-inch) oven bag. Place the oven bag in a baking dish large enough to hold the ham.
3. Score the ham by making ¼-inch diagonal cuts in a diamond pattern. Insert one clove in the center of each diamond.
4. Place the ham inside the bag, fat side up. Close the bag with a twist tie. Pierce the top of the bag with six to eight small slits.
5. Bake the ham for 12 minutes per pound, minus 30 minutes (see next step).
6. Thirty minutes before it is done, remove the ham from the oven.
7. Increase the oven temperature to 375°F.
8. Slit the bag down the center and open to the sides to completely expose the ham.
9. Brush the entire top of ham with Dijon mustard. Sprinkle with the Splenda brown sugar.
10. Bake for an additional 30 minutes at 375°F.

Step One = Yes (neutral)
Step Two = Yes (neutral)
Step Three = Yes (neutral)

OLD COUNTRY STEW

Steps Two and Three

Start to finish: 1 hour 15 minutes

Serves: 6 (1 cup/serving)

Baking this stew in the oven allows the flavors to meld into a wonderful comfort meal. The aroma will fill your kitchen and home with its mouthwatering fragrance.

Cooking oil spray

1 tablespoon olive oil

12 ounces lean boneless pork, cut into ½-inch cubes

1 large onion, chopped

2 medium carrots, chopped

2 cloves minced garlic

4 ounces smoked turkey sausage links, halved lengthwise and cut into ½-inch slices

2 (15-ounce) cans canned white kidney beans (cannellini), drained and rinsed

4 medium tomatoes, chopped

1 cup homemade (page 151) or canned chicken broth (low-sodium, if desired)

1 cup water

¼ cup white wine

½ teaspoon dried thyme, crushed

½ teaspoon dried rosemary, crushed

½ teaspoon salt

¼ teaspoon black pepper

1. Preheat the oven to 325°F. Lightly coat a Dutch oven–style pan with cooking oil spray.

2. Add the olive oil and heat over medium-high heat. Add pork cubes and cook, frequently turning the meat so all sides lightly brown, 10 to 12 minutes.

3. Add the onions, carrots, garlic, and smoked turkey sausage.

4. Cook until the onion is tender and translucent, 6 to 8 minutes.

5. Add the white beans, tomatoes, broth, water, wine, thyme, rosemary, salt, and pepper.

6. Bake, covered, for 50 minutes, until the pork cubes and carrots are tender.

Step One = No

Step Two = Yes (20 grams net carb, or one 11–20 gram carb serving)

Step Three = Yes (20 grams net carb, or one 11–20 gram carb serving)

GRILLED PORK KEBABS

Steps One, Two, and Three
Prep: 15 minutes
Start to finish: 3 hours
Makes: 8 skewers

The longer you marinate the meat, the more flavor it will retain after grilling. These pretty kebabs pair beautifully with Cauliflower "Rice" (page 245) for Step One or Brown Rice Pilaf (page 240) for Steps Two and Three.

1 pound pork tenderloin, cut into ½-inch cubes
¼ cup bottled Italian dressing (low-fat preferred)
2 cloves garlic, minced
¼ cup white wine
1 teaspoon dried oregano
¼ teaspoon salt
½ teaspoon black pepper
24 grape tomatoes
24 small mushrooms
24 pearl onions, peeled
24 large red seedless grapes
Olive oil cooking spray
8 (6-inch-long) wooden skewers, soaked in warm water for at least 1 hour

1. Combine the cubed pork tenderloin, dressing, garlic, wine, oregano, salt, and pepper in a zippered plastic bag placed inside a shallow dish. Seal the bag and refrigerate for at least 2 hours or even overnight.
2. Thread the pork cubes onto the skewers, alternating them with tomatoes, mushrooms, onions, and grapes. Lightly spray the filled skewer with olive oil cooking spray.
3. Heat your grill until medium hot. Place the skewers on the grill and cook for 15 to 18 minutes, turning frequently, until the pork is cooked through.

Step One = Yes (eliminate the grapes and it is a neutral food; with grapes, each skewer has 5 grams net carb ["Counter"])
Step Two = Yes (as above)
Step Three = Yes (as above)

Bacon-Wrapped Pork Loin

Steps One, Two, and Three
Start to finish: 60 minutes
Serves: 4

My friend's grandmother insisted on having pork on New Year's Day to ensure good luck for the coming year. With this recipe, the luck has already begun. The bacon adds its unique flavor and using turkey bacon helps lower the fat content! Some companies now make bacon without nitrites/nitrates (preservatives and flavor enhancers in cured/processed meats). Ask for it at your supermarket or butcher shop.

1 pork loin (1½ pounds)
Salt and pepper
1 tablespoon olive oil
2 tablespoons finely chopped fresh rosemary
2 tablespoons finely chopped fresh dill
¼ pound turkey bacon, thinly sliced
1 cup white wine
½ cup homemade or canned beef broth (low-sodium, if desired)
1 teaspoon cornstarch

1. Preheat the oven to 375°F.
2. Season the pork with salt and pepper.
3. Heat the oil in a large cast-iron skillet over medium-high heat.
4. Sear the pork on all sides until browned, about 10 minutes total. Remove from the heat.
5. Rub the pork loin with the chopped rosemary and dill; wrap with turkey bacon, overlapping the strips slightly. Tie the pork roast with kitchen twine.
6. Return the pork to the skillet and roast in the oven, basting occasionally with cooking juices, for 35 to 40 minutes, until the internal temperature is 145°F on a meat thermometer.
7. Remove from the oven. Transfer the pork to a serving dish. Cover the pork loosely with foil to keep warm.

(CONTINUES)

BACON-WRAPPED PORK LOIN (CONTINUED)

8. Make the sauce right in the pan! Place the roasting skillet on the stove top over low heat. Add the wine and stir to scrape up any brown bits from the pan bottom.

9. Pour the sauce through a fine-mesh sieve into a small saucepan. Skim off the fat.

10. Whisk together the broth and cornstarch, then add to the au jus mixture and stir constantly over medium heat until the sauce begins to thicken. Serve over the sliced pork.

Step One = Yes (neutral)
Step Two = Yes (neutral)
Step Three = Yes (neutral)

LAMB CHOPS WITH HERBED MUSHROOMS

Steps One, Two, and Three
Start to finish: 40 minutes
Serves: 4

Lamb is a primary meat from some of the world's best cooking traditions—think Greece, India, and Italy. It's true that lamb has a strong flavor, but instead of trying to hide it, complement it. Don't skimp on the spices; they blend well with the flavor of lamb.

Cooking oil spray
2 tablespoons olive oil
8 lamb loin chops, fat trimmed, cut 1 inch thick
1 medium onion, thinly sliced
2 cloves garlic, minced
2 cups sliced fresh mushrooms
¼ teaspoon salt
¼ teaspoon black pepper
¼ teaspoon dried thyme
¼ teaspoon dried basil
¼ teaspoon drilled rosemary
¼ teaspoon dried dill

1. Preheat the oven to 150°F. Spray a baking sheet with cooking oil spray.
2. In a large nonstick skillet over medium-high heat, heat the olive oil. Add the chops. Cook for 12 to 14 minutes for medium doneness (160°F), turning once.
3. Transfer the chops to prepared baking sheet and place in the oven to keep warm.
4. Stir the onion, garlic, and mushrooms into the drippings in the skillet. Cook, stirring, for 8 to 10 minutes, until the onions are golden and the mushrooms are soft.
5. Stir in the salt, pepper, and herbs, and let the flavors mix, 2 to 3 minutes.
6. Arrange the chops on a serving platter and spoon the mushroom mixture over the chops.

Step One = Yes (neutral)
Step Two = Yes (neutral)
Step Three = Yes (neutral)

RED WINE MARINADE

Steps One, Two, and Three

Start to finish: 5 minutes

Makes: 2 cups marinade (for up to 2 pounds of meat or poultry)

Try changing up plain old chicken, beef, or pork with a nice marinade—this recipe is quick and easy, yet big on flavor.

½ cup finely chopped onion
2 cloves garlic, minced
¼ cup olive oil
¼ cup chopped fresh parsley
1 teaspoon sucralose or stevia
¾ teaspoon salt
¼ teaspoon black pepper
1 teaspoon Italian seasoning
   mix
8 ounces red wine (not port)
2 tablespoons water

1. In a small bowl, whisk together all the ingredients.
2. Pour over your choice of meat, cover, and marinate, chilled, for at least 30 minutes, preferably for more than 2 hours or overnight.

Step One = Yes (neutral)
Step Two = Yes (neutral)
Step Three = Yes (neutral)

VEGETARIAN ENTRÉES

❍ Spinach-Feta Pie   194

❍ Quick Broccoli Pie   195

❍ Vegetarian Pot Luck   196

❍ Eggplant Parmesan   197

❍ Roma Tofu Bake   198

❍ Tofu and Veggies   199

❍ Tofu Marsala   200

❍ Bok Choy and Tofu Stir-Fry   201

❍ Mushroom-Cheese "Burgers"   202

❍ Portobello "Buns"   203

❍ White Bean–Stuffed Tomatoes   204

SPINACH-FETA PIE

Steps One, Two, and Three
Start to finish: 60 minutes
Serves: 6

Eliminating the phyllo dough from this Greek-style pie allows for the neutral status of this crustless creation. Makes a great light dinner and pairs beautifully with Very Berry Crème (page 282) for Steps Two and Three.

Cooking oil spray

2 (10-ounce) packages frozen chopped spinach, thawed

1 large onion, chopped

3 cloves garlic, minced

1 tablespoon olive oil

1 cup low-fat cottage cheese, drained

4 ounces feta cheese, crumbled

2 large eggs, beaten lightly with 2 tablespoons milk

1 teaspoon Italian seasoning

¼ teaspoon black pepper

½ cup grated Parmesan cheese

1 tablespoon butter, at room temperature

1. Preheat the oven to 350°F. Lightly coat a 9-inch pie plate with cooking oil spray.

2. Place the thawed spinach in a colander and squeeze out any excess water. Transfer the spinach to layered paper towels and press out any remaining water. Set aside.

3. In a medium saucepan over medium heat, cook the onion and garlic in the olive oil until translucent, about 8 minutes.

4. Stir the spinach, cottage cheese, feta cheese, eggs, and seasonings into the onion mixture. Mix well.

5. Spoon the mixture into the prepared pie plate. Sprinkle with the Parmesan cheese and dot with the butter.

6. Bake uncovered for 30 to 35 minutes, or until a knife inserted near the center comes out clean. To serve, cut into six wedges.

Step One = Yes (neutral)
Step Two = Yes (neutral)
Step Three = Yes (neutral)

QUICK BROCCOLI PIE

Steps One, Two, and Three
Start to finish: 55 minutes
Serves: 6

Low-fat cottage cheese gives this crustless pie a low-fat, high protein, high-calcium nutrient profile . . . the red peppers and deep green broccoli give it gorgeous eye appeal.

16 ounces 2% cottage cheese

10 ounces frozen chopped broccoli, thawed, well drained (absorb excess liquid in paper towels)

1 cup shredded part-skim mozzarella cheese

4 eggs, beaten

1 (7 ounces) jar roasted red peppers, drained and chopped

½ cup grated Parmesan cheese

1 teaspoon dried parsley

½ teaspoon salt

½ teaspoon black pepper

Cooking oil spray

1. Preheat the oven to 350°F.
2. In a large mixing bowl, mix all the ingredients and blend thoroughly.
3. Lightly coat a 9-inch pie plate with cooking oil spray. Pour the mixture into the pie plate.
4. Bake for 45 minutes, or until the center is set.

Step One = Yes (neutral)
Step Two = Yes (neutral)
Step Three = Yes (neutral)

VEGETARIAN POT LUCK

Steps Two and Three
Start to finish: 45 minutes
Serves: 4 to 5 (1^1/$_2$ cups/serving)

Shiitake mushrooms add depth to the sauces of many Asian dishes while bok choy adds crunch and B vitamins. If you're concerned about sodium, opt for a low-sodium soy sauce.

5 cups homemade or canned vegetable broth (low-sodium, if desired)

3 cloves garlic, peeled

2 teaspoons olive oil

6 ounces shiitake mushrooms, stemmed, wiped clean, and sliced

1 medium onion, chopped

1 small head bok choy (¾ pound) cut into ½-inch pieces, stems and greens separated

3½ ounces Chinese wheat noodles

1 (14- to 16-ounce) package firm tofu, drained, patted dry, and cut into ½-inch cubes

1 cup grated carrots

1 tablespoon rice vinegar

2 teaspoons soy sauce (low-sodium, if desired)

1 teaspoon toasted sesame oil

¼ cup chopped green onion, for garnish

1. Combine the broth and garlic in a Dutch oven; bring to a boil. Lower the heat to medium-low and let simmer, partially covered, for 20 minutes. Discard the garlic.

2. Meanwhile, heat the olive oil in a large non-stick skillet over medium-high heat. Add the onion and cook about 5 minutes. Add the mushrooms and continue to cook for another 5 minutes. Add the bok choy *stems* and cook, stirring often, until tender, about 5 minutes.

3. Add the mushroom mixture to the broth. Add the noodles, lower the heat to medium-low, and simmer for 3 minutes. Add the bok choy greens and tofu cubes. Simmer until heated through, about 3 minutes. Stir in the carrots, rice vinegar to taste, soy sauce, and sesame oil.

4. Serve garnished with green onion.

Step One = No
Step Two = Yes (16 grams net carb, or one 11–20 gram carb serving)
Step Three = Yes (16 grams net carb, or one 11–20 gram carb serving)

EGGPLANT PARMESAN

Steps One, Two, and Three
Start to finish: 60 minutes
Serves: 6 to 8

Making traditional eggplant Parmesan can be a messy, time-consuming process. This quick and easy alternative roasts the eggplant—producing wonderful flavor and is a neutral food choice. Mangia!

2 (14½-ounce) cans chopped or diced tomatoes
2 cloves garlic, minced
1 medium onion, chopped
½ cup white wine
¼ teaspoon crushed fresh basil
¼ teaspoon crushed fresh oregano
Salt and pepper
6 medium eggplants
Cooking oil spray
¼ cup olive oil
3 cups grated part-skim mozzarella cheese
½ cup grated Parmesan cheese

Step One = Yes (neutral)
Step Two = Yes (neutral)
Step Three = Yes (neutral)

1. Preheat the oven to 400°F.
2. Place the tomatoes, garlic, onion, wine, basil, oregano, salt, and pepper in a saucepan and bring to a boil. Lower the heat and simmer for 30 minutes.
3. Meanwhile, spray two large cookie sheets with cooking oil spray. Trim the eggplants and cut lengthwise into thick slices. Brush the slices with the olive oil and place on the prepared cookie sheets.
4. Roast at the top of the oven for about 8 minutes per side, until golden and tender. Set aside.
5. Spoon about ½ cup of the tomato sauce into the bottom of an 11 by 13-inch baking dish and top with a layer of roasted eggplant and shredded mozzarella. Continue with the layers of sauce, eggplant, and cheese, finishing with a layer of mozzarella on top.
6. Sprinkle the top with Parmesan cheese and bake for 30 to 40 minutes, until the cheese is bubbling and golden.

ROMA TOFU BAKE

Steps One, Two, and Three
Start to finish: 50 minutes
Serves: 4

The beauty of tofu is that it takes on the flavors of the ingredients that surround it. You'll taste the robust flavors of Italy in every bite of this hearty dish.

1 tablespoon olive oil

2 cloves garlic, minced

1 (14- to 16-ounce) package extra-firm tofu, rinsed and cut into bite-size cubes

10 ounces fresh spinach, washed well, trimmed, and chopped

Salt and pepper

Cooking oil spray

1 cup marinara sauce (no-sugar-added variety)

1 teaspoon Italian seasoning

1 cup part-skim ricotta cheese

1 cup shredded part-skim mozzarella cheese

1/4 cup grated Parmesan cheese

Step One = Yes (neutral)
Step Two = Yes (neutral)
Step Three = Yes (neutral)

1. Preheat the oven to 375°F. Lightly coat a 9 by 13-inch baking dish with cooking oil spray.

2. Heat oil in a large skillet over medium heat. Add the garlic and cook until softened, about 3 minutes. Add the cubed tofu to the skillet and cook until golden, 5 to 7 minutes. Remove the tofu and set aside. Add the spinach to the skillet, cover, and cook until tender, about 3 minutes. Season with salt and pepper and remove from heat.

3. Spoon about 1/2 cup of the marinara sauce into the bottom of the prepared baking dish to cover the bottom. Place the tofu in a single layer on top of the sauce. Sprinkle with the Italian seasoning. Top the tofu with a layer of cooked spinach, shredded mozzarella, and, using a spoon, place dollops of ricotta cheese on top.

4. Drizzle the remaining 1/2 cup of sauce over the ricotta. Sprinkle with the grated Parmesan cheese.

5. Cover with foil and bake until the tofu is hot and the cheese is melted and bubbling, about 15 minutes. Remove the foil and bake for 5 minutes uncovered.

TOFU AND VEGGIES

Steps One, Two, and Three

Start to finish: 20 minutes

Serves: 4 (1 cup/serving)

You can make this one-pot recipe in no time. Cook the tofu to a golden brown to give it a little extra texture.

- **2 tablespoons olive oil**
- **1 medium onion, chopped**
- **2 cloves garlic, minced**
- **1 (14- to 16-ounce) extra-firm tofu, rinsed, drained, blotted dry, and cut into bite-size pieces**
- **1 cup cooked spinach, chopped and squeezed dry**
- **1 cup crushed tomatoes, drained**
- **¼ teaspoon salt**
- **¼ teaspoon black pepper**
- **½ cup Parmesan cheese**

1. In a large skillet, heat the oil over medium-high heat. Add the onion and garlic. Cook, stirring, until golden brown.
2. Add the tofu and brown lightly on both sides, turning once. When the tofu is golden brown, add the cooked spinach and tomatoes, salt, pepper, and Parmesan. Cover and bring to a boil, lower the heat, and simmer for 5 minutes, stirring occasionally.

Step One = Yes (neutral)
Step Two = Yes (neutral)
Step Three = Yes (neutral)

TOFU MARSALA

Steps One, Two, and Three
Start to finish: 40 minutes
Serves: 4 (1 cup/serving)

Everyone is familiar with Chicken Marsala. This vegetarian version uses the same onion, mushroom, and Marsala wine base but replaces chicken with golden browned tofu. Serve over Cauliflower "Rice" (page 245), and the entire dish is only 5 grams of net carb!

¼ cup olive oil
1 (14- to 16-ounce) package extra-firm tofu, drained, rinsed, blotted dry, and cut into ½- or ¾-inch cubes
¾ teaspoon salt
½ teaspoon black pepper
1 medium onion, diced
1 carrot, thinly sliced
2 cloves garlic, minced
8 ounces mushrooms, sliced
1 tablespoon whole wheat flour
1 cup red wine, such as Marsala (not port wine)
1 cup homemade or canned vegetable broth (low-sodium, if desired)

Step One = Yes (5-gram net carb "Counter")
Step Two = Yes (5 grams net carb)
Step Three = Yes (5 grams net carb)

1. Heat 2 tablespoons of the oil in a large nonstick skillet over medium-high heat. Add the tofu and cook in a single layer, stirring every 1 to 2 minutes, until golden brown, about 10 minutes.
2. Transfer the tofu to a shallow dish big enough to fit in one layer. Sprinkle with salt and pepper, and gently toss to combine.
3. Heat the remaining 2 tablespoons of oil in the pan over medium heat. Add the onion, carrot, and garlic. Cook, stirring often, until the onion and garlic are beginning to turn golden, 5 to 7 minutes.
4. Add the mushrooms and cook, stirring, for 5 minutes more. Sprinkle the vegetables with the flour and stir to coat.
5. Add the wine and broth to the cooked vegetables to cook for 4 to 6 minutes more, stirring until the sauce has thickened. Return the tofu to the pan and stir until heated through, 1 to 2 minutes.

BOK CHOY AND TOFU STIR-FRY

Steps One, Two, and Three

Start to finish: 60 minutes (including marinating time)

Serves: 4

The Asian influence of rice vinegar, soy sauce, sesame oil, ginger, and garlic turn this colorful vegetarian dish into a treat for the taste buds.

¼ cup rice vinegar

¼ cup white wine

2 tablespoons soy sauce

1 tablespoon sesame oil

1 teaspoon ground ginger

1 clove garlic, minced

1 (14- to 16-ounce) package firm tofu, drained, rinsed, blotted dry, and cut into 4 slices

2 tablespoons olive oil

3 cups sliced mushrooms

1 red bell pepper, seeded and cut into strips

1 orange bell pepper, seeded and cut into strips

1 medium sweet onion, finely chopped

4 cup coarsely shredded bok choy

1 cup frozen shelled edamame, thawed

½ teaspoon cornstarch

2 tablespoons sesame seeds

1. To make the marinade, in a baking dish, combine the vinegar, white wine, soy sauce, sesame oil, ginger, and garlic.
2. Add the tofu slices, turning to coat. Marinate at room temperature for 30 minutes, turning the tofu once halfway through the marinating time.
3. Add 1 tablespoon of the olive oil to a skillet, heat the oil until hot, and add the tofu slices (reserving the marinade). Cook the tofu for 5 to 7 minutes, until heated through and golden in color, turning once halfway through the cooking.
4. Remove the tofu from the skillet and place one slice on each dinner plate. Cover to retain the heat.
5. Add the remaining tablespoon of olive oil to the skillet over medium-high heat. Add the mushrooms, bell peppers, and onion. Cook, stirring, for 6 to 8 minutes, or until the vegetables are becoming tender.

(CONTINUES)

BOK CHOY AND TOFU STIR-FRY (CONTINUED)

Step One = Yes (neutral)
Step Two = Yes (neutral)
Step Three = Yes (neutral)

6. Add the bok choy and edamame. Cook, stirring, for 2 to 3 minutes more, or until the bok choy is wilted.
7. Whisk the cornstarch into the reserved marinade; pour into the vegetable mixture. Cook, stirring, stir until thickened.
8. Cover each slice of tofu with the bok choy mixture. Serve immediately.

MUSHROOM-CHEESE "BURGERS"

Steps One, Two, and Three
Start to finish: 15 minutes
Serves: 4

Add a slice of cheese, some fresh tomato, a dash of low-carb ketchup, and a lettuce-leaf wrap, and you have an all-American cheeseburger (sans the beef).

4 portobello mushrooms
2 tablespoons olive oil
Salt and pepper
1 teaspoon dried Italian dressing, crushed
4 slices Provolone cheese

Step One = Yes (neutral)
Step Two = Yes (neutral)
Step Three = Yes (neutral)

1. With a sharp knife, scrape the gills from mushroom caps.
2. Drizzle the mushrooms with the olive oil. Sprinkle with salt, pepper, and Italian seasoning.
3. Cook the mushrooms on the rack of an uncovered charcoal grill, directly over medium-hot coals, for 6 to 8 minutes, turning halfway through cooking.
4. Top each mushroom with a cheese slice.

PORTOBELLO "BUNS"

Steps One, Two, and Three
Start to finish: 10 minutes
Serves: 1

Use these "buns" as a carb-free vegetarian holder for your garden burger creations . . . and meat eaters can use these portobello "buns" to hold their hamburger or turkey burger.

1 teaspoon olive oil
2 portobello mushroom caps

1. In a small nonstick skillet, heat the olive oil over medium heat.
2. Cook the mushroom caps, turning once with a wide spatula, until lightly browned, 3 minutes per side.
3. Place the browned mushroom caps on paper towels to absorb any excess oil.

> **Step One** = Yes (neutral)
> **Step Two** = Yes (neutral)
> **Step Three** = Yes (neutral)

WHITE BEAN–STUFFED TOMATOES

Steps Two and Three
Start to finish: 45 minutes
Serves: 4

A new twist on a "peak-of-the-season" summer staple . . . the succulent tomato!

4 large red tomatoes
1½ cups soft bread crumbs (from whole wheat bread)
1 (15-ounce) can white kidney beans (cannellini beans), drained and rinsed
½ cup grated Parmesan cheese
1 teaspoon Italian seasoning
1 tablespoon olive oil
2 cloves garlic, minced
⅛ teaspoon salt
⅛ teaspoon black pepper
Cooking oil spray
1 tablespoon butter, melted

1. Preheat the oven to 350°F.
2. Slice off ¾ inch from the top of each tomato. Finely chop the tomato tops to produce about ¾ cup of chopped tomato and set aside.
3. Using a melon baller or a spoon, remove and discard the seeds from each tomato. Put the hollowed-out tomatoes upside down on paper towels to drain.
4. In a large bowl, stir together the chopped tomato, ¾ cup of the bread crumbs, all the beans, ¼ cup of the Parmesan cheese, ¾ teaspoon of the Italian seasoning, salt, and pepper.
5. Spoon the bean mixture into the hollowed-out tomatoes.
6. Place the stuffed tomatoes in a 2-quart square baking dish lightly coated with cooking oil spray.
7. In a small bowl, stir together the remaining ¾ cup of bread crumbs, ¼ cup of Parmesan cheese, and ¼ teaspoon of Italian seasoning. Sprinkle evenly over the tomatoes and drizzle with the melted butter.

8. Bake uncovered for 20 to 30 minutes, or until the bread crumbs are golden brown and the tomatoes are heated through.

Step One = No
Step Two = Yes (16 grams net carb,
   or one 11–20 gram carb serving)
Step Three = Yes (16 grams net carb,
   or one 11–20 gram carb serving)

SEAFOOD

○ Miracle Crab Cakes   208
○ Shrimp Lo Mein   210
○ Bacon Scallops with Baby Spinach   211
○ Mediterranean Fish   212
○ Baked Cod au Gratin   213
○ Crunchy Oven-Fried Fish   214
○ Crusted Salmon   215
○ Grilled Rosemary Salmon   216
○ Grilled Snapper with Salsa   217
○ Broiled Flounder with Parmesan   218
○ Salmon Croquettes   219
○ Miracle Tuna Melt   220
○ BBQ Tilapia Sandwiches   221

MIRACLE CRAB CAKES

Steps Two and Three

Start to finish: 1¹/₂ hours (including 1 hour chilling time)

Serves: 5 (1 crab cake/serving)

The combination of tender crabmeat and fresh herbs makes these crab cakes an instant classic that any seafood lover will enjoy. Serve them with Snap Pea Salad (page 129) for a perfect dinner.

1½ cups fresh whole wheat bread crumbs (about 5 slices of bread)

12 ounces fresh or canned crab-meat (about 2 cups)

2 tablespoons chopped fresh dill

2 tablespoons chopped fresh flat-leaf parsley

1 medium onion, grated

2 teaspoons Old Bay seasoning mix

¼ teaspoon salt

⅛ teaspoon black pepper

1 large egg

¼ cup light mayonnaise

1 teaspoon lemon juice

2 teaspoons Dijon mustard

⅓ cup unseasoned dry bread crumbs

Cooking oil spray

4 teaspoons olive oil

1. Mix the bread crumbs and crabmeat in a large bowl. Add the dill, parsley, onion, Old Bay seasoning mix, salt, and pepper. Mix well.

2. Whisk the egg, mayonnaise, lemon juice, and mustard in a small mixing bowl until smooth. Stir it into the crabmeat mixture and mix well.

3. Using clean hands, form the mixture into six ½- to ¾-inch-thick patties (½ cup each).

4. Dredge the patties in the bread crumbs and place on a baking sheet covered with parchment or waxed paper. Refrigerate for 1 hour.

5. Preheat the oven to 450°F. Coat another baking sheet with cooking oil spray.

6. Heat 2 teaspoons of the olive oil in a large skillet over medium heat. Add three crab cakes and cook until their bottoms become golden, about 3 minutes. Transfer the crab cakes, bottom side up, to the oiled baking sheet.

Tip: To make the bread crumbs, trim the crusts from the low carb bread and gently crumble the slices into crumbs. Or, place coarsely torn slices into food processor and process until coarse.

7. Add the remaining 2 teaspoons of olive oil to the skillet and repeat the process for the remaining three crab cakes.

8. Bake the crab cakes until golden on the second side and heated through, about 20 minutes.

> **Step One** = No
>
> **Step Two** = Yes (20 grams net carb, or one 11–20 gram carb serving)
>
> **Step Three** = Yes (20 grams net carb, or one 11–20 gram carb serving)

SHRIMP LO MEIN

Steps One, Two, and Three

Start to finish: 30 minutes

Serves: 4

In the mood for Chinese take-out? This colorful and flavorful one-skillet meal hits the spot and fits all steps of the Metabolism Miracle. High-carb noodles are replaced with neutral tofu noodles, which give this dish the green light even during Step One.

16 ounces tofu noodles (such as *shirataki*), drained, rinsed thoroughly under cold water, and blotted dry

1 pound peeled frozen raw medium shrimp (31- to 40-count), thawed according to package directions and rinsed well

3 tablespoons light teriyaki sauce

18 ounces frozen Szechuan vegetable blend

1 cup frozen shelled edamame

½ cup vegetable broth (low-sodium if desired)

1 tablespoon cornstarch

Step One = Yes (5-gram net carb "Counter")

Step Two = Yes (5 grams net carb)

Step Three = Yes (5 grams net carb)

1. Place the noodles on a dinner plate. Microwave for 40 seconds on HIGH. Remove the plate from the microwave, fluff the noodles with a fork, and microwave for another 40 seconds on HIGH. Set aside.

2. Place the shrimp in a small bowl and toss with 2 tablespoons of the teriyaki sauce. Set aside.

3. Place the vegetables and shelled edamame in a large nonstick skillet with the vegetable broth. Cover and cook, stirring occasionally, over medium-high heat for 8 to 10 minutes, or until cooked through.

4. Stir the shrimp into the vegetable mixture. Cover and cook for 5 to 7 minutes, or until the shrimp are pink and cooked through.

5. Combine the remaining tablespoon of teriyaki sauce and the cornstarch, and add to the shrimp mixture, cooking and stirring until thickened. Gently add the tofu noodles to the skillet and cook, stirring, until warmed through.

BACON SCALLOPS WITH BABY SPINACH

Steps One, Two, and Three
Start to finish: 45 minutes
Serves: 4

In this dish, succulent scallops are made even more delectable by a wrap of crispy bacon. Served over fresh wilted spinach, this entrée would pair nicely with a glass of Pinot Grigio and a table full of friends on a warm summer night.

Cooking oil spray

16 large sea scallops, rinsed and blotted dry

½ teaspoon lemon pepper

16 strips uncooked bacon (turkey bacon without nitrates/nitrites preferred)

3 tablespoons extra-virgin olive oil

1 tablespoon lemon juice

¼ teaspoon salt

¼ teaspoon black pepper

12 ounces baby spinach

1. Place the rack in top section of oven for broiling. Turn on the broiler. Coat a large baking sheet with cooking oil spray.
2. Pat the scallops dry and sprinkle both sides with lemon pepper. Wrap one piece of bacon around each scallop.
3. Thread four scallops crosswise onto a 10-inch metal skewer (securing the bacon on the scallop) and place on the prepared baking sheet. Repeat with the other scallops and three additional metal skewers.
4. Broil until the scallops are just cooked through and the bacon is cooked, 6 to 7 minutes.
5. Meanwhile, whisk the oil, lemon juice, salt, and pepper in a medium bowl. Reserve 1 tablespoon of the vinaigrette in small bowl.
6. Place the spinach in a colander and rinse well under cold water. Do not dry.
7. Heat a large skillet over medium heat. When hot, add handfuls of wet spinach to the pan and cook, stirring, until just wilted, 2 to 3 minutes.

(CONTINUES)

BACON SCALLOPS WITH BABY SPINACH (CONTINUED)

Step One = Yes (neutral)
Step Two = Yes (neutral)
Step Three = Yes (neutral)

8. Drain the spinach and add to the medium bowl of vinaigrette, tossing to coat.
9. Divide the spinach equally among four salad plates. Top with four scallops per plate and drizzle the reserved vinaigrette on top.

MEDITERRANEAN FISH

Steps One, Two, and Three
Start to finish: 30 minutes
Serves: 4

Inspired by the Mediterranean, this white fish with just a hint of cinnamon is a snap to prepare and bakes in the oven, giving you the time to prepare Italian Garden Salad (page 135) or Garlic Zucchini (page 239).

2 tablespoons olive oil
1 medium onion, thinly sliced
1 clove garlic, minced
1 (14½-ounce) can stewed tomatoes
3 tablespoons medium-hot salsa
¼ teaspoon ground cinnamon
Cooking oil spray
1½ pounds firm fish (such as halibut or red snapper)
12 black olives, halved

1. Preheat the oven to 350°F.
2. In a medium skillet, heat the olive oil over medium-high heat. Add the onions and garlic, and cook until golden, 5 to 7 minutes.
3. Stir in the tomatoes, salsa, and cinnamon. Heat until warm, about 3 minutes.
4. Coat a baking dish with cooking oil spray. Rinse and dry the fish and place it in the dish.
5. Pour the sauce over the fish and sprinkle with the olive halves. Cover and bake until the fish is flaky, 20 to 25 minutes.

Step One = Yes (neutral)
Step Two = Yes (neutral)
Step Three = Yes (neutral)

BAKED COD AU GRATIN

Steps One, Two, and Three
Start to finish: 45 minutes
Serves: 4

There's something decadent about delicious fish in a wine-and-cheese sauce. Rich, creamy, and oh so flavorful.

¼ cup olive oil

2 medium onions, very thinly sliced

1 cup dry white wine

1½ pounds cod, cut into 1½-inch pieces

2 teaspoons chopped fresh thyme

½ teaspoon salt

½ teaspoon black pepper

3 slices low-carb bread (with 5 grams or less net carb per slice), cut into small cubes

½ teaspoon paprika

½ teaspoon garlic powder

1 cup shredded Swiss cheese

1. Preheat the oven to 400°F.
2. Heat 2 tablespoons of the olive oil in a large ovenproof skillet over medium-high heat. Add the onions and cook, stirring often, until just starting to soften, 5 to 7 minutes.
3. Add the wine. Turn up the heat to high and cook, stirring often, until the wine is slightly reduced, 2 to 4 minutes.
4. Place the cod on the onions and sprinkle with the thyme, salt, and pepper.
5. Cover the pan tightly with foil. Transfer to the oven and bake for 12 minutes.
6. While the fish is baking, toss the bread cubes with the remaining 2 tablespoons of oil, paprika, and garlic powder in a medium bowl. Spread the bread mixture over the fish and top with the cheese. Bake uncovered until the fish is opaque in the center, about 10 minutes more.

Step One = Yes (5-gram net carb "Counter")
Step Two = Yes (5 grams net carb)
Step Three = Yes (5 grams net carb)

CRUNCHY OVEN-FRIED FISH

Steps Two and Three
Start to finish: 25 minutes
Serves: 4 (1^1/$_2$ cups/serving)

Kids love this dish almost as much as adults do. Serve with a vegetable side or salad for Step Two, or as "fish and chips" by adding Grilled Sweet Potato Fries (page 228) for Step Three.

1½ pounds fresh or frozen
   skinless cod or flounder
½ cup low-fat milk
1 egg, slightly beaten
Salt and pepper
½ cup whole wheat flour
⅔ cup fine dried whole wheat
   bread crumbs
½ cup grated Parmesan cheese
½ teaspoon lemon pepper
¼ cup butter, melted
Cooking oil spray

Step One = No
Step Two = Yes (18 grams net
   carb, or one 11–20 gram carb
   serving)
Step Three = Yes (18 grams net
   carb, or one 11–20 gram carb
   serving)

1. Preheat the oven to 400°F.
2. Thaw the fish if frozen. Rinse the fish and pat dry with paper towels. Cut the fish into four pieces, if necessary.
3. Line up three small, shallow dishes. Whisk together the egg, milk, and a pinch of salt and pepper and pour into the first dish.
4. Place the flour in the second dish.
5. Mix together the bread crumbs, Parmesan, and lemon pepper, and place in the third dish. Drizzle the melted butter over the bread-crumb mixture and stir until well mixed.
6. Coat a baking pan or baking dish with cooking oil spray. One piece of fish at a time, dip both sides of the fillet into the egg mixture, coat both sides with flour, and then dip both sides into the bread-crumb mixture.
7. Place the fish in a single layer in the baking pan. Bake uncovered for 8 to 10 minutes, or until the fish flakes easily when tested with a fork.

CRUSTED SALMON

Steps One, Two, and Three
Start to finish: 45 minutes
Serves: 4

Crunchy on the outside and moist on the inside, this salmon dish will quickly become a favorite. Pairs nicely with Sweet Potato Latkes (page 236) for Steps Two and Three.

Cooking oil spray
2 tablespoons olive oil
1 medium onion, chopped
4 cloves garlic, minced
Salt and pepper
½ cup herb-seasoned whole wheat bread crumbs
¼ cup mayonnaise, or as needed
2 teaspoons dry mustard
4 salmon fillets (about 1 inch thick)

1. Preheat the oven to 350°F. Spray a baking sheet with cooking oil spray.
2. Heat the oil in a skillet over medium-high heat. Sauté the onion with the garlic, salt, and pepper until tender, 5 to 7 minutes.
3. Transfer the onion to a medium bowl and mix with bread crumbs, dry mustard, and mayonnaise.
4. Place the salmon fillets on the baking sheet, divide the crumb mixture into four portions, and press the crumb mixture on the top of each salmon fillet.
5. Bake for 10 minutes, until the salmon flakes easily with a fork, and then broil for 5 minutes to crisp the top.

Step One = Yes (5-gram net carb "Counter")
Step Two = Yes (5 grams net carb)
Step Three = Yes (5 grams net carb)

GRILLED ROSEMARY SALMON

Steps One, Two, and Three
Start to finish: 50 minutes
Serves: 4

In Greece, cooks know that fresh herbs such as rosemary can transform a simple piece of fish into delicate fare. This quick and easy recipe capitalizes on the use of fresh herbs, olive oil, and lemon juice. . . . Opa!

2 pounds salmon fillets
½ cup olive oil
½ cup lemon juice
4 green onions, thinly sliced
3 tablespoons chopped fresh parsley
1½ teaspoons chopped fresh rosemary
½ teaspoon salt
⅛ teaspoon black pepper

1. Place the salmon in a shallow dish.
2. Whisk together the olive oil and lemon juice in a medium bowl. Add the green onions, parsley, rosemary, salt, and pepper, and mix well. Set aside ¼ cup of the marinade for basting later.
3. Pour the remaining marinade over the salmon. Cover and refrigerate for 60 minutes, turning at the 30-minute mark.
4. Drain, discarding the marinade that has just been used for the fish. Grill the salmon over medium coals, skin side down, for 15 to 20 minutes, or until the fish flakes easily with a fork, basting occasionally with the reserved marinade.

Step One = Yes (neutral)
Step Two = Yes (neutral)
Step Three = Yes (neutral)

GRILLED SNAPPER WITH SALSA

Steps One, Two, and Three
Start to finish: 20 minutes
Serves: 4

The mild flavor of snapper topped with the freshness of salsa . . . a perfect pairing.

½ cup lime juice
½ cup olive oil
2 cloves garlic, minced
4 red snapper fillets (8 to 10 ounces each)
Salt and pepper

Salsa:
2 medium tomatoes, cored and diced
1 green bell pepper, seeded and finely chopped
1 small onion, finely chopped
1 jalapeño, seeded and chopped
1 clove garlic, minced
½ cup olive oil
¼ cup chopped fresh oregano

1. Whisk together lime juice, olive oil, and garlic in a small bowl.
2. In a shallow pan that can hold the fillets in a single layer, arrange the fillets and pour in the lime mixture. Cover and refrigerate for 1 hour, turning once or twice.
3. Remove the fillets and discard the mixture. Heat your grill to medium hot. Grill the fillets for 5 to 6 minutes per side. Check one fillet to make sure the fish is opaque and cooked through.
4. To make the salsa, mix together all the salsa ingredients. Serve the salsa on top of the snapper.

Step One = Yes (neutral)
Step Two = Yes (neutral)
Step Three = Yes (neutral)

BROILED FLOUNDER WITH PARMESAN

Steps One, Two, and Three
Start to finish: 30 minutes
Serves: 4

This is a delicious way to prepare flounder or any other mild white fish. Pair it with Sautéed Brussels Sprouts (page 235).

Cooking oil spray
½ cup light mayonnaise
½ cup Parmesan cheese
1 tablespoon lemon juice
½ teaspoon Worcestershire sauce
2 small cloves garlic, minced
1½ pounds flounder fillets
Salt and pepper
1 tablespoon coarsely chopped fresh flat-leaf parsley

1. Position a rack for broiling. Turn on the broiler. Coat a broiler pan with cooking oil spray.
2. Whisk the mayonnaise, Parmesan, lemon juice, Worcestershire sauce, and garlic in a small bowl and set aside.
3. Lightly season both sides of the fillets with salt and pepper to taste. Broil until the flounder is lightly browned, 7 to 8 minutes.
4. When the tops of the fillets are lightly browned, remove the fish from the broiler. Spread equal amounts of the mayonnaise mixture over the top of each fillet. Return to the broiler and cook until the topping is bubbling, 1½ to 2 minutes.
5. Transfer the fillets to four dinner plates and sprinkle with the parsley. Serve immediately.

Step One = Yes (neutral)
Step Two = Yes (neutral)
Step Three = Yes (neutral)

SALMON CROQUETTES

Steps One, Two, and Three
Start to finish: 45 minutes
Serves: 6 (1 croquette/serving)

You can't get enough salmon, as far as I'm concerned. High in protein and omega-3 essential fatty acids, these croquettes make it easy to stay healthy. Serve with Broccoli with Cheese Sauce (page 227) for a wonderful meal on all steps of the Metabolism Miracle.

Optional tartar sauce:
  ½ cup light mayonnaise
  2 teaspoons dill pickle relish

Croquettes:
  1 (15- to 16-ounce) can red salmon, not drained
  2 eggs, beaten lightly
  ½ cup quick-cooking oats
  ½ medium onion, finely chopped
  ½ cup finely chopped celery
  ¼ teaspoon salt
  ¼ teaspoon black pepper
  Cooking oil spray
  ¼ teaspoon hot pepper sauce (optional)

1. Combine the mayonnaise and dill pickle relish in a small dish, if using. Mix well and chill it in the refrigerator.
2. Place the salmon and the liquid from the can in a medium bowl. Remove and discard any dark skin or bones (or crush and add back the bones if you want the added calcium). Add the eggs, oats, onion, celery, salt, and pepper. Mix well.
3. Shape the mixture into six ½-inch-thick patties.
4. Coat a large nonstick skillet with cooking oil spray. Place three patties in the skillet. Cook over medium heat for 5 to 6 minutes per side, or until thoroughly cooked and set. Repeat with the remaining patties.
5. Serve the salmon cakes with the chilled sauce, if desired.

Step One = Yes (5-gram net carb "Counter")
Step Two = Yes (5 grams net carb)
Step Three = Yes (5 grams net carb)

MIRACLE TUNA MELT

Steps Two and Three
Start to finish: 30 minutes
Serves: 4 (1 sandwich/serving)

I often use this modified tuna melt recipe as a quick lunch or dinner entrée. By replacing buttered and grilled white bread with a light multigrain English muffin, this melted sandwich is a low-glycemic, low-carb, high-fiber treat.

2 (6-ounce) cans water-packed white tuna, drained and flaked

¾ cup chopped celery

3 tablespoons finely chopped onion

⅓ cup low-fat mayonnaise

¼ teaspoon sucralose or stevia

¼ teaspoon salt

¼ teaspoon black pepper

4 light multigrain English muffins, split and lightly toasted

8 slices tomato

1 cup shredded low-fat Cheddar cheese

1. Preheat the oven to 350°F.
2. Combine the tuna, celery, onion, mayonnaise, sweetener, salt, and pepper in a medium bowl. Mix well.
3. Spread one-eighth of the tuna salad mixture on each English muffin half and top each with a tomato slice. Sprinkle with the Cheddar cheese. Place on an ungreased cookie sheet.
4. Bake for 8 to 10 minutes, or until the cheese is melted and the sandwiches are thoroughly heated.

Step One = No
Step Two = Yes (17 grams net carb, or one 11–20 gram carb serving)
Step Three = Yes (17 grams net carb, or one 11–20 gram carb serving)

BBQ TILAPIA SANDWICHES

Steps Two and Three
Start to finish: 20 minutes
Serves: 4 (1 sandwich/serving)

Tilapia, a mild white fish, is inexpensive and easy to prepare. This is a complete meal when topped with coleslaw on an English muffin. The added drizzle of zero-carb barbecue sauce gives it the extra zing to take this sandwich to the height of flavor.

4 fresh or frozen skinless tilapia fillets (4 to 5 ounces each)
Cooking oil spray
¼ cup light mayonnaise
2 teaspoons lemon juice
2 cups bagged coleslaw mix
4 light multigrain English muffins, halved
2 tablespoons zero-carb barbecue sauce

1. Thaw the fish, if frozen. Rinse the fish and pat it dry with paper towels. Lightly coat both sides of each fillet with cooking oil spray.
2. Place the fish in a large nonstick skillet. Cook over medium heat for 4 to 5 minutes per side, until golden brown.
3. Combine the mayonnaise and lemon juice in a medium bowl. Add the coleslaw mix and toss to coat.
4. Toast the English muffin halves. To assemble, spoon the dressed coleslaw mixture onto the English muffin halves. Top with the fish fillets. Drizzle the fish with carb-free barbecue sauce.

Step One = No
Step Two = Yes (18 grams net carb, or one 11–20 gram carb serving)
Step Three = Yes (18 grams net carb, or one 11–20 gram carb serving)

15 VEGETABLES AND SIDE DISHES

○ Not Your Mom's Green Bean
  Side Dish   224
○ Summer Squash Casserole   225
○ Caribbean Corn on the Cob   226
○ Broccoli with Cheese Sauce   227
○ Grilled Sweet Potato "Fries"   228
○ Roasted Sweet Potato "Fries"   229
○ Sweet-and-Sour Coleslaw   230
○ Pineapple Coleslaw   231
○ Carrot-Parsnip Latkes   232
○ Tabbouleh with Grilled
  Vegetables   233
○ Herbed Mashed Parsnips   234

○ Sautéed Brussels Sprouts   235
○ Sweet Potato Latkes   236
○ Mini Zucchini Pancakes   237
○ Fresh and Crunchy Spring
  Vegetables   238
○ Garlic Zucchini   239
○ Brown Rice Pilaf   240
○ Winter Squash Soufflé   241
○ Almond-Topped Artichokes   242
○ Asparagus with Goat Cheese   243
○ Snow Peas and Water Chestnuts   244
○ Cauliflower "Rice"   245

NOT YOUR MOM'S GREEN BEAN SIDE DISH

Steps One, Two, and Three

Prep: 10 minutes

Start to finish: 30 minutes

Serves: 6 (1 cup/serving)

This green bean dish has just a taste of French-fried onions along with the added surprise of fresh thyme and shallots. Add to a grilled chicken or fish dish for a delicious and unique side dish.

1½ pounds fresh green beans, trimmed and cut into bite-size pieces

1 tablespoon olive oil

6 ounces sliced fresh mushrooms

4 shallots, chopped

3 cloves garlic, finely minced

2 teaspoons chopped fresh thyme

½ teaspoon salt

1 (2.8-ounce) can French-fried onions

Step One = Yes (neutral)

Step Two = Yes (neutral)

Step Three = Yes (neutral)

1. Add the green beans to a large pot of boiling, salted water. Cook for 10 minutes or until tender, and drain in a colander.

2. Meanwhile, heat 2 teaspoons of the olive oil in a large nonstick skillet over medium-high heat. Add the sliced mushrooms and chopped shallots, stirring occasionally, just until tender (about 5 minutes). Add the garlic, thyme, and salt. Cook, stirring constantly, until fragrant (about 2 minutes). Stir in the drained green beans and heat through.

3. To make the topping, heat the remaining 1 teaspoon of olive oil in a small nonstick skillet over medium heat. Add the French-fried onions and cook, stirring occasionally, until lightly toasted, 1 to 2 minutes.

4. Transfer the beans to a large bowl, sprinkle with the French-fried onions, and serve immediately.

SUMMER SQUASH CASSEROLE

Steps One, Two, and Three
Start to finish: 40 minutes
Serves: 8

At high summer everyone is trying to give away their bounty of summer squash. Here's a great way to keep your garden under control and your dinner table delicious.

2 medium yellow summer squash, diced

2 medium zucchini, diced

8 ounces fresh mushrooms, sliced

1 medium red onion, finely chopped

2 tablespoons olive oil

8 ounces shredded low-fat Cheddar cheese

1 (10¾-ounce) can condensed cream of mushroom soup, undiluted (low-sodium, if desired)

½ cup light sour cream

½ cup homemade (page 151) or canned chicken broth (low-sodium, if desired)

Cooking oil spray

1. Preheat the oven to 350°F.
2. In a large skillet, sauté the summer squash, zucchini, mushrooms, and onion in olive oil until tender, about 10 minutes. Place in a colander and drain the excess liquid.
3. Whisk together the mushroom soup, sour cream, and broth until smooth and creamy.
4. In a large bowl, combine the vegetable mixture, mushroom soup mixture, and shredded Cheddar cheese. Mix well.
5. Coat a 9 by 11-inch baking dish with cooking oil spray. Spoon the vegetable mixture into the dish and bake uncovered for 30 minutes, or until bubbly.

Step One = Yes (5-gram net carb "Counter")
Step Two = Yes (5 grams net carb)
Step Three = Yes (5 grams net carb)

CARIBBEAN CORN ON THE COB

Steps Two and Three
Start to finish: 40 minutes
Serves: 8 ($^1/_2$ ear corn/serving)

Sweet corn is hard to beat in high summer, but add a little lime and chili pepper and you'll think you're in the tropics.

4 tablespoons (¼ cup) salted butter, at room temperature
1 teaspoon grated lime zest
1 tablespoon lime juice
1 teaspoon chili powder
4 ears fresh corn on the cob, unhusked

Step One = No
Step Two = Yes (15 grams net carb, or one 11–20 gram carb serving)
Step Three = Yes (15 grams net carb, or one 11–20 gram carb serving)

1. Combine the butter with lime zest, lime juice, and chili powder. Cover and allow to stand at room temperature for 30 minutes.

2. Remove the outer leaves of the corn husk, leaving the inner leaves and as much corn silk as possible. Rinse in cold water and place all four ears in zippered plastic bag. Close the bag, leaving about 1 inch unsealed.

3. Place the bagged corn on a microwave-safe plate and microwave on HIGH for 5 minutes. Carefully turn over the bag and cook on HIGH for 5 more minutes. If you'd prefer to cook your corn on the stovetop rather than the microwave, remove the husks, break the ears in half, place the corn in a large pot of boiling and salted water, and cook for 10 minutes. Serve hot with 1 teaspoon of butter mixture per serving.

4. Wearing oven mitts, remove the plate from the microwave and let the corn cool briefly. Peel off the husks and break each ear of corn in half. Serve hot with 1 teaspoon of the butter mixture per serving.

BROCCOLI WITH CHEESE SAUCE

Steps One, Two, and Three
Start to finish: 15 minutes
Serves: 4

Steaming your broccoli until it is just tender helps it retain most of the nutrition. That little bit of extra crunch is wonderful when covered in light cheese sauce.

1½ pounds fresh broccoli, cut into florets

¾ cup homemade (page 151) or canned chicken or vegetable broth (low-sodium, if desired)

⅓ cup light sour cream

½ cup shredded low-fat Cheddar cheese

2 teaspoons lemon juice

2 teaspoons Dijon mustard

1. Place the broccoli florets and broth in a large microwave-safe bowl. Cover and microwave on HIGH for 5 to 6 minutes or until fork tender. Drain, reserving ½ cup broth, and keep warm.

2. For the sauce, combine the sour cream, shredded Cheddar, reserved broth, lemon juice, and mustard in a small microwave-safe bowl. Whisk until smooth. Cover and microwave on HIGH for 2 to 3 minutes or until warmed. Serve over the broccoli.

Step One = Yes (neutral)
Step Two = Yes (neutral)
Step Three = Yes (neutral)

GRILLED SWEET POTATO "FRIES"

Steps Two and Three
Start to finish: 25 minutes
Serves: 4 ($^1/_2$ sweet potato/serving)

Once they've had sweet potato fries, most people enjoy them as much or more than regular old white potato fries. Sweet potatoes have so much flavor, color, and vitamins! That's great news for anyone with Met B for whom sweet potatoes are a much healthier choice.

**2 medium sweet potatoes,
    scrubbed**
$^1/_2$ teaspoon salt
**$^1/_2$ teaspoon dried oregano,
    crushed**
$^1/_2$ teaspoon garlic powder
$^1/_2$ teaspoon ground cinnamon
Pinch of black pepper
Cooking oil spray

Step One = No
Step Two = Yes (15 grams net
    carb, or one 11–20 gram carb
    serving)
Step Three = Yes (15 grams net
    carb, or one 11–20 gram carb
    serving)

1. Cut the sweet potatoes in half lengthwise and then again crosswise. Cut each piece into 1-inch-thick wedges. In a covered medium saucepan, cook the potato wedges in enough boiling, salted water to cover them. Boil for 8 to 10 minutes, or just until tender. Drain well. Pat dry with paper towels.

2. In a small bowl, combine the salt, oregano, garlic powder, and cinnamon, along with a pinch of pepper, and place in large zippered plastic bag.

3. Coat the sweet potato wedges with cooking oil spray. Add the wedges to the bag and shake until all pieces are coated with the seasoning mix.

4. Place the potato wedges on the rack of an uncovered grill directly over medium coals or, for a gas grill, over medium heat. Cover and grill for 3 to 5 minutes or until the potato wedges are lightly browned, turning once halfway through the grilling.

ROASTED SWEET POTATO "FRIES"

Steps Two and Three
Start to finish: 60 minutes
Serves: 4 ($^{1}/_{2}$ sweet potato/serving)

When it's too cold to fire up the grill for Grilled Sweet Potato "Fries," this oven interpretation is a wonderful substitute. Play with different spice combinations to find the one that you like best.

Cooking oil spray
1 pound sweet potatoes, scrubbed and sliced
½ teaspoon salt
½ teaspoon garlic powder
½ teaspoon onion powder
¼ teaspoon black pepper
Pinch of ground nutmeg

1. Preheat the oven to 425°F. Lightly coat a 9 by 13-inch baking pan or a cookie sheet with cooking oil spray.
2. Scrub the potatoes. Slice them lengthwise into quarters and cut each quarter in half. Set aside.
3. In a small bowl, combine the salt, garlic powder, onion powder, and nutmeg, and place in a large zippered plastic bag.
4. Coat the sweet potato wedges with cooking oil spray. Add the wedges to the bag and shake until all pieces are coated with the seasoning mix.
5. Arrange the seasoned sweet potato wedges in a single layer on the prepared baking pan.
6. Bake for 30 to 35 minutes, until brown and tender, turning once during the baking.

Step One = No
Step Two = Yes (15 grams net carb, or one 11–20 gram carb serving)
Step Three = Yes (15 grams net carb, or one 11–20 gram carb serving)

SWEET-AND-SOUR COLESLAW

Steps One, Two, and Three
Start to finish: 5 minutes
Serves: 4 (1$\frac{1}{2}$ cups/serving)

This is a great salad to accompany grilled foods or sandwich fare. Using coleslaw mix makes the process so simple, and the tang and sweetness combination in this recipe makes this side dish a favorite!

5$\frac{1}{2}$ cups bagged coleslaw mix
$\frac{1}{2}$ cup light mayonnaise
$\frac{1}{4}$ cup half-and-half or light cream
$\frac{1}{4}$ cup sucralose
3 tablespoons white vinegar
$\frac{1}{2}$ teaspoon salt
$\frac{1}{4}$ teaspoon celery seeds
$\frac{1}{4}$ teaspoon dried dill

1. Place the coleslaw mix in a large serving bowl and fluff it with two forks.
2. In a medium bowl, whisk together the mayonnaise, half-and-half, sweetener, vinegar, salt, celery seeds, and dill.
3. Pour the dressing over the coleslaw mix and toss to coat. Chill until ready to serve.

Step One = Yes (neutral)
Step Two = Yes (neutral)
Step Three = Yes (neutral)

PINEAPPLE COLESLAW

Steps Two and Three
Prep: 20 minutes
Start to finish: 1 hour 20 minutes
Serves: 4 ($^3/_4$ cup/serving)

The surprise flavor of pineapple in this tropical version of coleslaw makes it a dish to remember. It's a quick and easy side dish that pairs perfectly with BBQ Chicken (page 166) or Mushroom-Cheese "Burgers" (page 202).

2 cups shredded cabbage or bagged coleslaw mix

1½ cups crushed pineapple, drained

2 tablespoons seeded and finely chopped green bell pepper

2 tablespoons grated onion

1 teaspoon dried dill

¼ cup light sour cream

¼ cup light mayonnaise

1. Toss the coleslaw mix, pineapple, green pepper, onion, and dill together in a medium bowl.
2. Combine the sour cream and mayonnaise in a small bowl. Toss the mayo mixture with the cabbage mixture.
3. Chill for at least 1 hour before serving.

Step One = No
Step Two = Yes (14 grams net carb, or one 11–20 gram carb serving)
Step Three = Yes (14 grams net carb, or one 11–20 gram carb serving)

CARROT-PARSNIP LATKES

Steps Two and Three

Prep: 20 minutes

Start to finish: 50 minutes

Serves: 5 (3 latkes/serving)

When I make these latkes, they're gone within minutes. They are crispy on the outside and moist on the inside and full of beta-carotene and fiber from the sweet root vegetables. Three latkes are a one-carb serving for Step Two or Three.

1 pound carrots, peeled

1 pound parsnips, peeled

1 medium onion, peeled

3 large egg whites, beaten lightly

⅓ cup plain dried bread crumbs (whole wheat preferred)

2 teaspoons chopped fresh thyme

½ teaspoon salt

¼ teaspoon black pepper

Cooking oil spray

Step One = No

Step Two = Yes (17 grams net carb, or one 11–20 gram carb serving)

Step Three = Yes (17 grams net carb, or one 11–20 gram carb serving)

1. Preheat the oven to 200°F. Set a cookie sheet on an oven rack to warm.

2. Coarsely grate the carrots, parsnips, and onion into a medium bowl; stir to mix. Add the egg whites, bread crumbs, thyme, salt, and pepper. Mix well.

3. Spray a large nonstick skillet with cooking oil spray and set over medium heat. Drop the batter by ¼ cupfuls onto the hot skillet and press each mound into a 3-inch-diameter pancake.

4. Cook the latkes until browned and cooked through, about 8 minutes per side, flipping once to brown the other side.

5. Transfer the cooked latkes to the warmed cookie sheet in the oven. Spray the nonstick skillet again with cooking oil spray before you begin browning the next batch of latkes.

TABBOULEH WITH GRILLED VEGETABLES

Steps Two and Three
Start to finish: 60 minutes
Serves: 6 (1 cup/serving)

Grilled veggies bring a completely different texture and flavor to this tabbouleh dish. Fresh mint and toasted walnuts make it an unforgettable addition to your summer picnic or outdoor barbecue.

1 cup uncooked bulgur
¾ teaspoon salt
1 cup boiling water
¼ cup olive oil
2 medium zucchini, cut lengthwise into ½-inch strips
2 sweet onions, such as Vidalia, cut into ½-inch-thick rounds
3 large portobello mushroom caps, wiped clean
1 green bell pepper, seeded and cut into ½-inch strips
2 cups cherry tomatoes
½ cup walnut halves
Black pepper
3 tablespoons lemon juice
½ cup chopped fresh parsley
½ cup chopped fresh mint

1. Place the bulgur and ½ teaspoon of the salt in a large mixing bowl. Add the boiling water and stir. Cover the bowl tightly with plastic wrap and let the bulgur soak until tender and the liquid has been absorbed, about 30 minutes.

2. Meanwhile, in a large skillet over medium heat, cook the zucchini and onions in 1 tablespoon of the olive oil for 8 minutes and set aside. Cook the mushrooms in 1 additional tablespoon of the olive oil for 8 minutes and set aside. Cook the tomatoes in 1 tablespoon of olive oil for 3 minutes and set aside.

3. Toast the walnuts in a small, dry skillet over medium-low heat, stirring constantly, until fragrant, 2 to 3 minutes. When the vegetables are cool enough to handle, coarsely chop the zucchini, onions, mushrooms, and green pepper. Cut the cherry tomatoes in half.

4. When the bulgur is tender, add to it the remaining tablespoon of olive oil, remaining

(CONTINUES)

TABBOULEH WITH GRILLED VEGETABLES (CONTINUED)

Step One = No
Step Two = Yes (17 grams net carb, or one 11–20 gram carb serving)
Step Three = Yes (17 grams net carb, or one 11–20 gram carb serving)

¼ teaspoon salt, and the lemon juice, parsley, mint, and black pepper to taste and toss to mix.

5. Add the vegetables to the bulgur bowl and toss. Place in a large serving bowl and sprinkle with the toasted walnuts.

HERBED MASHED PARSNIPS

Steps Two and Three
Start to finish: 30 minutes
Serves: 4 (³/₄ cup/serving)

Parsnips are a hugely underappreciated vegetable. A great substitute for the carb-dense white potato, they work well in many of the same dishes. Before you announce the substitution, see if anybody notices the new flavor in the mashed "potatoes."

2 pounds parsnips, peeled and cut into 2-inch pieces
½ teaspoon dried chives
½ teaspoon dried parsley
½ teaspoon dried dill
¾ cup half-and-half
2 tablespoons butter
Salt and pepper

Step One = No
Step Two = Yes (18 grams net carb, or one 11–20 gram carb serving)
Step Three = Yes (18 grams net carb, or one 11–20 gram carb serving)

1. Bring a large pot of salted water to a boil. Add the parsnips and cook until tender when pierced with a fork, 15 to 18 minutes.

2. Drain the parsnips in a colander and return them to the pot. Add the chives, parsley, and dill.

3. Mash the parsnips with a potato masher or hand mixer, leaving them rather rough. Stir in the half-and-half and butter. Mash until the parsnips reach your desired texture. Season to taste with salt and pepper.

SAUTÉED BRUSSELS SPROUTS

Steps One, Two, and Three
Start to finish: 30 minutes
Serves: 4 ($^3/_4$ cup/serving)

A simple dish with big flavor, these little cabbages sautéed in onion and simmered in chicken broth will end the "broccoli every night" blues.

1 tablespoon olive oil

1 tablespoon butter

1 medium red onion, finely chopped

1 pound (about 4 cups) fresh Brussels sprouts, halved vertically

1 cup homemade (page 151) or canned chicken broth or vegetable broth (low-sodium, if desired)

Salt and pepper

1. Heat the oil and butter in a large nonstick skillet over medium heat until melted. Add the onion. Cook, stirring, for 5 to 7 minutes, until the onion becomes translucent and soft. Set aside.

2. In the same skillet that onion was cooked in, sauté the Brussels sprouts for 5 minutes.

3. Add the broth to the Brussels sprouts. Cover and cook for about 20 minutes, or until the sprouts are crisp-tender.

4. Drain the broth and return the Brussels sprouts to the pan. Mix in the onion mixture. Add salt and pepper to taste and serve warm.

Step One = Yes (neutral)
Step Two = Yes (neutral)
Step Three = Yes (neutral)

SWEET POTATO LATKES

Steps Two and Three
Start to finish: 45 minutes
Serves: 3 (3 latkes/serving)

The bright orange of these latkes hints that they are rich in beta-carotene, making them more nutritious than the traditional white potato latke. Dip them in light sour cream for an unforgettable taste sensation. Three of these light pancakes count as an 11–20 gram carb serving during Step Two or Three.

1 slice low-carb bread (with 5 grams or less net carb)
1 medium sweet potato
½ medium sweet onion (such as Vidalia)
1 egg white, lightly beaten
⅛ teaspoon baking powder
⅛ teaspoon salt
Black pepper
Olive oil cooking spray
¼ cup light sour cream (optional)

Step One = No
Step Two = Yes (20 grams net carb, or one 11–20 gram carb serving)
Step Three = Yes (20 grams net carb, or one 11–20 gram carb serving)

1. Toast the bread until dark in tone. On a hand-held grater, grate the toasted bread into crumbs and set aside.
2. Grate the sweet potato and onion. Place in a medium bowl. Stir in the egg white, bread crumbs, baking powder, salt, and pepper to taste.
3. Coat a nonstick skillet with olive oil cooking spray and preheat over medium heat. Drop ¼ cup of the potato mixture at a time into the skillet. Flatten the pancake with a fork or the back of a spatula. Cook for 5 to 6 minutes per side, turning only once when golden brown on the bottom. Spray the bottom of the pan with more cooking oil spray before you flip each pancake.
4. Serve immediately, accompanied by a dollop of light sour cream, if desired.

MINI ZUCCHINI PANCAKES

Steps One, Two, and Three
Start to finish: 45 minutes
Serves: 3 (4 mini pancakes/serving)

Have you ever had potato pancakes? To have a similar taste treat without the carbs, use zucchini as the star ingredient. Crispy on the outside and tender on the inside, these delicacies are both irresistible and neutral!

1 large egg plus 1 egg white
⅔ cup finely chopped shallots
1 tablespoon chopped fresh flat-leaf parsley
¼ teaspoon salt
¼ teaspoon black pepper
2 cups seeded zucchini
⅔ cup freshly grated Parmesan cheese
2 tablespoons whole wheat flour
2 tablespoons olive oil
Low-fat sour cream (optional)

Tip: To remove seeds, cut squash in half lengthwise and use a spoon to scrape seeds.

Step One = Yes (5-gram net carb "Counter")
Step Two = Yes (5 grams net carb)
Step Three = Yes (5 grams net carb)

1. Preheat the oven to 400°F.
2. Beat the egg and egg white in a large bowl. Stir in the shallots, parsley, salt, and pepper.
3. Grate the zucchini directly into a colander. Press down on the zucchini to remove excess liquid. When all the squash is shredded, place it in the center of a clean kitchen towel, gather up the ends, and twist to squeeze out any remaining liquid.
4. Add the squash, Parmesan cheese, and flour to the bowl containing the eggs and stir until mixed.
5. Heat the oil in a large, ovenproof skillet over medium heat. Drop ¼ cup of the squash mixture into the pan and press down with a spatula to form a pancake. Cook until browned and crispy on the bottom. Gently turn over the cakes and transfer the pan to the oven.
6. Bake, uncooked side up, for 8 to 10 minutes.
7. Serve immediately. Add a dollop of sour cream, if desired.

FRESH AND CRUNCHY SPRING VEGETABLES

Steps One, Two, and Three
Start to finish: 25 minutes
Serves: 6 to 8

For a little member of the onion family, shallots provide a tremendous boost in flavor to any dish. Eat this delicious spring medley freely and you'll add vitamins and fiber to your day!

¼ **pound string beans, ends removed**
¼ **pound snap peas, ends and strings removed**
½ **pound broccoli florets**
¼ **pound asparagus, ends removed**
2 **tablespoons butter**
1 **tablespoon olive oil**
3 **large shallots, sliced**
Salt and pepper

1. Blanch the green beans, snap peas, broccoli florets, and asparagus in a large pot of salted boiling water for 4 minutes. They will be al dente. Lift the veggies from the water with a slotted spoon or sieve and immerse them in a large bowl of ice water to immediately stop the cooking process.
2. When all the vegetables in the ice water are cold, drain well.
3. Before serving, heat the butter and oil in a large skillet or pot and sauté the shallots over medium heat for 5 minutes, tossing occasionally until lightly browned. Add the drained vegetables to the shallots and add salt and pepper to taste. Cook until the vegetables are just heated through and retain their crunch.

Step One = Yes (neutral)
Step Two = Yes (neutral)
Step Three = Yes (neutral)

GARLIC ZUCCHINI

Steps One, Two, and Three
Start to finish: 25 minutes
Serves: 4 (1 cup/serving)

This zucchini sauté is easy to put together at the last minute. Serve with a simple dish such as Miracle Tuna Melt (page 220) and have a balanced meal within thirty minutes!

- 1 tablespoon olive oil
- 4 cups thinly sliced, unpeeled zucchini
- 4 cloves garlic, thinly sliced
- ¼ cup white wine
- ¾ cup homemade (page 151) or canned chicken broth (low-sodium, if desired)
- 1 teaspoon paprika
- Salt and pepper
- ¼ cup chopped fresh parsley
- 1 tablespoon grated Parmesan cheese (optional)

1. Heat the oil in a large skillet over medium heat. Add the zucchini slices and garlic, and cook until golden brown, stirring frequently, about 8 minutes.
2. Add the wine, broth, paprika, and salt and pepper to taste, and bring to a boil. Lower the heat and simmer for 2 minutes. Spoon out any excess liquid.
3. Pour the zucchini into a serving bowl and sprinkle with the parsley. Sprinkle with the Parmesan, if desired.

Step One = Yes (neutral)
Step Two = Yes (neutral)
Step Three = Yes (neutral)

BROWN RICE PILAF

Steps Two and Three
Start to finish: 40 minutes
Serves: 4 ($^2/_3$ cup/serving)

You can pair this versatile brown rice pilaf with so many of the chicken, meat, and seafood entrées in this cookbook. Brown rice is naturally high in B vitamins and its natural fiber improves its glycemic index!

1 cup uncooked brown rice

2 cups homemade (page 151) or canned chicken broth (low-sodium, if desired)

1 cup sliced mushrooms

½ cup shredded carrot

¼ cup thinly sliced green onions

¼ teaspoon black pepper

¼ teaspoon dried marjoram, crushed

1 tablespoon finely chopped fresh parsley

1 tablespoon butter

Step One = No
Step Two = Yes (20 grams net carb, or one 11–20 gram carb serving)
Step Three = Yes (20 grams net carb, or one 11–20 gram carb serving)

1. Rinse the rice in a strainer under cold running water for 30 seconds, swirling the rice around with your hand.
2. Pour the rice into a large bowl of water and let soak for 60 minutes to soften. Strain in a colander.
3. Meanwhile, bring the chicken broth to a boil in a large pot over high heat. When the broth boils, add the mushrooms, carrot, green onions, pepper, marjoram, parsley, and butter. Return the broth to a boil. Add the rice, stirring once.
4. When the broth returns to a full boil, lower the heat to medium-low, cover tightly with a lid, and cook for about 40 minutes. Do not stir the rice.
5. After 40 minutes, remove the rice from the heat and let stand, covered, for 10 minutes.
6. Uncover the rice and fluff with a fork before serving.

Winter Squash Soufflé

Steps Two and Three
Start to finish: 1 hour 15 minutes (including sitting time)
Serves: 4

Winter squash add a bright splash to any table. You can use fresh squash, but the frozen cubes of winter squash are affordable, delicious, and so very convenient. An elegant soufflé made with a base of this vitamin A–rich vegetable is both beautiful and healthful.

Cooking oil spray
All-purpose flour
2 (12-ounce) packages frozen cooked winter squash
4 eggs
¼ cup butter, melted
2 tablespoons Splenda brown sugar
½ teaspoon salt
⅛ teaspoon ground nutmeg
⅛ teaspoon ground cinnamon

Step One = No
Step Two = Yes (19 grams net carb, or one 11–20 gram carb serving)
Step Three = Yes (19 grams net carb, or one 11–20 gram carb serving)

1. Coat a 1½-quart soufflé dish with cooking oil spray and lightly sprinkle it with flour.
2. Prepare the frozen squash according to the package directions. When cooked, drain in a colander and place in a large mixing bowl.
3. Meanwhile, separate the eggs, placing the yolks in a small bowl and the whites in a large bowl. Let the eggs and squash stand at room temperature for about 30 minutes.
4. Preheat the oven to 350°F.
5. In a large bowl, using a hand mixer, combine the egg yolks, squash, butter, Splenda brown sugar, salt, nutmeg, and cinnamon.
6. Using the hand mixer (with clean beaters), beat the egg whites separately until stiff peaks form.
7. With a spatula, gently stir one-quarter of the beaten whites into the squash mixture until no white streaks remain. Gently fold in the remaining whites just until incorporated.
8. Transfer to the prepared soufflé dish. Bake for 55 to 60 minutes, or until the top is puffed and the center appears set. Serve immediately.

ALMOND-TOPPED ARTICHOKES

Steps One, Two, and Three
Start to finish: 20 minutes
Serves: 4

I love artichokes, but I don't like the heavy sauces that often accompany them. In this recipe, a crunchy topping makes the hearts low in fat, high in flavor, and extra memorable.

Cooking oil spray
2 (9-ounce) packages frozen artichoke hearts, thawed completely
1 tablespoon lemon juice
¼ cup ground almonds
½ cup grated Parmesan cheese
¼ cup Italian bread crumbs
1 teaspoon Italian seasoning
½ teaspoon garlic powder
2 tablespoons olive oil

1. Preheat the oven to 375°F. Coat a 9-inch pie plate with cooking oil spray.
2. Place the artichoke hearts in a colander and rinse well with cold water. Drain well, then pat dry with paper towels. Place them in the prepared pie plate and sprinkle with the lemon juice.
3. In a small bowl, combine the almonds, cheese, bread crumbs, Italian seasoning, and garlic powder. Sprinkle the mixture evenly over the artichokes.
4. Drizzle the olive oil over the coated artichoke hearts. Bake for 15 minutes, or until the topping is golden.

Step One = Yes (5-gram net carb "Counter")
Step Two = Yes (5 grams net carb)
Step Three = Yes (5 grams net carb)

ASPARAGUS WITH GOAT CHEESE

Steps One, Two, and Three
Start to finish: 10 minutes
Serves: 4 (4 to 6 spears/serving)

Asparagus shines in the spring when it is one of the first vegetables out of the garden. Take care not to overcook the asparagus. You want the stalks to have bright color and a tender bite for perfection. If you don't have pine nuts on hand, try pecans.

Cooking oil spray
2 tablespoons pine nuts
2 tablespoons olive oil
1 pound asparagus spears,
    ends removed
⅛ teaspoon salt
⅛ teaspoon black pepper
¼ cup crumbled goat cheese

1. Coat a large skillet with cooking oil spray.
2. Toast the pine nuts in a small, dry skillet over medium-high heat, stirring constantly, about 2 minutes. Set aside.
3. Pour the olive oil into the skillet and turn up the heat to medium. When the oil is hot, place the asparagus spears in the skillet. Sprinkle with salt and pepper. Sauté the asparagus on all sides until crisp-tender, turning occasionally.
4. Arrange the asparagus spears on a warmed serving plate. Sprinkle the goat cheese over all and top with toasted pine nuts. Serve immediately.

Step One = Yes (neutral)
Step Two = Yes (neutral)
Step Three = Yes (neutral)

SNOW PEAS AND WATER CHESTNUTS

Steps One, Two, and Three
Start to finish: 10 minutes
Serves: 4 (1 cup/serving)

Two main ingredients make this vegetable stir-fry a "snap" to make! Makes a nice side dish with Broiled Flounder with Parmesan (page 218).

1 tablespoon olive oil
24 ounces frozen snow pea pods
1 cup sliced water chestnuts, drained
1 cup homemade (page 151) or canned chicken broth (low-sodium, if desired)
2 teaspoons soy sauce (low-sodium, if desired)
2 teaspoons cornstarch

1. Heat the olive oil in a large skillet over medium-high heat.
2. Add the snow peas, water chestnuts, and broth. Bring to a boil. Cover and cook for 2 minutes, or until the vegetables are crisp-tender.
3. In a cup, whisk the soy sauce and cornstarch together; add to the vegetable mixture. Cook uncovered over medium heat, stirring constantly, until thickened, about 2 minutes.

Step One = Yes (neutral)
Step Two = Yes (neutral)
Step Three = Yes (neutral)

CAULIFLOWER "RICE"

Steps One, Two, and Three
Start to finish: 15 minutes
Makes: 1 head of cauliflower "rice"

Cauliflower "rice" can be bland on its own but it absorbs the flavor of stir-fries or sauces and becomes a wonderful substitute for white rice. You can also add butter, Parmesan cheese, and parsley, and serve as a side dish. It's a neutral food, so you can eat as much as you want!

1 head fresh cauliflower
Salt

1. Using a food processor or even a hand grater, grate or chop the cauliflower until it is the size of rice (usc a plain steel blade or shredder blade).
2. Add a sprinkling of salt to taste and microwave on HIGH in a covered dish for 4 minutes. *Do not add water.* To keep it fluffy, just let the moisture in the cauliflower do its work.

Step One = Yes (neutral)
Step Two = Yes (neutral)
Step Three = Yes (neutral)

16

BREAKFAST

○ Tex-Mex Eggs   248
○ Fruit-Filled Avocado Boats   249
○ Vegetable Frittata   250
○ Broccoli-Mushroom Frittata   251
○ Sausage and Egg Casserole   252
○ Crustless Quiche   253
○ Carrot and Oat Muffins   254
○ Oat-Nut Muffins   255
○ Banana Muffins   256
○ Legal Pancakes   257
○ Blueberry French Toast   258
○ Faux Breakfast Hash Browns   259
○ "Miracle" Granola   260
○ Baked Ham Omelet Cups   261
○ Peanut Butter Hot "Cereal"   262

TEX-MEX EGGS

Steps One, Two, and Three
Start to finish: 25 minutes
Serves: 4

Chili powder is a beloved staple in the southwest. It jazzes up just about any dish and you'll often find it added to eggs. This satisfying egg dish contains the high-quality protein that will fill you up and fuel all of your Saturday errands! You may serve this dish with a dip of guacamole, if you like.

Cooking oil spray
1 tablespoon olive oil
½ yellow bell pepper, seeded and sliced into thin strips
½ red bell pepper, seeded and sliced into thin strips
½ green bell pepper, seeded and sliced into thin strips
1 medium onion, chopped
6 medium tomatoes, peeled and chopped
1 teaspoon chili powder
¼ teaspoon salt, plus extra (optional)
4 eggs
Black pepper (optional)

1. Coat a large skillet with cooking oil spray. Add the olive oil, peppers, and onion, and cook for 5 minutes, until tender.
2. Add the tomatoes, chili powder, and the ¼ teaspoon of salt. Bring to a boil. Lower the heat and simmer covered for 10 minutes.
3. Carefully break each egg over the simmering tomato mixture and allow to gently rest on top of the mixture. Try to break the eggs so that they do not touch. Sprinkle with a little extra salt and pepper, if desired.
4. Cover and simmer over medium-low heat for 3 to 5 minutes, or until the whites are completely set and the yolks begin to thicken but are not hard.

Step One = Yes (neutral)
Step Two = Yes (neutral)
Step Three = Yes (neutral)

FRUIT-FILLED AVOCADO BOATS

Steps Two and Three

Start to finish: 20 minutes

Serves: 4

Sweet oranges, apples, and pineapples make a surprisingly appealing contrast to the creamy avocado in this unusual dish. Use it for a special brunch.

2 large ripe avocados, halved and pitted

2 teaspoons lemon juice

3 tablespoons olive oil

2 teaspoons balsamic vinegar

⅛ teaspoon black pepper

1 teaspoon sucralose or stevia

2 teaspoons rum (optional)

Salt

1 cup diced fresh pineapple

1 orange, membranes and seeds removed, diced

1 apple, peeled, cored, and cubed

1. Sprinkle the exposed flesh of the avocados with 1 teaspoon of the lemon juice and set aside.

2. To make the dressing, whisk together olive oil, remaining teaspoon of lemon juice, balsamic vinegar, black pepper, sweetener, and rum in a small bowl. Add salt to taste and set aside.

3. Add the fruit to the dressing and mix well so that all the fruit is coated.

4. Fill the avocado halves with the dressed fruit and serve.

Step One = No

Step Two = Yes (12 grams net carb, or one 11–20 gram carb serving)

Step Three = Yes (12 grams net carb, or one 11–20 gram carb serving)

VEGETABLE FRITTATA

Steps One, Two, and Three

Start to finish: 60 minutes (including standing time)

Serves: 8

Also known as my "hodgepodge" frittata, I often substitute vegetables that happen to be in the fridge or freezer for any of the vegetables listed below. Cauliflower, spinach, green beans, broccoli, and Brussels sprouts all work well, as do any cooked greens.

Cooking oil spray

1 (9-or 10-ounce) package frozen asparagus tips, or 1 cup cooked "hodgepodge" neutral veggies

1 medium yellow bell pepper, seeded and cut into strips

1 medium red bell pepper, seeded and cut into strips

1 medium onion, finely chopped

1 medium zucchini, chopped

12 eggs, beaten well, or 3 cups liquid egg substitute

½ cup half-and-half

½ cup low-fat milk

1 tablespoon chopped fresh dill

1 tablespoon chopped fresh parsley

1 teaspoon salt

½ teaspoon black pepper

1 cup shredded low-fat Cheddar cheese

1. Preheat the oven to 350°F. Coat an 8-inch square or 7 by 11-inch baking pan with cooking oil spray.
2. Bring 4 cups of salted water to a boil in a large saucepan. Add the asparagus tips. Cover and bring to a boil, then lower the heat and simmer for 3 minutes.
3. Add the bell peppers and onion. Cover and bring again to a boil, then lower the heat and simmer for about 2 minutes more.
4. Drain the boiled veggies in a colander. Add the chopped zucchini to the vegetable mixture and stir.
5. Spread the vegetable mixture evenly in the prepared baking pan and set aside.
6. Whisk together the eggs, half-and-half, milk, dill, parsley, salt, and black pepper in a large bowl. Pour the egg mixture over the vegetables. Top with the Cheddar cheese.
7. Bake uncovered for 30 to 40 minutes, or until a knife inserted in the center comes out clean.

Step One = Yes (neutral)
Step Two = Yes (neutral)
Step Three = Yes (neutral)

BROCCOLI-MUSHROOM FRITTATA

Steps One, Two, and Three
Start to finish: 45 minutes
Serves: 4 (¹⁄₄ frittata/serving)

This frittata is sophisticated enough to feed your visiting relatives, but easy enough to feed your family as a quick weeknight dinner or a "different" weekend breakfast.

8 eggs, or 2 cups liquid egg substitute
¹⁄₂ cup low-fat milk
¹⁄₄ teaspoon salt
¹⁄₄ teaspoon black pepper
6 ounces shredded Monterey Jack cheese
Cooking oil spray
1 tablespoon olive oil
2 cups chopped broccoli florets
2 cups sliced fresh mushrooms
¹⁄₄ cup finely chopped green onions (green part only)
2 cups cherry tomatoes, halved

1. Preheat the oven to 350°F.
2. Whisk together the eggs, milk, salt, and pepper in a large bowl. Stir in the shredded cheese. Set aside.
3. Coat a large skillet with cooking oil spray. Add the olive oil, broccoli, mushroom, and green onions. Cook over medium heat for 10 minutes, stirring occasionally, until the broccoli becomes tender.
4. Coat an 8-inch square or 7 by 11-inch baking pan with cooking oil spray. Spread the broccoli mixture evenly in the baking pan. Pour the egg mixture over the broccoli mixture. Bake uncovered for 30 minutes.
5. Sprinkle the quartered cherry tomatoes over the top of the frittata. Broil 5 inches from heat for about 3 minutes. Remove from the oven and let sit for 5 minutes before serving.

Step One = Yes (neutral)
Step Two = Yes (neutral)
Step Three = Yes (neutral)

SAUSAGE AND EGG CASSEROLE

Steps One, Two, and Three
Start to finish: 5 hours (including chilling time)
Serves: 6

Don't panic about the use of flour in a "neutral food." The amount used in this recipe, distributed over six servings, is negligible. Make the casserole the night before, place it in the refrigerator, and cook the next morning. Add a slice of lightly buttered low-carb toast and your breakfast is complete!

6 lean breakfast sausage links (preferably lean or low-fat)

6 eggs plus 2 egg whites, beaten well

¼ cup half-and-half

¼ cup milk (nonfat or low-fat)

¼ teaspoon salt

¼ teaspoon black pepper

8 ounces low-fat Cheddar cheese, shredded

1 tablespoon whole wheat flour

4 ounces Monterey Jack cheese, shredded

Step One = Yes (neutral)
Step Two = Yes (neutral)
Step Three = Yes (neutral)

1. Cook the sausage links according to the package directions. Drain the fat and set the sausages aside.

2. Beat the eggs, egg whites, half-and-half, milk, salt, and pepper until well blended in a medium bowl. Set aside.

3. Toss together the Cheddar cheese and flour in a medium bowl. Place in the bottom of an ungreased 1½-quart, shallow round baking dish. Evenly sprinkle with the Monterey Jack.

4. Pour the egg mixture over the cheese. Arrange the sausage links like "spokes" on top. Cover and refrigerate for 4 to 24 hours.

5. Uncover the dish and let stand at room temperature for 30 minutes. Preheat the oven to 350°F.

6. Bake the casserole for 40 to 50 minutes, or until puffed and the egg custard is set when the dish is shaken. Cut into six wedges and serve.

CRUSTLESS QUICHE

Steps One, Two, and Three
Start to finish: 60 minutes
Serves: 6

This quiche is so cheesy, rich, and filling no one will miss the crust. Serve it with Very Berry Crème (page 282) during Steps Two and Three for a very appealing and antioxidant-rich breakfast.

4 tablespoons (¼ cup) butter
¼ cup whole wheat flour
¾ cup low-fat milk
1 cup low-fat cottage or ricotta cheese
4 ounces light cream cheese, at room temperature
½ teaspoon baking powder
½ teaspoon salt
½ teaspoon Dijon mustard
5 eggs plus 2 egg whites
6 ounces Swiss or low-fat Cheddar cheese, shredded
¼ cup grated Parmesan cheese
Cooking oil spray
1 small onion, finely chopped
2 tablespoons seeded and chopped green bell pepper
6 cherry tomatoes, halved

Step One = Yes (5-gram net carb "Counter")
Step Two = Yes (5 grams net carb)
Step Three = Yes (5 grams net carb)

1. Preheat the oven to 350°F.
2. Melt the butter over medium heat in a medium saucepan. Stir in the flour; cook, stirring until bubbly. Add the milk and heat, stirring until the sauce thickens. Remove from the heat; set aside to cool.
3. In a mixing bowl, mix together the cottage cheese, cream cheese, baking powder, salt, and mustard.
4. In a large mixing bowl, beat the eggs and egg whites. Slowly add the cream cheese mixture and the flour mixture.
5. Fold in the Swiss and Parmesan cheeses.
6. Liberally coat a 10-inch pie plate with cooking oil spray. Pour the mixture into pie plate. Sprinkle the onion and bell pepper over the top. Arrange the cherry tomatoes, cut side up, around the top.
7. Bake for about 50 minutes, until puffy and lightly browned. A knife inserted in the center of the quiche should come out clean.
8. Let rest for 15 minutes before serving; cut in 6 to 8 slices.

CARROT AND OAT MUFFINS

Steps Two and Three
Start to finish: 45 minutes
Makes: 12 muffins (1 muffin/serving)

You'll notice two types of flour are often used in the baked goods in The Metabolism Miracle Cookbook. Using all whole wheat flour would cause the product to be too dense and doughy. I usually use equal amounts of two flours, and the end result of this recipe will provide adequate fiber! Enjoy these muffins with an Instant Espresso Chiller (page 104).

Cooking oil spray
½ cup milk (nonfat or low-fat preferred)
½ cup unsweetened natural applesauce
1 tablespoon olive oil
2 eggs, beaten, or ½ cup liquid egg substitute
½ cup shredded carrot (1 large carrot)
¾ cup whole wheat flour
¾ cup all-purpose flour
1 cup old-fashioned rolled oats
⅓ cup sucralose
1 teaspoon ground cinnamon
1½ teaspoons baking powder
½ teaspoon baking soda
¼ teaspoon salt
½ cup finely chopped walnuts (optional)

Step One = No
Step Two = Yes (20 grams net carb, or one 11–20 gram carb serving)
Step Three = Yes (20 grams net carb, or one 11–20 gram carb serving)

1. Preheat the oven to 350°F. Coat twelve cups of a muffin pan with cooking oil spray.
2. In a large bowl, beat together the milk, applesauce, oil, and eggs. Stir in the shredded carrots.
3. In another large bowl, combine the whole wheat flour, all-purpose flour, oats, sucralose, cinnamon, baking powder, baking soda, and salt in a separate bowl. Stir well.
4. Add the flour mixture to the applesauce mixture. Stir just until the batter is moistened; do not beat.
5. Spoon the batter into the muffin cups, filling two-thirds to three-quarters full. Sprinkle the walnuts over the top of the muffin batter, if desired. Fill any empty muffin cups halfway with water.
6. Bake for 20 to 25 minutes, or until muffins are golden brown. Let cool in the pan on a wire rack for 5 minutes and then let cool directly on the rack.

OAT-NUT MUFFINS

Steps Two and Three
Start to finish: 40 minutes
Makes: 12 muffins (1 muffin/serving)

The secret ingredient in these muffins is natural applesauce, which replaces much of the oil, butter, and other fats used in most muffin recipes. You'll find these muffins to be tender, moist, and delicious on their own or with a smear of light cream cheese or whipped butter.

Cooking oil spray
½ cup unsweetened natural applesauce
1 cup old-fashioned rolled oats
½ cup whole wheat flour
¼ cup all-purpose flour
1 teaspoon baking powder
¼ teaspoon baking soda
¼ teaspoon salt
1 cup pecans or walnuts
1 large egg
¼ cup sucralose
2 tablespoons oil
1 teaspoon vanilla extract

Step One = No
Step Two = Yes (20 grams net carb, or one 11–20 gram carb serving)
Step Three = Yes (20 grams net carb, or one 11–20 gram carb serving)

1. Preheat the oven to 350°F. Coat twelve cups of a muffin pan with cooking oil spray.
2. Coat a baking sheet with cooking oil spray. Spread the oats on the baking sheet and bake, stirring twice, until light golden and fragrant, 10 to 15 minutes. Let cool.
3. Mix the flour, baking powder, baking soda, and salt in a large bowl.
4. Grind the nuts in a food processor until they are finely ground.
5. Add the egg, sucralose, oil, and vanilla to the food processor. Process until smooth, stopping to scrape down the sides.
6. Add the egg mixture to the dry ingredients along with applesauce and oats. Stir just until combined.
7. Scoop the batter into the prepared muffin cups. Fill any empty muffin cups halfway with water. Bake until the tops spring back when touched lightly, 12 to 15 minutes. Let cool in the pan on a wire rack for 5 minutes.

BANANA MUFFINS

Steps Two and Three

Start to finish: 35 minutes

Makes: 12 muffins (1 muffin/serving)

When bananas get a smidge too ripe for my liking I peel them, place them in a zippered plastic bag, and freeze them until I'm ready to make this recipe. Let them defrost overnight in the refrigerator before you put them in the batter.

Cooking oil spray

1½ cups old-fashioned rolled oats

1 tablespoon baking powder

½ teaspoon baking soda

⅛ teaspoon salt

1 cup mashed bananas

2 tablespoons sucralose

¼ cup unsweetened natural applesauce

½ teaspoon vanilla extract

1 egg, beaten lightly

Step One = No

Step Two = Yes (15 grams net carb, or one 11–20 gram carb serving)

Step Three = Yes (15 grams net carb, or one 11–20 gram carb serving)

1. Preheat the oven to 350°F. Spray twelve cups of a muffin pan with cooking oil spray.
2. In a blender or food processor, grind oats into a flourlike consistency. After grinding, you need 1 cup of "oat" flour.
3. Mix together the oat flour, baking powder, baking soda, and salt.
4. In a small bowl, beat together the banana, egg, and sucralose. Stir in the applesauce and vanilla. Fold the banana mixture into the flour mixture until just combined.
5. Scoop the batter into prepared muffin cups. Fill any empty muffin cups halfway with water.
6. Bake for 15 to 20 minutes, or until a toothpick inserted into center of a muffin comes out clean. Let cool in the pan on a wire rack for 5 minutes, then remove from the pan and let cool on the wire rack.

LEGAL PANCAKES

Steps One, Two, and Three
Start to finish: 15 minutes
Serves: 4

The number of eggs and the use of almond flour make these pancakes higher in protein and lower in carb than your average stack of cakes. Imagine that. . . "neutral pancakes!"

1. Combine all ingredients, except the cooking oil spray, and mix well in a large bowl.

- **1 cup almond flour**
- **2 individual serving packets sucralose**
- **4 eggs, beaten**
- **⅔ cup seltzer**
- **2 tablespoons half-and-half**
- **½ teaspoon salt**
- **Pinch of ground cinnamon**
- **Cooking oil spray**

2. Coat a griddle or large skillet with cooking oil spray and heat over medium-high heat.
3. Drop the batter onto the hot skillet. The pancakes can be made silver-dollar or 4-inch pancake size. Flip only once.
4. Serve with whipped butter, sugar-free syrup, sugar-free jam, or light whipped cream.

Step One = Yes (neutral)
Step Two = Yes (neutral)
Step Three = Yes (neutral)

BLUEBERRY FRENCH TOAST

Steps Two and Three
Start to finish: 60 minutes
Serves: 6

This is the solution for anyone who doesn't like standing over the skillet all morning, flipping every piece of French toast until they are browned on both sides. Using the casserole approach here, you can sit down and enjoy the Sunday paper and a cup Ginger-Lemon Green Tea (page 98) while the French toast bakes to perfection.

Cooking oil spray
6 slices whole wheat bread, cut
  into 1-inch pieces
1 cup fresh blueberries
½ cup sucralose
½ cup milk (preferably low-fat)
2 eggs plus 4 egg whites
½ teaspoon vanilla extract
¼ teaspoon salt

1. Preheat the oven to 350°F. Coat an 8-inch square baking dish with cooking oil spray.
2. Alternate layering the bread cubes with the blueberries in the baking dish. Toss gently to combine. Set aside.
3. Whisk the sucralose into milk in a medium bowl until dissolved. Whisk in the eggs, egg whites, vanilla, and salt.
4. Pour the mixture over the bread. Toss to coat. Let stand for 5 minutes.
5. Bake for 40 to 45 minutes, or until top of bread is browned and the center is almost set. Let stand for 5 minutes before serving.

Step One = No
Step Two = Yes (18 grams net carb, or one 11–20 gram carb serving)
Step Three = Yes (18 grams net carb, or one 11–20 gram carb serving)

FAUX BREAKFAST HASH BROWNS

Steps One, Two, and Three
Start to finish: 25 minutes
Serves: 4

Cauliflower can become a welcome friend, as it can take the place of high-carb potatoes in some of your favorite recipes. Here it substitutes for the potatoes in this delectable version of a classic diner favorite. Neutral hash browns! Priceless.

1 medium onion, chopped
8 slices cooked turkey bacon, chopped
1 medium head fresh cauliflower, grated
2 tablespoons olive oil (plus more as needed)
Salt and pepper

1. In a large skillet over medium-high heat, cook the onion and bacon until the onion is golden and the bacon is cooked. Transfer the bacon to paper towels and remove any excess fat. Chop the bacon and return it to the skillet.
2. Add the cauliflower and the 2 tablespoons of olive oil, and stir until the cauliflower is tender and browned all over. Add oil as needed to assist in cooking.
3. Season to taste with salt and pepper.

Step One = Yes (neutral)
Step Two = Yes (neutral)
Step Three = Yes (neutral)

"MIRACLE" GRANOLA

Steps One, Two, and Three
Start to finish: 35 minutes
Serves: 6 (about ½ cup/serving)

Full of protein and healthful oils, nuts make a great alternative to high-carb breakfast cereals. Don't go overboard by eating this delicious mix by the handful all day long, as it packs a lot of fat in its punch. Consider half a cup to be a reasonable serving.

½ cup flaxseeds
½ cup sunflower seed kernels
½ cup unsweetened shredded coconut
½ cup chopped walnuts
½ cup chopped pecans
½ cup chopped almonds
Cooking oil spray
4 tablespoons (¼ cup) butter, melted
1 teaspoon vanilla extract
1½ teaspoons ground cinnamon
2 individual serving packets sucralose or stevia

1. Preheat the oven to 325°F.
2. Combine the seeds, coconut, and nuts in a medium bowl and mix well.
3. Lightly coat a baking sheet with cooking oil spray. Spread the mixture evenly on the baking sheet and set aside.
4. Melt the butter in a small saucepan and add the vanilla, cinnamon, and sweetener. Drizzle the butter mixture over the granola.
5. Bake for about 30 minutes, stirring every 5 minutes to avoid burning. Let cool. Store in a tightly sealed container.

Step One = Yes (neutral)
Step Two = Yes (neutral)
Step Three = Yes (neutral)

BAKED HAM OMELET CUPS

Steps One, Two, and Three
Start to finish: 30 minutes
Serves: 4

These ham-and-egg packages are fun to put together. Make up a larger batch on the weekend, freeze, and reheat them in the microwave for a quick weekday breakfast!

- 6 slices Virginia baked ham (deli-sliced to medium thickness)
- 4 large eggs, or 1 cup liquid egg substitute
- 3 tablespoons milk (nonfat or low-fat)
- ¼ teaspoon salt
- 2 tablespoons green onion, chopped
- 4 slices low-fat cheese, cut into thin strips

1. Preheat the oven to 350°F.
2. Place a nonstick skillet over medium-high heat. Heat the ham until it becomes warm and slightly browned. Remove from the heat.
3. Chop two slices of the heated ham into pieces, reserving four slices.
4. Place a slice of the heated ham in its own muffin cup and press down to form a "wrapper" for the omelet.
5. Beat the eggs with the milk and salt in a small bowl. Stir in the chopped ham and green onion.
6. Pour the egg mixture into the ham cups. Bake uncovered for 15 minutes, until the eggs are set.
7. Layer the strips of cheese over the omelet cups and bake for a few minutes longer, or until the whites are completely set and the yolks begin to thicken but are not hard.

Step One = Yes (neutral)
Step Two = Yes (neutral)
Step Three = Yes (neutral)

PEANUT BUTTER HOT "CEREAL"

Steps One, Two, and Three
Start to finish: 5 minutes
Serves: 1

Flaxseed is one of this century's great rediscoveries. Full of omega-3 fatty acids that keep your arteries limber by reducing inflammation, these seeds often appear in the top ten lists of foods to eat for good health. Like oats, they're high in soluble fiber that helps to lower cholesterol.

½ cup boiling water
¼ cup flaxseed meal
2 tablespoons natural peanut butter
½ teaspoon ground cinnamon
1 individual serving packet sucralose or stevia
Unsweetened soy or almond milk (optional)

1. In a cereal bowl, pour the boiling water over the flaxseed meal and stir well.
2. Immediately stir in the peanut butter, cinnamon, and sweetener.
3. Let thicken for 1 to 2 minutes and then stir. You may add soy or almond milk as desired to keep this a neutral choice.

Step One = Yes (neutral)
Step Two = Yes (neutral)
Step Three = Yes (neutral)

17

SNACKS

○ Sweet and Crunchy Nuts   264
○ Dark Chocolate Chips on a Log   265
○ Cheesy Chips   266
○ Miracle Mozzarella Sticks   267
○ Pepperoni Pizza Dip for Fresh Veggies   268
○ 15 Other Snack Food Ideas   269

SWEET AND CRUNCHY NUTS

Steps One, Two, and Three
Start to finish: 35 minutes
Serves: 4 ($^1/_2$ cup/serving)

Nuts make a great snack. They have the crunch factor and give you a satisfying feeling of fullness. This mix adds a sweet touch to a trio of my favorite nuts. The cinnamon smells heavenly as you roast them slowly in the oven.

Cooking oil spray
¾ cup pecan halves
¾ cup walnut halves
½ cup whole almonds
1 egg white, lightly beaten
½ cup sucralose or stevia
½ teaspoon ground cinnamon
2 tablespoons butter

1. Preheat the oven to 250°F. Coat a cookie sheet with cooking oil spray.
2. Combine the nuts in a medium bowl. Add egg white and toss to coat the nuts.
3. In a microwave-safe cup, combine the sweetener and cinnamon with the butter. Cover and microwave for 10 seconds, or until the butter is melted. Stir. Drizzle over the nuts, tossing to coat.
4. Spread the nut mixture evenly on the prepared cookie sheet. Bake for 20 to 30 minutes, or until the nuts are toasted, stirring every 10 minutes. Let cool on waxed paper. Store in an airtight container.

Step One = Yes (neutral)
Step Two = Yes (neutral)
Step Three = Yes (neutral)

DARK CHOCOLATE CHIPS ON A LOG

Steps One, Two, and Three
Start to finish: 15 minutes
Serves: 4 (4 pieces/serving)

This recipe could have been titled "ants on a log," but we are replacing the typical raisins with dark chocolate morsels to keep this a 5-gram food choice. You'll love the combo of PB, banana, and chocolate . . . yummy and nutritious!

½ cup whipped cream cheese

3 tablespoons natural creamy peanut butter

½ banana, mashed

4 stalks celery, each cut width-wise into 4 equal pieces

2 tablespoons dark chocolate chips

1. Combine the cream cheese, peanut butter, and banana in a small mixing bowl. Mix until smooth.
2. Spoon the spread into the celery stalks.
3. Top each filled stalk portion with a few dark chocolate chips.

Step One = Yes (5-gram net carb "Counter")
Step Two = Yes (5 grams net carbs)
Step Three = Yes (5 grams net carbs)

CHEESY CHIPS

Steps One, Two, and Three
Start to finish: 3 minutes
Serves: 1

Sometimes you just "need a chip"! This easy-to-make treat is more heart sensible if you use low-fat cheese and well-cooked, drained turkey bacon. It will match your desire for something crunchy as a neutral side with your healthy salad or 5-gram sandwich.

Cooking oil spray
6 tablespoons shredded low-fat Cheddar cheese
2 tablespoons well-cooked crumbled turkey bacon, drained and blotted to reduce fat
Salsa, for dipping (optional)

1. Lightly coat a nonstick frying pan with cooking oil spray. Heat over medium heat until hot.
2. Place six mounds of the cheese (about 1 tablespoon each) on the hot pan surface, spaced well apart. Sprinkle with pepper, if desired. Sprinkle the top of each mound with bacon crumbles.
3. Cook for 1 minute, or until the outer edges begin turning light brown and are crispy on the bottom. Flip and crisp the other side for about 1 minute.
4. Remove from the pan and place on paper towels to remove any excess fat. The chips are ready to eat, and delicious with a dip of salsa!

Step One = Yes (neutral)
Step Two = Yes (neutral)
Step Three = Yes (neutral)

MIRACLE MOZZARELLA STICKS

Steps One, Two, and Three
Start to finish: 3 minutes
Serves: 1

This easy recipe will remind you of gooey, chewy mozzarella sticks, without the high carbs and fat. They are great as an appetizer before dinner or as your bedtime snack. Use them anywhere you can use a 5-gram carb.

Cooking oil spray
1 slice low-carb bread (with 5 grams or less net carb)
¼ cup shredded part-skim mozzarella cheese
Black pepper (optional)
Garlic powder (optional)
Salsa, for dipping (optional)

1. Very lightly coat a nonstick pan with cooking oil spray and place over medium heat. Place the slice of bread in the pan.
2. Sprinkle the mozzarella over the top of the bread to coat it. Lightly sprinkle with pepper and garlic powder, if desired.
3. Cover with a lid and allow the cheese to melt for 1 to 2 minutes, until the bottom of the bread is crisp and golden brown.
4. Remove from the pan and slice into 4-inch sticks. Dip in salsa, if desired.

Step One = Yes (5-gram net carb "Counter")
Step Two = Yes (5 grams net carb)
Step Three = Yes (5 grams net carb)

PEPPERONI PIZZA DIP FOR FRESH VEGGIES

Steps One, Two, and Three
Start to finish: 10 minutes
Serves: 5 (¹/₂ cup/serving)

Served warm, this dip provides an easy way to increase your neutral veggie intake. Dip fresh bell pepper slices, broccoli florets, mushrooms, celery sticks, cauliflower, cucumbers, or even fresh green beans into this delicious dip, and before you know it, the veggies are gone.

8 ounces light cream cheese
¹/₂ cup light sour cream
1 teaspoon light Italian seasoning
¹/₄ teaspoon garlic powder
¹/₂ cup seasoned crushed tomatoes
¹/₂ cup chopped turkey pepperoni
¹/₂ cup chopped red onion
¹/₂ cup seeded and chopped green bell pepper
1 cup shredded part-skim mozzarella cheese

1. Preheat the oven to 350°F.
2. Mix the cream cheese, sour cream, Italian seasoning, and garlic powder in a large bowl until smooth. Spread into a 9-inch pie pan.
3. Spoon the tomatoes over the cream cheese mixture. Sprinkle with the turkey pepperoni, onion, and green pepper. Bake for 10 minutes.
4. Remove from the oven and top with the mozzarella cheese. Bake for 5 minutes more, or until the cheese is melted and the dip is heated through.
5. Serve with your choice of fresh crudités.

Step One = Yes (neutral)
Step Two = Yes (neutral)
Step Three = Yes (neutral)

15 OTHER SNACK FOOD IDEAS

NEUTRALS

1. **Fresh veggie plate** (bell pepper strips, mushrooms, cucumbers, broccoli florets, celery sticks) with light ranch dressing as a dip
2. **Dry-roasted edamame** (find them packaged near the nuts in the supermarket)
3. **Ricotta "pudding"**

    ½ cup part skim ricotta cheese

    1 tablespoon low-fat sour cream

    ¼ teaspoon vanilla extract

    1 individual serving packet sucralose or stevia

    Mix together and chill! (Makes one serving.)
4. **Celery sticks** filled with natural almond butter or light cream cheese spread
5. **"Fruity" mousse**

    1 (4-serving) package of sugar-free gelatin (cherry, raspberry, lime, or lemon)

    1 (8-ounce) container light cream cheese, at room temperature

    ½ cup light sour cream

    1 cup light whipping cream

    2 tablespoons sucralose

    Prepare the gelatin as directed and let set in the refrigerator for 75 minutes. Beat the gelatin until creamy, then add and beat together with cream cheese and sour cream. In another bowl, whip together the whipping cream and sucralose until peaks form. Gently fold the "whipped cream" into the gelatin mixture until it looks marbled. Spoon into dessert dishes (or leave in a large bowl) and refrigerate for at least 2 hours. (Makes four servings.)

5-GRAM "COUNTER"S

1. **Party Mix I:** Combine an individual portion of nuts, sunflower seed kernels, dried soybeans or dry-roasted edamame, along with ¼ cup goldfish crackers (now made with fiber)

2. **One "Coco Pop" popcorn cake** spread with low-fat cream cheese or natural nut butter and sprinkled with ground cinnamon

3. **Dip of low-fat ricotta cheese** mixed with sugar-free fruit spread (don't exceed 5 grams' worth of fruit spread!)

4. **½ cup low-fat Greek yogurt** mixed with 1 individual serving packet sucralose or stevia, ground cinnamon, and walnuts

5. **Five baked tortilla chips** with ¼ cup of salsa

ONE-CARB SERVINGS

1. **One fresh apple,** cored and sliced, spread with natural almond butter = **11–20 grams net carb, or 1 carb serving**

2. **¾ cup blueberries or 7 sliced strawberries** atop a dip of "ricotta pudding" = **11–20 grams net carb, or 1 carb serving**

3. **½ sliced banana** in a bowl, topped with cooled liquid flavored gelatin. Chill until firm and serve with some light whipped cream = **11–20 grams net carb, or 1 carb serving**

4. **Party Mix II:** ¾ cup goldfish crackers + mixed nuts + 1 tablespoon of dark chocolate chip morsels = **11–20 grams net carb, or 1 carb serving**

5. **½ cup sugar-free pudding** or sugar-free ice cream with a topping of light whipped cream and chopped nuts = **11–20 grams net carb, or 1 carb serving**

18

DESSERTS

○ Crustless Pumpkin Pie   272
○ Cheesecake Cupcakes   273
○ Butter-Rum Cupcakes   274
○ Chocolate Cupcakes   275
○ Gingerbread Cake   276
○ Chocolate Mousse   277
○ Watermelon Sorbet   278
○ Fruit Pie with Coconut Crust   278
○ Ice-Cream Pie   280
○ Cherries with Ricotta and Toasted Almonds 281
○ Very Berry Crème   282
○ Apple-Walnut Custards   282
○ Pumpkin Custards   284
○ Spiced Apples   285
○ Pumpkin Bread Pudding   286
○ Almond Meringue Kisses   287
○ Peanut Butter Cookies   288
○ Coconut Macaroons   289
○ "DE"licious Chocolate Chip Cookies   290

CRUSTLESS PUMPKIN PIE

Steps One, Two, and Three
Start to finish: 50 minutes
Serves: 8

You won't miss the crust in this luscious version of pumpkin pie. If you don't have pumpkin pie spice, combine 1 teaspoon of ground cinnamon, ¾ teaspoon of nutmeg, and ¾ teaspoon of allspice.

Cooking oil spray
1¾ cups pure pumpkin (not pumpkin pie mix)
3 eggs
¾ cup sucralose
½ teaspoon salt
1 teaspoon ground cinnamon
1¾ teaspoons pumpkin pie spice
¾ cup light cream or half-and-half
Light whipped cream, for topping (optional)

1. Preheat the oven to 350°F. Liberally coat a 9-inch pie pan with cooking oil spray.
2. Whisk together all ingredients, except the light whipped cream, in a medium bowl until well blended.
3. Pour the mixture into the prepared pie pan and bake for 35 to 40 minutes. To test for doneness, stick a toothpick in the center. If it comes out clean, the pie is done.
4. Let cool and then chill in the refrigerator. Top with light whipped cream before serving, if desired. Keep leftover pie in the refrigerator.

Step One = Yes (5-gram net carb "Counter")
Step Two = Yes (5 grams net carb)
Step Three = Yes (5 grams net carb)

CHEESECAKE CUPCAKES

Steps One, Two, and Three
Prep: 35 minutes
Start to finish: 2 hours 35 minutes
Makes: 6 cupcakes (1 cupcake/serving)

The muffin tins keep portion sizes uniform for these lovely little desserts. If you opt for a dot of jelly on top, make sure it's carb-free to keep the neutral price tag for these cupcakes.

6 ounces light cream cheese, at room temperature
½ cup part-skim ricotta cheese
2 tablespoons sucralose
1 large egg plus 1 large egg yolk
½ teaspoon vanilla extract
Carb-free fruit spread (optional)

Step One = Yes (neutral)
Step Two = Yes (neutral)
Step Three = Yes (neutral)

1. Preheat the oven to 350°F. Line six cups of a muffin tin with paper or foil liners.
2. Combine the cream cheese and ricotta in a food processor or use a hand mixer to beat until creamy. Add the sweetener, egg, egg yolk, and vanilla, and process until smooth.
3. Divide the mixture equally among the prepared muffin cups. Fill any empty muffin cups halfway with water.
4. Place the muffin tin in a large roasting pan filled with hot water halfway up the side of the tin, to prevent burning the delicate cheesecake. Bake for 18 to 20 minutes, until the cakes are puffed and set.
5. Remove the muffin tins from the water and let cool to room temperature.
6. Cover with plastic wrap and refrigerate for about 2 hours, until chilled.
7. After chilling, top the cheesecake cupcakes with carb-free jelly, if desired.

BUTTER-RUM CUPCAKES

Steps One, Two, and Three
Start to finish: 45 minutes
Makes: 4 cupcakes (1 cupcake/serving)

These tender cupcakes with their hint of rum bring thoughts of the holidays. Use whey protein powder or low-carb protein powder to keep each muffin in the neutral range.

Cooking oil spray
¼ cup soy flour
¼ cup sesame seeds, ground
¼ cup whey protein powder
2 large eggs, beaten lightly
3 tablespoons light sour cream
1 tablespoon butter, at room temperature
1 teaspoon rum or rum extract
3 tablespoons sucralose
1½ teaspoons vanilla extract
½ teaspoon baking powder

1. Preheat the oven to 350°F. Spray four cups of a muffin tin with cooking oil spray.
2. Combine the soy flour, sesame seeds, whey protein, eggs, sour cream, butter, rum, sweetener, vanilla, and baking powder in a large bowl and mix, using an electric mixer or food processor, for 2 to 3 minutes, until smooth.
3. Divide the batter evenly among the prepared muffin cups, filling each about half full. Fill any empty muffin cups halfway with water.
4. Bake for 20 to 25 minutes. To test for doneness, stick a toothpick in the center of a cupcakes. If it comes out clean, the cupcakes are done.
5. Let the cupcakes cool for 5 minutes. Remove from the tins and place on rack to cool completely.

Step One = Yes (neutral)
Step Two = Yes (neutral)
Step Three = Yes (neutral)

Chocolate Cupcakes

Steps One, Two, and Three
Start to finish: 30 minutes
Makes: 16 cupcakes (1 cupcake/serving)

Using almond flour keeps these delicious cupcakes in the "neutral" zone, suitable for all steps of the Metabolism Miracle program. Neutral chocolate cupcakes? Yummy!

5 eggs, separated
⅛ teaspoon cream of tartar
6 tablespoons butter, at room temperature
1 teaspoon vanilla extract
1 cup sucralose
2 cups almond flour
2 teaspoons baking powder
5 tablespoons unsweetened cocoa powder
Light whipped cream, for topping (optional)

Step One = Yes (neutral)
Step Two = Yes (neutral)
Step Three = Yes (neutral)

1. Preheat the oven to 325°F. Line six cups of a muffin tin with paper or foil liners.
2. Whisk the egg whites and cream of tartar in a mixing bowl until stiff. Set aside.
3. In a separate bowl, with clean beaters, cream the butter and egg yolks until light yellow and fluffy. Add the vanilla and sweetener. Beat until mixed.
4. Add about one-third of beaten egg whites to the egg yolk mixture and mix gently. Fold the mixture into the remaining egg whites.
5. Fold in 1 cup of the almond flour. Gently but thoroughly fold in the remaining almond flour, the baking powder, and the cocoa, being careful not to break down the egg whites.
6. Fill the lined muffin tins about half full. Fill any empty muffin cups halfway with water. Bake for 15 to 20 minutes, until the tops begin to crack. Remove from the oven and let stand for 5 minutes before removing the cupcakes from the tin. Let cool on a rack.
7. The cupcakes can be topped with light whipped cream immediately prior to serving.

Gingerbread Cake

Step Three
Start to finish: 45 minutes
Makes: 8 servings

Whole wheat flour in this American classic improves its glycemic index and increases the fiber. Because it's so tender and moist, no one will ever know. Use it only during Step Three, as it contains molasses!

Cooking oil spray
½ cup whole wheat flour
½ cup all-purpose flour
1 teaspoon baking powder
½ teaspoon baking soda
2 teaspoons ground cinnamon
½ teaspoon ground ginger
8 tablespoons (½ cup) butter, at room temperature
¼ cup light molasses
2 eggs, beaten, or ½ cup liquid egg substitute
1 teaspoon vanilla extract
1 cup sucralose
½ cup unsweetened natural applesauce

1. Preheat the oven to 350°F. Coat an 8-inch square metal cake pan with cooking oil spray.
2. Combine the flours, baking powder, baking soda, cinnamon, and ginger in a small bowl and set aside.
3. In a large mixing bowl, beat the butter and molasses with an electric mixer on high speed for about 1 minute.
4. Add the eggs and vanilla and blend on high speed for 30 seconds. The mixture will be very liquid.
5. Add the sweetener and beat on medium speed until very smooth, about 1½ minutes. Add the flour mixture and applesauce, and beat on low speed until mixed.
6. Spread the batter evenly in the prepared pan and bake for 30 to 35 minutes.

Step One = No
Step Two = No
Step Three = Yes (20 grams net carb, or one 11–20 gram carb serving)

CHOCOLATE MOUSSE

Steps One, Two, and Three
Start to finish: 1 hour 15 minutes (includes 1 hour chilling time)
Serves: 5

Don't tell the kids that there is tofu in this luscious dessert that helps to keep it in the 5-gram carb range!

1 (12-ounce) package **soft tofu**
1 (4-serving size) package **sugar-free chocolate-flavored instant pudding mix**
1 heaping tablespoon **unsweetened cocoa powder**
8 ounces **whipping cream**
1 teaspoon **vanilla extract**

1. Combine the tofu, pudding mix, and cocoa powder in a large mixing bowl. Set aside.
2. In a separate bowl, whip the cream until stiff and then add the vanilla.
3. Add the whipped cream mixture to the other ingredients and mix just until combined. Do not overwhip or the texture will become buttery instead of light and fluffy.
4. Pour into individual dishes and chill until ready to serve.

Step One = Yes (5-gram net carb "Counter")
Step Two = Yes (5 grams net carb)
Step Three = Yes (5 grams net carb)

WATERMELON SORBET

Steps Two and Three
Start to finish: 3 hours 10 minutes (includes freezing time)
Serves: 4 (1 cup/serving)

A cup of this sweet, icy cold sorbet makes a perfect finish to a hot summer day. Tuck a sprig of mint leaves on the dish to make it even prettier.

4 cups cubed and seeded watermelon

2 tablespoons sucralose or stevia

1 tablespoon lemon juice

1 tablespoon lime juice

1. Place the watermelon in a blender or food processor.
2. Add the sweetener, lemon juice, and lime juice. Blend until smooth.
3. Pour the mixture into a covered freezer container and freeze for 3 hours.
4. Scoop into four dessert dishes to serve.

Step One = No
Step Two = Yes (15 grams net carb)
Step Three = Yes (15 grams net carb, or one 11–20 gram carb serving)

FRUIT PIE WITH COCONUT CRUST

Steps Two and Three
Start to finish: 40 minutes
Serves: 4

A golden coconut crust cradles a bounty of fresh fruit and whipped cream. It's great to have a neutral crust to use for this and other desserts!

FRUIT PIE WITH COCONUT CRUST (CONTINUED)

Cooking oil spray

4 tablespoons (¼ cup) salted butter

2 cups shredded unsweetened coconut

¾ cup blueberries

8 strawberries, hulled and sliced

1 banana, sliced

Light whipped cream

Note: The crust alone is a neutral food.

1. Coat an 8- or 9-inch pie pan with cooking oil spray.
2. Melt the butter in a small saucepan over medium heat. Add the coconut and stir constantly until the coconut becomes light golden brown, 7 to 8 minutes.
3. Spoon the mixture into the pie pan. Using your fingers, press it firmly to cover the bottom and sides of the pan.
4. Before adding the filling, let the pie shell cool at room temperature for about 30 minutes or chill it for 10 to 15 minutes.
5. Fill the cooled pie shell with the blueberries, strawberries, and banana.
6. Top with the whipped cream. Cut into four pieces and serve immediately.

Step One = No
Step Two = Yes (17 grams net carb, or one 11–20 gram carb serving)
Step Three = Yes (17 grams net carb, or one 11–20 gram carb serving)

ICE-CREAM PIE

Steps Two and Three
Start to finish: 1 hour 45 minutes (including 1 hour freezing time)
Serves: 8

The coconut crust turns a plain dip of ice cream into something special. Be sure to temper the pie for 15 minutes out of the freezer, to soften the ice cream slightly before serving.

Cooking oil spray
4 tablespoons (¼ cup) salted butter
2 cups shredded coconut
1 quart sugar-free ice cream (any flavor)
Light whipped cream

Step One = No
Step Two = Yes (17 grams net carb, or one 11–20 gram carb serving)
Step Three = Yes (17 grams net carb, or one 11–20 gram carb serving)

1. Coat an 8- or 9-inch pie pan with cooking oil spray.
2. Melt the butter in a small saucepan over medium heat. Add the coconut and stir constantly until the coconut becomes light golden brown, 7 to 8 minutes.
3. Spoon the mixture into the pie pan. Press it firmly, using your fingers, to cover the bottom and sides of the pan.
4. Before adding the filling, let the shell cool at room temperature for 30 minutes or chill it for 15 minutes.
5. Place the ice cream in a mixing bowl and let it soften until you can mix it with a large spoon into a soft consistency.
6. Spoon the softened ice cream into the cooled coconut shell. Cover and place in the freezer until the ice cream hardens (at least 1 hour).
7. Cut into eight slices and top with a dollop of whipped cream to serve.

Note: The crust alone is a neutral food.

CHERRIES WITH RICOTTA AND TOASTED ALMONDS

Steps Two and Three
Start to finish: 5 minutes
Serves: 1

Using frozen cherries means that you don't have to wait for cherry season to make this special treat. It's a very pretty dish to serve to friends and family.

12 frozen pitted cherries
¼ cup part-skim ricotta cheese
1 tablespoon toasted slivered almonds

1. Microwave the cherries on HIGH for 30 seconds in a small microwave-safe bowl.
2. Top the warm cherries with a dollop of ricotta and the almonds.

Step One = No
Step Two = Yes (17 grams net carb, or one 11–20 gram carb serving)
Step Three = Yes (17 grams net carb, or one 11–20 gram carb serving)

VERY BERRY CRÈME

Steps Two and Three
Start to finish: 15 minutes
Serves: 4 (³/₄ cup/serving)

The smooth and creamy sauce is a lovely addition to the sweet berries. All berries are chock-full of healthful, natural antioxidants and have a low glycemic index.

3 cups berries (any combination of blueberries, raspberries, sliced strawberries, or blackberries)

2 tablespoons sucralose or stevia

½ teaspoon vanilla extract

¼ teaspoon ground ginger

1 cup light sour cream

1. Place ¾ cup of berries in each of four bowls.
2. Whisk together the sweetener, vanilla, ginger, and light sour cream in a medium mixing bowl.
3. Spoon ¼ cup of mixture over each bowl of berries and serve.

Step One = No
Step Two = Yes (15 grams net carb, or one 11–20 gram carb serving)
Step Three = Yes (15 grams net carb, or one 11–20 gram carb serving

APPLE-WALNUT CUSTARDS

Steps Two and Three
Start to finish: 45 minutes
Serves: 4

Apples, walnuts, oats . . . who could ask for more? Consider toasting the nuts to enhance their flavor.

APPLE-WALNUT CUSTARDS (CONTINUED)

Cooking oil spray

½ cup unsweetened natural applesauce

⅓ cup skim or low-fat milk

1 egg, beaten lightly

3 tablespoons Splenda brown sugar

1 tablespoon butter, melted

½ teaspoon vanilla extract

½ teaspoon maple flavoring

¾ cup peeled, cored, and chopped cooking apple (1 medium)

⅓ cup old-fashioned rolled oats

¼ cup chopped walnuts (toasting optional)

1. Preheat the oven to 375°F. Lightly coat four 6-ounce ramekins with cooking oil spray. Place the ramekins in a baking pan.
2. In a medium bowl, combine the applesauce, milk, egg, Splenda brown sugar, butter, vanilla, and maple flavoring. Stir in the apples and oats.
3. Divide the apple mixture evenly among the ramekins.
4. Slowly add hot water to the baking pan until the water level is about one-third up the side of the ramekins.
5. Bake for 25 minutes, or until a knife inserted near the centers comes out clean.
6. Cool for 15 minutes on a wire rack. Sprinkle with chopped walnuts.

Step One = No
Step Two = Yes (16 grams net carb, or one (11–20 gram carb serving)
Step Three = Yes (16 grams net carb, or one 11–20 gram carb serving)

PUMPKIN CUSTARDS

Steps Two and Three
Start to finish: 60 minutes
Serves: 8

The spices in pumpkin custards make them unforgettable. I like to linger over this dessert with a cup of coffee and good conversation.

Cooking oil spray
1 (15-ounce) can pure pumpkin (not pumpkin pie mix)
12 ounces evaporated skim milk
2 large eggs plus 2 large egg whites
½ cup sucralose
3 tablespoons Splenda brown sugar
1½ teaspoons ground cinnamon
½ teaspoon ground ginger
¼ teaspoon ground cloves
Light whipped cream, as desired
¼ teaspoon ground nutmeg

1. Preheat the oven to 350°F. Spray eight oven-proof custard cups with cooking oil spray. Place the cups in a large baking pan.
2. In a large bowl, whisk together the pumpkin, evaporated milk, eggs, egg whites, sweeteners, cinnamon, ginger, and ground cloves.
3. Pour ½ cup of the custard mixture into each prepared cup.
4. Place a baking pan in the oven. Pour hot water into the baking pan—enough to reach halfway up the side of the custard cups—to form a "water bath" for the custard cups so they don't stick and burn.
5. Bake for 40 to 45 minutes, or until center of the custard puffs up.
6. Wearing oven mitts, remove the cups from the hot water. Let cool at room temperature and then refrigerate until chilled.
7. When ready to serve, top with whipped cream and a pinch of nutmeg.

Step One = No
Step Two = Yes (20 grams net carb, or one 11–20 gram carb serving)
Step Three = Yes (20 grams net carb, or one 11–20 gram carb serving)

SPICED APPLES

Steps Two and Three
Start to finish: 15 minutes
Serves: 4 (1 apple/serving)

Just a smidge of cocoa on the apple slices adds a special touch to this creation. You can use all different types of apples, although I'm partial to crisp varieties such as Empire or Fuji.

¼ cup sucralose or stevia
1 teaspoon ground cinnamon
1 teaspoon unsweetened cocoa
  powder
4 apples, cored and quartered
¼ cup sugar-free, fat-free hot
  fudge topping
20 pecans, ground

1. Mix the sweetener, cinnamon, and cocoa powder together in a small bowl.
2. Place the apple quarters on a plate. Sprinkle half the sweetener mixture on top of the apples. Turn over apple slices and coat the other sides.
3. Drizzle each apple quarter with the fudge topping. Sprinkle with the ground pecans.
4. Chill for at least 15 minutes before serving.

   Step One = No
   Step Two = Yes (20 grams net carb,
     or one 11–20 gram carb serving)
   Step Three = Yes (20 grams net carb,
     or one 11–20 gram carb serving)

PUMPKIN BREAD PUDDING

Steps Two and Three
Start to finish: 40 minutes
Serves: 4

By using low-carb bread and pumpkin, typically "off limits" bread pudding fits as an 11–20 gram carb serving for Steps Two and Three! Top with a spritz of whipped cream.

Cooking oil spray
5 slices low-carb bread (with 5 grams or less net carb per slice)
1 (15-ounce) can pure pumpkin (not pumpkin pie mix)
2 eggs, or ½ cup liquid egg substitute
1 teaspoon ground cinnamon
2 teaspoons vanilla extract
¼ cup sucralose or stevia
Whipped topping (optional)

1. Preheat the oven to 375°F. Lightly coat four 6-ounce ovenproof ramekins with cooking oil spray. Place the ramekins in a baking pan.
2. Toast the bread and cut into 1-inch cubes. Set aside.
3. Using an electric mixer, beat the pumpkin, egg substitute, cinnamon, vanilla, and sweetener together in a medium bowl. Fold in the toast cubes.
4. Spread the batter evenly in the ramekins. Slowly add hot water to the baking pan and fill until the water level is one-third up the side of the ramekins.
5. Bake for 30 minutes.
6. Serve warm with whipped topping, if desired.

Step One = No
Step Two = Yes (13 grams net carb, or one 11–20 grams net carb serving)
Step Three = Yes (13 grams net carb, or one 11–20 gram carb serving)

ALMOND MERINGUE KISSES

Steps One, Two, and Three
Start to finish: 2¹/₂ hours (includes 2 hours cooling time)
Serves: 7 (5 mini cookies/serving)

These meringues are as light as angel wings. They offer a sweet conclusion to a dinner any time of the year.

2 egg whites
1 teaspoon almond extract
¼ teaspoon cream of tartar
⅛ teaspoon salt
½ cup sucralose
1 tablespoon cornstarch
Unsweetened cocoa powder, for dusting

Step One = Yes (5-gram net carb "Counter")
Step Two = Yes (5 grams net carb)
Step Three = Yes (5 grams net carb)

1. Preheat the oven to 300°F.
2. Let the egg whites stand in a medium bowl at room temperature for 30 minutes. Line two large baking sheets with parchment paper and set aside.
3. Add the almond extract, cream of tartar, and salt to the egg whites. Beat with an electric mixer on medium to high speed until soft peaks form.
4. Combine the sweetener and cornstarch. Add to the egg mixture, about 1 tablespoon at a time, beating on high speed until stiff peaks form.
5. Transfer the egg mixture to a piping bag with a large closed star tip. Pipe small "kisses" 1 inch apart on cookie sheets.
6. Place the cookie sheets on separate oven racks; bake for 12 minutes. Turn off the heat and allow the cookies to dry for 1 hour in the oven with the door closed.
7. Carefully lift the cookies off the parchment paper. Transfer to wire racks and let cool completely.
8. Sprinkle lightly with cocoa powder, if desired.

PEANUT BUTTER COOKIES

Steps One, Two, and Three
Start to finish: 30 minutes
Makes: 12 cookies (1 large cookie/serving)

You'll be amazed that this delicious cookie is made without flour. These peanut butter creations are so satisfying you only need one to satisfy the desire for something sweet.

Cooking oil spray
1 cup sucralose, plus extra for dipping the fork
1 large egg
1 teaspoon vanilla extract
1 cup creamy or chunky natural peanut butter
1 teaspoon baking soda

Note: Natural peanut butter should be stirred well and at room temperature before you begin this recipe.

1. Preheat the oven to 350°F. Coat a cookie sheet with cooking oil spray.
2. Mix the sweetener, egg, and vanilla with an electric mixer on low for 3 minutes in a medium bowl. Add the peanut butter and baking soda. Mix on medium speed until the dough comes together, about 30 seconds.
3. Form the dough into walnut-size ball and place 2 inches apart on the baking sheet.
4. Dip a fork in additional sweetener and flatten the cookies with crisscross marks.
5. Bake for 10 to 12 minutes, until lightly browned on bottom. Transfer to a wire rack and let cool completely.

Step One = Yes (neutral)
Step Two = Yes (neutral)
Step Three = Yes (neutral)

COCONUT MACAROONS

Steps One, Two, and Three
Start to finish: 30 minutes
Makes: about 36 macaroons

Funny name for an easy cookie. A macaroon is a chewy cookie made with sugar, egg whites, and coconut. By replacing the sugar with sucralose, this simple treat is a neutral food! Enjoy with a cup of coffee and a good book!

2 large egg whites
¼ teaspoon cream of tartar
⅓ cup sucralose
1 teaspoon almond extract
2¼ cups grated unsweetened coconut

1. Preheat the oven to 375°F.
2. Place the egg whites and cream of tartar in a large bowl. Beat until stiff peaks form.
3. Continue beating, adding the sweetener. Fold in the almond extract. Fold in the grated coconut; the mixture will be stiff.
4. Drop by spoonfuls onto a nonstick cookie sheet.
5. Bake for 20 minutes. Transfer the macaroons to a wire rack to let cool.

Step One = Yes (neutral)
Step Two = Yes (neutral)
Step Three = Yes (neutral)

"DE"LICIOUS CHOCOLATE CHIP COOKIES

Steps One, Two, and Three
Start to finish: 30 minutes
Makes: 24 to 28 cookies (1 cookie/serving)

Chocolate chip cookies during Step One as a 5-gram net carb "Counter"? Remember that these cookies do have a teeny bit of carb, so one cookie at a time will do it. Enjoy!

Cooking oil spray
1½ cups soy flour
½ teaspoon baking soda
½ teaspoon salt
8 tablespoons (½ cup) butter
1 cup sucralose
1 egg
¾ cup light sour cream
1 tablespoon vanilla extract
4 ounces sugar-free chocolate chip morsels
½ cup pecans or walnuts, chopped (optional)

1. Preheat the oven to 350°F. Spray a cookie sheet with cooking oil spray.
2. In a large bowl, mix together the soy flour, baking soda, and salt. Set aside.
3. In a medium bowl, cream the butter with the sweetener, adding the egg, sour cream, and vanilla, and beating until mixed.
4. Slowly add the dry ingredients and mix well. Fold in the chocolate chips and nuts (if using).
5. Drop the dough by the teaspoonful onto the cookie sheet.
6. Bake for about 12 minutes, until golden brown. Let cool before removing the cookies from the baking sheet.

Step One = Yes (5-gram net carb "Counter")
Step Two = Yes (5 grams net carb)
Step Three = Yes (5 grams net carb)

ACKNOWLEDGMENTS

Special Thanks To:

Diana Kresefski: For your fresh perspective, reality checks, organizational ability, and 24/7 help with this project and all of your help at Miracle Enterprises.

Michael Scott Simon, Esq.: Heartfelt thanks once again for all you do regarding The Miracle. Thanks for sharing my vision and for helping make miracles unfold . . . what an amazing ride.

To all those at Da Capo Press/Perseus Books Group who have helped to make the Metabolism Miracle program an international success! Special thanks to **John Radziewcz**, publisher; **Katie McHugh**, senior editor; **Kate Burke** and publicity; **Lindsey Treibel**, **Kevin Hanover**, and marketing; **Peter Costanza**, online marketing; the sales department; **Cisca L. Schreefel**, associate director of editorial services; and **Carla Thompson**, publicity at Perseus Book Group (UK). You have all been very supportive, positive, and helpful in this process, and I have once again enjoyed working with all of you. Onward and upward.

Susan Burgoin, food photographer; and **Mary Holloway**, food stylist, for the outstanding job with the recipe photos.

Jimmy L.: For shining the "light" so I could clearly see the way . . .

Lynn Merritt: My soul sister and kindred spirit.

Diana Orlando: Louise to my Thelma, I'm very blessed that you are in my life.

Greg B.: For being there at that moment. Thank you.

The Metabolism Miracle readers from around the world and my patients at the Nutrition Center of Morristown: For requesting (demanding!!!) this cookbook and for your input in many of the recipes! Also, thank you for all your support, for keeping me posted regarding your progress, and for spreading The Miracle. . . . xo

APPENDIX I: SHOPPING LIST

Shopping List for All Recipes

BREAD

(All steps) Low-carb bread, bread products, cereal bars, and crackers containing 2–5 grams net carb

(Steps Two and Three) Bread, bread products, cereals, cereal bars, crackers, tortillas, and wraps that have 11–20 grams net carb and 2 grams fiber or more

BEVERAGES

Sugar-free or diet beverages containing sucralose or stevia, including club soda, coffee (including decaf), diet soda, green tea (including decaf), seltzer (including flavored seltzer), sugar-free flavored water, sugar-free tonic water, tea (including decaf), water

Alcohol: ask physician. Champagne; light beer; liquor (no sweetened liqueurs); red, rosé, or white wine (no port or sangria). Use carb-free mixers only.

FATS

Nuts, seeds, and snacking legumes: almonds, cashews, coconut, edamame, macadamia, peanuts, pecans, pistachios, pumpkin seeds, sesame seeds, sunflower seeds, walnuts, coconut, and all other nuts or seeds that do not include added sugar in their ingredients

Cream cheese: low-fat or whipped preferred

Butter: low-fat or whipped preferred

Margarine: low-fat or whipped preferred, without hydrogenation or trans fats

Cream and creamers: cream, half-and-half (including nonfat), heavy cream, light cream, sour cream (low-fat or light preferred), whipping cream

Salad dressing: low-fat or light preferred, or oil and vinegar (flavored vinegar is okay). Avoid fat-free dressings and those with added sugar or honey, as they are high in carbohydrate content.

Oils: canola, corn, olive, peanut, safflower, sunflower, vegetable, as well as cooking oil spray

Mayonnaise: low-fat or light preferred

MILK

Low-carb milk (2–5 grams net carb) can be used as a 5-gram "Counter" during Step One. Fat-free milk, lactose-free milk, low-fat milk, skim milk with 11–20 grams carb for Steps Two and Three.

DAIRY

Yogurt: (all steps) low-carb or Greek yogurt with 2–5 grams net carb; (Steps Two and Three) light or Greek yogurt with 11–20 grams net carb

PROTEIN

Turkey: turkey (white meat preferred), sliced turkey breast, turkey sausage, turkey bacon

Beef: 85–93% ground beef, ground round, flank steak, sliced roast beef, sirloin, T-bone steak trimmed, Porterhouse steak trimmed, filet mignon, round steak, London broil, tenderloin, rib roast, rump roast, chuck roast

Chicken: chicken breast, precooked chicken strips, white meat of chicken preferred

Other poultry: duck (skinless), pheasant (skinless)

Fish and seafood: flounder, shrimp, tilapia, cod, tuna, trout, snapper, herring, whiting, haddock, sardines, salmon, sea bass, pollock, halibut, swordfish, mahi-mahi, clams, crab, oysters, lobster, scallops (all fish and shellfish are allowed)

Pork: baked ham, loin chops, pork tenderloin, Canadian bacon, trimmed chops, fresh ham, deli ham (no honey)

Eggs: eggs (organic preferred), liquid egg substitute, egg whites

Lamb: roast lamb, lamb chop, leg of lamb

Veal: lean veal chop, veal roast

Game: deer, buffalo, rabbit

Soy products: meat substitutes (check label for net carb 5 grams or less and then treat as a neutral food), tofu, unsweetened soy milk

Protein shakes or protein bars:

> Those with less than 1 gram net carb are neutral.
>
> Those with 2–5 grams net carb count as 5-gram "Counters."
>
> Those with 11–20 grams net carb count as a 1-carb serving.

Cheeses: (low-fat or part skim preferred) American, Cheddar, cottage, feta, grated, Lorraine, Parmesan, Provolone, ricotta, Romano, string, and Swiss cheese, as well as any other variety of cheese

Nut butters: natural almond butter, natural peanut butter. Check the ingredient list and make sure the contents are simply nuts, oil, and salt (optional) . . . no form of sugar.

SUPPLEMENTS

Multivitamin/multimineral supplement, fish oil (1,000–1,200 mg/capsule), B complex (B-50), calcium with vitamin D (500–600 mg calcium with 200 mg vitamin D per capsule)

SWEETS, MUNCHIES, AND CONDIMENTS

Jelly: (all steps) jellies with 1 gram net carb or less

Syrup: (Step One) syrups with 1 gram net carb or less; (Step Two and Three) syrups with 2–5 grams net carb

Broth or bouillon

Lemon or lime juice

Mustard, hot sauce, soy sauce

Spices: all are allowed that don't contain added sugar

Ketchup: low-carb or low-sugar ketchup

Sweeteners: sucralose and stevia are recommended (all FDA-approved sweeteners such as aspartame and saccharin are allowed but not recommended)

Other sweets and munchies: dark chocolate squares (2–5 grams/portion), ice pops (carb-free or with 2–5 grams carb), low-carb cookies or other baked goods (with 2–5 grams net carb), sugar-free gelatin. Packaged products with 2–5 grams net carb/serving can be used as a 5-gram "Counter," such as 1 cup popcorn or 5 stone-ground crackers, or a serving of low-carb (5-gram) pudding.

Crackers, pretzels, snacks, in a serving that contains 11–20 grams carb and 2 grams fiber or more.

VEGETABLES

(All steps) Artichokes, artichoke hearts, asparagus, Brussels sprouts, green beans, wax beans, bean sprouts, broccoli, cabbage, cauliflower, celery, cucumber, eggplant, greens (chard, collards, kale, mustard greens, turnip greens), escarole, endive, lettuce (any variety), jicama, mushrooms, onions and green onions, okra, peppers (all colors), dill pickles, radishes, salsa, sauerkraut, snap peas, spaghetti squash, spinach, summer squash, tomatoes (including canned), tomato juice, turnips, vegetable juice, water chestnuts, zucchini, and summer squash

(Steps Two and Three) Above, plus beets, carrots, corn, legumes (black beans, black-eyed peas, cannellini beans, chickpeas [garbanzo beans], kidney beans, lentils, lima beans, peas, white beans), rutabaga, sweet potato, winter squash (acorn, butternut, pumpkin, etc.)

APPENDIX II: METRIC CONVERSIONS

Metric Conversions

General Formula for Metric Conversion	
Ounces to grams	**Multiply ounces by 28.35**
Grams to ounces	Multiply grams by 0.035
Pounds to grams	**Multiply pounds by 453.5**
Pounds to kilograms	Multiply pounds by 0.45
Cups to liters	**Multiply cups by 0.24**
Fahrenheit to Celsius	Subtract 32 from Fahrenheit temperature, multiply by 5, divide by 9
Celsius to Fahrenheit	**Multiply Celsius temperature by 9, divide by 5, add 32**

Volume (Liquid) Measurements				
1 teaspoon	=	**$1/6$ fluid ounce**	=	**5 milliliters**
1 tablespoon	=	$1/2$ fluid ounce	=	15 milliliters
2 tablespoons	=	**1 fluid ounce**	=	**30 milliliters**
$1/4$ cup	=	2 fluid ounces	=	60 milliliters
$1/3$ cup	=	**$2^2/3$ fluid ounces**	=	**79 milliliters**
$1/2$ cup	=	4 fluid ounces	=	118 milliliters
1 cup or $1/2$ pint	=	**8 fluid ounces**	=	**250 milliliters**
2 cups or 1 pint	=	16 fluid ounces	=	500 milliliters
4 cups or 1 quart	=	**32 fluid ounces**	=	**1,000 milliliters**
1 gallon	=	4 liters		

Volume (Dry) Measurements

$1/4$ teaspoon	=	1 milliliter
$1/2$ teaspoon	=	2 milliliters
$3/4$ teaspoon	=	4 milliliters
1 teaspoon	=	5 milliliters
1 tablespoon	=	15 milliliters
$1/4$ cup	=	59 milliliters
$1/3$ cup	=	79 milliliters
$1/2$ cup	=	118 milliliters
$2/3$ cup	=	158 milliliters
$3/4$ cup	=	177 milliliters
1 cup	=	225 milliliters
4 cups or 1 quart	=	1 liter
$1/2$ gallon	=	2 liters
1 gallon	=	4 liters

Weight (Mass) Measurements

1 ounce	=	30 grams		
2 ounces	=	55 grams		
3 ounces	=	85 grams		
4 ounces	=	$1/4$ pound	=	125 grams
8 ounces	=	$1/2$ pound	=	240 grams
12 ounces	=	$3/4$ pound	=	375 grams
16 ounces	=	1 pound	=	454 grams

Linear Measurements

$1/2$ inch	=	$1 1/3$ cm
1 inch	=	$2 1/2$ cm
6 inches	=	15 cm
8 inches	=	20 cm
10 inches	=	25 cm
12 inches	=	30 cm
20 inches	=	50 cm

Oven Temperature Equivalents, Fahrenheit (F) and Celsius (C)

100°F = 38°C
200°F = 95°C
250°F = 120°C
300°F = 150°C
350°F = 180°C
400°F = 205°C
450°F = 230° C

INDEX

Alcohol, 46
Almond flour
    Chocolate Cupcakes, 275
    Legal Pancakes, 257
Almond Meringue Kisses, 287
Almonds
    Almond-Topped Artichokes, 242
    Cherries with Ricotta and
        Toasted Almonds, 281
    "Miracle" Granola, 260
    Sweet and Crunchy Nuts, 264
Appetizers
    Avocado Tomatoes, 115
    Chicken Quesadillas, 121
    Cocktail Sauce, 125
    Crab-Stuffed Tomatoes, 114
    Dijon Deviled Eggs, 119
    Edamame-Feta Spread, 117
    Grilled Portobellos, 112
    Ham and Pickle Spirals, 122
    Mini Meat Loaves, 123
    Miracle Guacamole, 116
    Miracle Mozzarella Sticks, 267
    Mushrooms Stuffed with Three
        Cheeses, 111
    Pesto Cherry Tomatoes, 113
    Savory Lettuce Bowls, 124
    Smoked Salmon with Herb
        Sauce, 120
    Spinach Party Dip, 118
    Stuffed Jalapeños, 110
Apples
    Apple-Walnut Custards, 282–283
    Frozen Cranberry-Apple
        Slushies, 100
    Fruit-Filled Avocado Boats, 249
    one-carb serving, 270
    Spiced Apples, 285
    Turkey Waldorf Salad, 139
Arrow Sheet foods chart, 38–39

Artichokes
    Almond-Topped Artichokes, 242
    Baby Artichoke Salad, 131
    Tabbouleh with Artichokes, 133
Asian Shrimp Salad, 143
Asparagus
    Asparagus with Goat Cheese, 243
    Fresh and Crunchy Spring
        Vegetables, 238
    Lemony Scallop and Shrimp
        Soup, 157
    Vegetable Frittata, 250
Avocados
    Avocado Tomatoes, 115
    Chicken Quesadillas, 121
    Fruit-Filled Avocado Boats, 249
    Miracle Guacamole, 116
    My Favorite Cobb Salad, 141
    Shrimp Salad with Fruit, 144

B-complex supplements, 20
Baby Artichoke Salad, 131
Bacon
    Bacon Scallops with Baby
        Spinach, 211–212
    Bacon-Wrapped Pork Loin,
        189–190
    Cheesy Chips, 266
    Faux Breakfast Hash Browns, 259
    My Favorite Cobb Salad, 141
    Split Pea Soup in a Hurry, 150
Baked Beef Tenderloin with Brown
    Sauce, 181
Baked Cod au Gratin, 213
Baked Ham Omelet Cups, 261
Bananas
    Banana Muffins, 256
    Dark Chocolate Chips on a Log,
        265

Fruit Pie with Coconut Crust,
    278–279
one-carb serving, 270
Basil
    Basil Chicken with Vegetables,
        169
    Pesto Cherry Tomatoes, 113
BBQ Chicken, 166
BBQ Tilapia Sandwiches, 221
Beans and legumes. See also Peanut
        butter; Peas
    Asian Shrimp Salad, 143
    Bok Choy and Tofu Stir-Fry,
        201–202
    Edamame-Feta Spread, 117
    Fresh and Crunchy Spring
        Vegetables, 238
    Minestrone, 149
    Not Your Mom's Green Bean
        Side Dish, 224
    Old Country Stew, 187
    Pantry-Ready Tuna Niçoise, 142
    Shrimp Lo Mein, 210
    Vegetable-Lentil Soup, 148
    White Bean–Stuffed Tomatoes,
        204–205
Beef
    Baked Beef Tenderloin with
        Brown Sauce, 181
    Broken Noodles, 185
    Ginger Flank Steak, 179–180
    Mediterranean Meat Loaf, 183
    Mini Meat Loaves, 123
    Mini Meatball Soup, 159–160
    Savory Lettuce Bowls, 124
    Sloppy Joes, 184
    Steak with Sherry Sauce, 178
    Stuffed Jalapeños, 110
    Veal Stroganoff (substitution),
        183

Bell peppers
Bok Choy and Tofu Stir-Fry,
201–202
Crab-Stuffed Tomatoes, 114
Grilled Portobellos, 112
Savory Lettuce Bowls, 124
Tex-Mex Eggs, 248
Veal Stroganoff, 183
Vegetable Frittata, 250
Berries
Berry Dreamer, 106
Blueberry French Toast, 258
Chocolate-Strawberry Smoothie,
103
Fruit Pie with Coconut Crust,
278–279
Melon and Ricotta Salad, 136
Mixed Berry Smoothie, 102–103
Very Berry Crème, 282
Beverages
Berry Dreamer, 106
Chocolate-Strawberry Smoothie,
103
Chocolate–Peanut Butter
Smoothie, 100–101
Cranberry Spritzer, 105
Dark Chocolate Dreamer, 104–
105
Frozen Cranberry-Apple
Slushies, 100
Ginger Chai Refresher, 106–107
Ginger-Lemon Green Tea, 98
Icy Melon Tea, 99
Instant Espresso Chiller, 104
Miracle Mojito, 107–108
Mixed Berry Smoothie, 102–103
Orange Dreamsicle Smoothie,
102
Pineapple Smoothie, 101
shopping list, 293
Blood tests indicating Metabolism
B, 15–16
Blue cheese
Broccoli Rabe Salad with Orzo,
132
My Favorite Cobb Salad, 141
Blueberries
Blueberry French Toast, 258
Fruit Pie with Coconut Crust,
278–279
Mixed Berry Smoothie, 102–103
one-carb serving, 270
Very Berry Crème, 282

Bok choy
Bok Choy and Tofu Stir-Fry,
201–202
Vegetarian Pot Luck, 196
"Bookend" eating, 18–19
Bread crumbs
Parmesan Bread Crumbs, 168
to make (tip), 208
Bread Pudding, Pumpkin, 286
Breakfasts
Baked Ham Omelet Cups, 261
Banana Muffins, 256
Blueberry French Toast, 258
Broccoli-Mushroom Frittata, 251
Carrot and Oat Muffins, 254
Crustless Quiche, 253
Faux Breakfast Hash Browns, 259
Fruit-Filled Avocado Boats, 249
Legal Pancakes, 257
menus for Step One, 48–49
menus for Step Two, 65–66
menus for Step Three, 90–91
"Miracle" Granola, 260
Oat-Nut Muffins, 255
Peanut Butter Hot "Cereal," 262
Sausage and Egg Casserole, 252
Tex-Mex Eggs, 248
Vegetable Frittata, 250
Broccoli
Broccoli-Mushroom Frittata, 251
Broccoli with Cheese Sauce, 227
Chicken Strata, 167
Fresh and Crunchy Spring
Vegetables, 238
Italian Garden Salad, 135
Quick Broccoli Pie, 195
Broccoli Rabe Salad with Orzo, 132
Broiled Flounder with Parmesan, 218
Broken Noodles, 185
Brown Rice Pilaf, 240
Brussels Sprouts, Sautéed, 235
Bulgur
Minestrone, 149
Tabbouleh with Artichokes, 133
Tabbouleh with Grilled
Vegetables, 233–234
"Buns," Portobello, 203
"Burgers," Mushroom-Cheese, 202
Butter-Rum Cupcakes, 274

Cabbage. See Coleslaw mix
Cakes and cupcakes
Butter-Rum Cupcakes, 274
Cheesecake Cupcakes, 273

Chocolate Cupcakes, 275
Gingerbread Cake, 276
Calcium with vitamin D
supplements, 20
Calories in–calories out program, 6,
8
Canadian bacon, in Turkey Melts,
176
Cannellini beans
Old Country Stew, 187
White Bean–Stuffed Tomatoes,
204–205
Cantaloupe
Icy Melon Tea, 99
Melon and Ricotta Salad, 136
Carbohydrates. See also Step One;
Step Two; Step Three
effect on insulin production, 12
5-gram "Counter" carbs, 41–44,
63, 269–270
fueling forward for upcoming
exercise, 28
net carb formula, 72
one-carb servings, 270
Caribbean Corn on the Cob, 226
Caribbean Watermelon Salad, 134
Carrots
Carrot and Oat Muffins, 254
Carrot-Parsnip Latkes, 232
Chicken and Wild Rice Soup,
154
Creamy Vegetable Soup, 146
Old Country Stew, 187
Postholiday Turkey Soup, 155
Split Pea Soup in a Hurry, 150
Vegetable-Lentil Soup, 148
Vegetarian Pot Luck, 196
Cauliflower
Cauliflower "Rice," 245
Cauliflower Salad, 130
Faux Breakfast Hash Browns, 259
Italian Garden Salad, 135
Celery
Avocado Tomatoes, 115
celery stick snack, 269
Chicken and Wild Rice Soup,
154
Creamy Shrimp Chowder, 158
Dark Chocolate Chips on a Log,
265
Manhattan-Style Clam
Chowder, 156
Miracle Tuna Melt, 220
Postholiday Turkey Soup, 155

Smoked Sausage Gumbo, 175
Turkey Salad with Pistachios
    and Grapes, 140
"Cereal," Peanut Butter Hot, 262
Chai Refresher, Ginger, 106–107
Cheddar cheese
    Broccoli with Cheese Sauce, 227
    Cheesy Chips, 266
    Chicken Fajitas, 173
    Chicken Quesadillas, 121
    Crustless Quiche, 253
    Miracle Tuna Melt, 220
    Sausage and Egg Casserole, 252
    Stuffed Jalapeños, 110
    Summer Squash Casserole, 225
    Vegetable Frittata, 250
Cheese (see also by specific type)
    Almond-Topped Artichokes, 242
    Asparagus with Goat Cheese, 243
    Baked Cod au Gratin, 213
    Baked Ham Omelet Cups, 261
    Broccoli-Mushroom Frittata, 251
    Broccoli Rabe Salad with Orzo,
        132
    Broccoli with Cheese Sauce, 227
    Broiled Flounder with
        Parmesan, 218
    Broken Noodles, 185
    Cheesecake Cupcakes, 273
    Cheesy Chips, 266
    Cherries with Ricotta and
        Toasted Almonds, 281
    Chicken Fajitas, 173
    Chicken Quesadillas, 121
    Chicken Strata, 167
    Chicken with Mozzarella, 170
    Crunchy Oven-Fried Fish, 214
    Crustless Quiche, 253
    Easy French Onion Soup, 147
    Easy Pesto Chicken, 165
    Edamame-Feta Spread, 117
    Eggplant Parmesan, 197
    "fruity" mousse, 269
    Grilled Portobellos, 112
    Ham and Pickle Spirals, 122
    Italian Garden Salad, 135
    Lemon-Garlic Chicken, 162
    Melon and Ricotta Salad, 136
    Mesclun and Sweet Potato
        Salad, 137–138
    Mini Zucchini Pancakes, 237
    Miracle Mozzarella Sticks, 267
    Miracle Tuna Melt, 220
    Mushroom-Cheese "Burgers,"
        202

Mushrooms Stuffed with Three
    Cheeses, 111
My Favorite Cobb Salad, 141
Parmesan Bread Crumbs, 168
Pear and Goat Cheese Salad, 128
Pepperoni Pizza Dip for Fresh
    Veggies, 268
Pesto Cherry Tomatoes, 113
Quick Broccoli Pie, 195
ricotta "pudding," 269
Roma Tofu Bake, 198
Sausage and Egg Casserole, 252
Spinach-Feta Pie, 194
Spinach Party Dip, 118
Stuffed Jalapeños, 110
Summer Squash Casserole, 225
Tofu and Veggies, 199
Turkey Melts, 176
Vegetable Frittata, 250
White Bean–Stuffed Tomatoes,
    204–205
Cheesecake Cupcakes, 273
Cheesy Chips, 266
Cherries with Ricotta and Toasted
    Almonds, 281
Chicken
    Basil Chicken with Vegetables,
        169
    BBQ Chicken, 166
    Chicken and Wild Rice Soup,
        154
    Chicken Fajitas, 173
    Chicken Marsala, 163–164
    Chicken Quesadillas, 121
    Chicken Stock, 151
    Chicken Strata, 167
    Chicken with Mozzarella, 170
    Easy Pesto Chicken, 165
    Grilled Lime Chicken, 171
    Hot and Sour Soup with
        Chicken, 153
    Lemon-Garlic Chicken, 162
    My Favorite Cobb Salad, 141
Chips, Cheesy, 266
Chocolate
    Chocolate Cupcakes, 275
    Chocolate Mousse, 277
    Chocolate-Strawberry Smoothie,
        103
    Chocolate–Peanut Butter
        Smoothie, 100–101
    Dark Chocolate Chips on a Log,
        265
    Dark Chocolate Dreamer, 104–
        105

"DE"licious Chocolate Chip
    Cookies, 290
Clam Chowder, Manhattan-Style,
    156
Cocktail Sauce, 125
Coconut
    Caribbean Watermelon Salad,
        134
    Coconut Macaroons, 289
    Fruit Pie with Coconut Crust,
        278–279
    "Miracle" Granola, 260
Cod
    Baked Cod au Gratin, 213
    Crunchy Oven-Fried Fish, 214
Coleslaw mix
    BBQ Tilapia Sandwiches, 221
    Hot and Sour Soup with
        Chicken, 153
    Pineapple Coleslaw, 231
    Sweet-and-Sour Coleslaw, 230
    Turkey Waldorf Salad, 139
Cookies
    Almond Meringue Kisses, 287
    Coconut Macaroons, 289
    "DE"licious Chocolate Chip
        Cookies, 290
    Peanut Butter Cookies, 288
Corn
    Caribbean Corn on the Cob, 226
    Minestrone, 149
Cottage cheese
    Crustless Quiche, 253
    Melon and Ricotta Salad, 136
    Quick Broccoli Pie, 195
    Spinach-Feta Pie, 194
    Spinach Party Dip, 118
"Counter" carbs, 41–44, 63, 269–270
Crabmeat
    Crab-Stuffed Tomatoes, 114
    Miracle Crab Cakes, 208–209
Cranberry-Apple Slushies, Frozen, 100
Cranberry Spritzer, 105
Cream cheese
    Cheesecake Cupcakes, 273
    Crustless Quiche, 253
    "fruity" mousse, 269
    Ham and Pickle Spirals, 122
    Pepperoni Pizza Dip for Fresh
        Veggies, 268
    Stuffed Jalapeños, 110
Creamy Shrimp Chowder, 158
Creamy Vegetable Soup, 146
Croquettes, Salmon, 219
Crunchy Oven-Fried Fish, 214

Crusted Salmon, 215
Crustless Quiche, 253
Cucumbers
    Caribbean Watermelon Salad,
        134
    Cauliflower Salad, 130
Cupcakes
    Butter-Rum Cupcakes, 274
    Cheesecake Cupcakes, 273
    Chocolate Cupcakes, 275
Custards
    Apple-Walnut Custards, 282–283
    Pumpkin Custards, 284

Dark Chocolate Dreamer, 104–105
"DE"licious Chocolate Chip
    Cookies, 290
Desserts
    Almond Meringue Kisses, 287
    Apple-Walnut Custards, 282–283
    Butter-Rum Cupcakes, 274
    Cheesecake Cupcakes, 273
    Cherries with Ricotta and
        Toasted Almonds, 281
    Chocolate Cupcakes, 275
    Chocolate Mousse, 277
    Coconut Macaroons, 289
    Crustless Pumpkin Pie, 272
    "DE"licious Chocolate Chip
        Cookies, 290
    Fruit Pie with Coconut Crust,
        278–279
    "fruity" mousse, 269
    Gingerbread Cake, 276
    Ice-Cream Pie, 280
    Peanut Butter Cookies, 288
    Pumpkin Bread Pudding, 286
    Pumpkin Custards, 284
    ricotta "pudding," 269
    shopping list, 296
    Spiced Apples, 285
    Very Berry Crème, 282
    Watermelon Sorbet, 278
Dijon Deviled Eggs, 119
Dips and spreads
    Cocktail Sauce, 125
    Edamame-Feta Spread, 117
    Miracle Guacamole, 116
    Pepperoni Pizza Dip for Fresh
        Veggies, 268
    Salsa, 217
    Smoked Salmon with Herb
        Sauce, 120
    Spinach Party Dip, 118
Dreamsicle Smoothie, Orange, 102

Easy French Onion Soup, 147
Easy Pesto Chicken, 165
Edamame
    Asian Shrimp Salad, 143
    Bok Choy and Tofu Stir-Fry,
        201–202
    Edamame-Feta Spread, 117
    Shrimp Lo Mein, 210
Egg dishes
    Baked Ham Omelet Cups, 261
    Broccoli-Mushroom Frittata, 251
    Crustless Quiche, 253
    Dijon Deviled Eggs, 119
    Egg Drop Soup, 152
    Quick Broccoli Pie, 195
    Sausage and Egg Casserole, 252
    Tex-Mex Eggs, 248
    to hard-boil eggs (tip), 119
    Vegetable Frittata, 250
    Winter Squash Soufflé, 241
Eggplant Parmesan, 197
Espresso Chiller, Instant, 104
Exercise
    benefits and guidelines, 22–23
    excessive tiredness from, 27–28
    fueling forward for, 28
    in Metabolism Miracle program,
        19

Fajita Seasoning Mix, 174
Fajitas, Chicken, 173
Faux Breakfast Hash Browns, 259
Fennel bulb, in Baby Artichoke
    Salad, 131
Feta cheese
    Edamame-Feta Spread, 117
    Pesto Cherry Tomatoes, 113
    Spinach-Feta Pie, 194
Fish
    Baked Cod au Gratin, 213
    BBQ Tilapia Sandwiches, 221
    Broiled Flounder with
        Parmesan, 218
    Crunchy Oven-Fried Fish, 214
    Crusted Salmon, 215
    Grilled Rosemary Salmon, 216
    Grilled Snapper with Salsa, 217
    Mediterranean Fish, 212
    Miracle Tuna Melt, 220
    Pantry-Ready Tuna Niçoise, 142
    Salmon Croquettes, 219
    Smoked Salmon with Herb
        Sauce, 120
Fish oil supplements, 20

5-gram "Counter" carbs, 41–44, 63,
    269–270
Flaxseed meal, in Peanut Butter
    Hot "Cereal," 262
Flaxseeds, in Granola, 260
Flounder
    Broiled Flounder with
        Parmesan, 218
    Crunchy Oven-Fried Fish, 214
French Onion Soup, Easy, 147
French Toast, Blueberry, 258
Fresh and Crunchy Spring
    Vegetables, 238
Fresh Herb Marinade, 172
"Fries," Grilled Sweet Potato, 228
"Fries," Roasted Sweet Potato, 229
Frozen Cranberry-Apple Slushies,
    100
Fruit Pie with Coconut Crust,
    278–279
"Fruity" mousse, 269

Garlic Zucchini, 239
Ginger Chai Refresher, 106–107
Ginger Flank Steak, 179–180
Ginger-Lemon Green Tea, 98
Gingerbread Cake, 276
Glazed Ham, 186
Goat cheese
    Asparagus with Goat Cheese, 243
    Mesclun and Sweet Potato
        Salad, 137–138
    Pear and Goat Cheese Salad, 128
    Pesto Cherry Tomatoes, 113
Granola, "Miracle," 260
Grapes
    Grilled Pork Kebabs, 188
    Shrimp Salad with Fruit, 144
    Turkey Salad with Pistachios
        and Grapes, 140
Green beans
    Fresh and Crunchy Spring
        Vegetables, 238
    Not Your Mom's Green Bean
        Side Dish, 224
    Pantry-Ready Tuna Niçoise, 142
    Vegetable Lentil Soup, 148
Green tea
    Ginger-Lemon Green Tea, 98
    in Metabolism Miracle program,
        21
Grilled Lime Chicken, 171
Grilled Pork Kebabs, 188
Grilled Portobellos, 112
Grilled Rosemary Salmon, 216

Grilled Snapper with Salsa, 217
Grilled Sweet Potato "Fries," 228
Grocery list, 293
Guacamole, Miracle, 116
Gumbo, Smoked Sausage, 175

Ham
    Baked Ham Omelet Cups, 261
    Glazed Ham, 186
    Ham and Pickle Spirals, 122
    Mesclun and Sweet Potato
        Salad, 137–138
Hash Browns, Faux Breakfast, 259
Herb Marinade, Fresh, 172
Herbed Mashed Parsnips, 234
Honeydew
    Icy Melon Tea, 99
    Melon and Ricotta Salad, 136
Hot and Sour Soup with Chicken,
    153
Hydration, 18

Ice-Cream Pie, 280
Icy Melon Tea, 99
Instant Espresso Chiller, 104
Insulin imbalance, 10, 11–12
Italian Garden Salad, 135

Jalapeños, Stuffed, 110
Japanese Pork and Spinach Soup, 160

Kebabs, Grilled Pork, 188
Kisses, Almond Meringue, 287

Lamb Chops with Herbed
    Mushrooms, 191
Latkes, Carrot-Parsnip, 232
Latkes, Sweet Potato, 236
Legal Pancakes, 257
Lemon-Garlic Chicken, 162
Lemony Scallop and Shrimp Soup,
    157
Lentil Soup, Vegetable, 148
Lettuce Bowls, Savory, 124
Lime Chicken, Grilled, 171

Manhattan-Style Clam Chowder,
    156
Marinade, Fresh Herb, 172
Marinade, Red Wine, 192
Marsala, Chicken, 163–164
Marsala, Tofu, 200
Meat Loaf, Mediterranean, 183
Meat Loaves, Mini, 123
Mediterranean Fish, 212

Mediterranean Meat Loaf, 183
Melon
    Caribbean Watermelon Salad,
        134
    Icy Melon Tea, 99
    Melon and Ricotta Salad, 136
    Watermelon Sorbet, 278
Menus
    portion sizes, 44
    Step One, 48–53
    Step Two, 65–69
    Step Three, 90–93
Meringue Kisses, Almond, 287
Mesclun and Sweet Potato Salad,
    137–138
Metabolism B
    blood tests indicating, 15–16
    family and personal indicators,
        14–15
    insulin imbalance, 10, 11–12
    symptoms, 13–14
Metabolism Miracle program. *See
    also* Step One; Step Two;
    Step Three
    dietary supplements, 19–21
    evidence of progress, 23–24, 27
    exercise, 19, 22–23, 27–28
    fat-loss expectations, 25–27
    for children, 89
    guidelines, 17–21
    ideal weight, 27
    steps in, 17–18
Minestrone, 149
Mini Meat Loaves, 123
Mini Meatball Soup, 159–160
Mini Zucchini Pancakes, 237
Miracle Crab Cakes, 208–209
Miracle Guacamole, 116
Miracle Mojito, 107–108
Miracle Mozzarella Sticks, 267
Miracle Tuna Melt, 220
Mixed Berry Smoothie, 102–103
Mojito, Miracle, 107–108
Monterey Jack cheese
    Broccoli-Mushroom Frittata, 251
    Mushrooms Stuffed with Three
        Cheeses, 111
    Sausage and Egg Casserole, 252
Mousse, Chocolate, 277
Mozzarella cheese
    Broken Noodles, 185
    Chicken with Mozzarella, 170
    Easy Pesto Chicken, 165
    Eggplant Parmesan, 197
    Miracle Mozzarella Sticks, 267

Pepperoni Pizza Dip for Fresh
    Veggies, 268
Quick Broccoli Pie, 195
Roma Tofu Bake, 198
Muffins
    Banana Muffins, 256
    Carrot and Oat Muffins, 254
    Oat-Nut Muffins, 255
Mushrooms
    Basil Chicken with Vegetables,
        169
    Bok Choy and Tofu Stir-Fry,
        201–202
    Broccoli-Mushroom Frittata, 251
    Brown Rice Pilaf, 240
    Chicken Marsala, 163–164
    Chicken Strata, 167
    Grilled Pork Kebabs, 188
    Grilled Portobellos, 112
    Hot and Sour Soup with
        Chicken, 153
    Lamb Chops with Herbed
        Mushrooms, 191
    Lemony Scallop and Shrimp
        Soup, 157
    Mushroom-Cheese "Burgers,"
        202
    Mushrooms Stuffed with Three
        Cheeses, 111
    Not Your Mom's Green Bean
        Side Dish, 224
    Steak with Sherry Sauce, 178
    Summer Squash Casserole, 225
    Tabbouleh with Grilled
        Vegetables, 233–234
    Tofu Marsala, 200
    Vegetarian Pot Luck, 196
My Favorite Cobb Salad, 141

Navy beans, in Minestrone, 149
Net carb formula, 72
Noodles and pasta
    Broccoli Rabe Salad with Orzo,
        132
    Broken Noodles, 185
    Shrimp Lo Mein, 210
    Vegetarian Pot Luck, 196
Nuts
    Almond-Topped Artichokes, 242
    Apple-Walnut Custards, 282–283
    Asparagus with Goat Cheese,
        243
    Carrot and Oat Muffins, 254
    Cherries with Ricotta and
        Toasted Almonds, 281

Nuts *(continued)*
  "DE"licious Chocolate Chip
    Cookies, 290
  "Miracle" Granola, 260
  Oat-Nut Muffins, 255
  Pear and Goat Cheese Salad, 128
  Pesto Cherry Tomatoes, 113
  Spiced Apples, 285
  Sweet and Crunchy Nuts, 264
  Tabbouleh with Grilled
    Vegetables, 233–234
  Turkey Salad with Pistachios
    and Grapes, 140
  Turkey Waldorf Salad, 139

Oats
  Apple-Walnut Custards, 282–283
  Banana Muffins, 256
  Carrot and Oat Muffins, 254
  Oat-Nut Muffins, 255
Old Country Stew, 187
Olives
  Italian Garden Salad, 135
  Mediterranean Fish, 212
  Pantry-Ready Tuna Niçoise, 142
Omelet Cups, Baked Ham, 261
Onions
  Baked Cod au Gratin, 213
  Easy French Onion Soup, 147
  Grilled Pork Kebabs, 188
  Not Your Mom's Green Bean
    Side Dish, 224
Oranges
  Asian Shrimp Salad, 143
  Fruit-Filled Avocado Boats, 249
  Orange Dreamsicle Smoothie,
    102
  Shrimp Salad with Fruit, 144
Orzo, Broccoli Rabe Salad with, 132
Oven-Fried Fish, Crunchy, 214

Pancakes, Legal, 257
Pantry-Ready Tuna Niçoise, 142
Parmesan cheese
  Almond-Topped Artichokes, 242
  Broiled Flounder with
    Parmesan, 218
  Broken Noodles, 185
  Crunchy Oven-Fried Fish, 214
  Crustless Quiche, 253
  Eggplant Parmesan, 197
  Grilled Portobellos, 112
  Italian Garden Salad, 135
  Lemon-Garlic Chicken, 162

Mini Zucchini Pancakes, 237
Mushrooms Stuffed with Three
  Cheeses, 111
Parmesan Bread Crumbs, 168
Roma Tofu Bake, 198
Spinach-Feta Pie, 194
Tofu and Veggies, 199
White Bean–Stuffed Tomatoes,
  204–205
Parsnips
  Carrot-Parsnip Latkes, 232
  Creamy Vegetable Soup, 146
  Herbed Mashed Parsnips, 234
  Manhattan-Style Clam
    Chowder, 156
Party Mix, 269, 270
Pasta and noodles
  Broccoli Rabe Salad with Orzo, 132
  Broken Noodles, 185
  Shrimp Lo Mein, 210
  Vegetarian Pot Luck, 196
Peanut butter
  Dark Chocolate Chips on a Log,
    265
  Peanut Butter Cookies, 288
  Peanut Butter Hot "Cereal," 262
Pear and Goat Cheese Salad, 128
Peas
  Cauliflower Salad, 130
  Fresh and Crunchy Spring
    Vegetables, 238
  Snap Pea Salad, 129
  Snow Peas with Water
    Chestnuts, 244
  Split Pea Soup in a Hurry, 150
Pecans
  "DE"licious Chocolate Chip
    Cookies, 290
  "Miracle" Granola, 260
  Oat-Nut Muffins, 255
  Spiced Apples, 285
  Sweet and Crunchy Nuts, 264
Pepperoni Pizza Dip for Fresh
  Veggies, 268
Peppers, bell
  Bok Choy and Tofu Stir-Fry,
    201–202
  Crab-Stuffed Tomatoes, 114
  Grilled Portobellos, 112
  Savory Lettuce Bowls, 124
  Tex-Mex Eggs, 248
  Veal Stroganoff, 183
  Vegetable Frittata, 250

Peppers, roasted red
  Mediterranean Meat Loaf, 183
  Quick Broccoli Pie, 195
Pesto Cherry Tomatoes, 113
Pesto Chicken, Easy, 165
Pickle and Ham Spirals, 122
Pies, dessert
  Crustless Pumpkin Pie, 272
  Fruit Pie with Coconut Crust,
    278–279
  Ice-Cream Pie, 280
Pies, savory
  Crustless Quiche, 253
  Quick Broccoli Pie, 195
  Spinach-Feta Pie, 194
Pine nuts
  Asparagus with Goat Cheese, 243
  Pesto Cherry Tomatoes, 113
Pineapple
  Fruit-Filled Avocado Boats, 249
  Pineapple Coleslaw, 231
  Pineapple Smoothie, 101
Pistachios and Grapes, Turkey
  Salad with, 140
Pork. *See also* Ham
  Bacon-Wrapped Pork Loin, 189–
    190
  Grilled Pork Kebabs, 188
  Ham and Pickle Spirals, 122
  Japanese Pork and Spinach
    Soup, 160
  Mini Meat Loaves, 123
  Mini Meatball Soup, 159–160
  Old Country Stew, 187
Portion sizes, 44
Portobello "Buns," 203
Portobellos, Grilled, 112
Postholiday Turkey Soup, 155
Provolone cheese, in Mushroom-
  Cheese "Burgers," 202
Puddings and custards
  Apple-Walnut Custards, 282–283
  one-carb serving, 270
  Pumpkin Bread Pudding, 286
  Pumpkin Custards, 284
  ricotta "pudding," 269
Pumpkin
  Crustless Pumpkin Pie, 272
  Pumpkin Bread Pudding, 286
  Pumpkin Custards, 284

Quesadillas, Chicken, 121
Quiche, Crustless, 253
Quick Broccoli Pie, 195

Red snapper
    Grilled Snapper with Salsa, 217
    Mediterranean Fish, 212
Red Wine Marinade, 192
"Rice," Cauliflower, 245
Rice Pilaf, Brown, 240
Ricotta cheese
    Broken Noodles, 185
    Cheesecake Cupcakes, 273
    Cherries with Ricotta and
        Toasted Almonds, 281
    Crustless Quiche, 253
    Melon and Ricotta Salad, 136
    Mushrooms Stuffed with Three
        Cheeses, 111
    ricotta "pudding," 269
    Roma Tofu Bake, 198
Roasted red peppers
    Mediterranean Meat Loaf, 183
    Quick Broccoli Pie, 195
Roasted Sweet Potato "Fries," 229
Roma Tofu Bake, 198
Rosemary Salmon, Grilled, 216

Salads
    Asian Shrimp Salad, 143
    Baby Artichoke Salad, 131
    Broccoli Rabe Salad with Orzo,
        132
    Caribbean Watermelon Salad,
        134
    Cauliflower Salad, 130
    Italian Garden Salad, 135
    Melon and Ricotta Salad, 136
    Mesclun and Sweet Potato
        Salad, 137–138
    My Favorite Cobb Salad, 141
    Pantry-Ready Tuna Niçoise, 142
    Pear and Goat Cheese Salad, 128
    Pineapple Coleslaw, 231
    Shrimp Salad with Fruit, 144
    Snap Pea Salad, 129
    Sweet-and-Sour Coleslaw, 230
    Tabbouleh with Artichokes, 133
    Turkey Salad with Pistachios
        and Grapes, 140
    Turkey Waldorf Salad, 139
Salmon
    Crusted Salmon, 215
    Grilled Rosemary Salmon, 216
    Salmon Croquettes, 219
    Smoked Salmon with Herb
        Sauce, 120
Salsa, Grilled Snapper with, 217

Sandwiches
    BBQ Tilapia Sandwiches, 221
    Miracle Tuna Melt, 220
    Portobello "Buns" for, 203
    Turkey Melts, 176
Sausage
    Broken Noodles, 185
    Old Country Stew, 187
    Pepperoni Pizza Dip for Fresh
        Veggies, 268
    Sausage and Egg Casserole, 252
    Smoked Sausage Gumbo, 175
Sautéed Brussels Sprouts, 235
Savory Lettuce Bowls, 124
Scallop and Shrimp Soup, Lemony,
    157
Scallops, Bacon, with Baby
    Spinach, 211–212
Seafood. See Fish; Shellfish
Seasoning Mix, Fajita, 174
Sesame seeds
    Bok Choy and Tofu Stir-Fry,
        201–202
    Butter-Rum Cupcakes, 274
    Snap Pea Salad, 129
Shellfish
    Asian Shrimp Salad, 143
    Bacon Scallops with Baby
        Spinach, 211–212
    Crab-Stuffed Tomatoes, 114
    Creamy Shrimp Chowder, 158
    Lemony Scallop and Shrimp
        Soup, 157
    Manhattan-Style Clam
        Chowder, 156
    Miracle Crab Cakes, 208–209
    Shrimp Lo Mein, 210
    Shrimp Salad with Fruit, 144
Shopping list, 293
Shrimp
    Asian Shrimp Salad, 143
    Creamy Shrimp Chowder, 158
    Lemony Scallop and Shrimp
        Soup, 157
    Shrimp Lo Mein, 210
    Shrimp Salad with Fruit, 144
Side dishes
    Almond-Topped Artichokes, 242
    Asparagus with Goat Cheese,
        243
    Broccoli with Cheese Sauce, 227
    Brown Rice Pilaf, 240
    Caribbean Corn on the Cob, 226
    Carrot-Parsnip Latkes, 232

Cauliflower "Rice," 245
    Fresh and Crunchy Spring
        Vegetables, 238
    Garlic Zucchini, 239
    Grilled Sweet Potato "Fries," 228
    Herbed Mashed Parsnips, 234
    Mini Zucchini Pancakes, 237
    Not Your Mom's Green Bean
        Side Dish, 224
    Pineapple Coleslaw, 231
    Roasted Sweet Potato "Fries," 229
    Sautéed Brussels Sprouts, 235
    Snow Peas with Water
        Chestnuts, 244
    Summer Squash Casserole, 225
    Sweet-and-Sour Coleslaw, 230
    Sweet Potato Latkes, 236
    Tabbouleh with Grilled
        Vegetables, 233–234
    Winter Squash Soufflé, 241
Slip-ups in eating program
    during Step One, 48
    during Step Two, 64–65
    during Step Three, 86
Sloppy Joes, 184
Smoked Salmon with Herb Sauce,
    120
Smoked Sausage Gumbo, 175
Smoothies
    Chocolate-Strawberry Smoothie,
        103
    Chocolate–Peanut Butter
        Smoothie, 100–101
    Mixed Berry Smoothie, 102–103
    Orange Dreamsicle Smoothie,
        102
    Pineapple Smoothie, 101
Snacks
    Cheesy Chips, 266
    Dark Chocolate Chips on a Log,
        265
    15 snack food ideas, 269–270
    Miracle Mozzarella Sticks, 267
    Pepperoni Pizza Dip for Fresh
        Veggies, 268
    shopping list, 296
    suggestions, 52–53, 69
    Sweet and Crunchy Nuts, 264
Snap peas
    Fresh and Crunchy Spring
        Vegetables, 238
    Snap Pea Salad, 129
Snow Peas with Water Chestnuts,
    244

Sorbet, Watermelon, 278
Soups and stews
    Chicken and Wild Rice Soup,
        154
    Chicken Stock, 151
    Creamy Shrimp Chowder, 158
    Creamy Vegetable Soup, 146
    Easy French Onion Soup, 147
    Egg Drop Soup, 152
    Hot and Sour Soup with
        Chicken, 153
    Japanese Pork and Spinach
        Soup, 160
    Lemony Scallop and Shrimp
        Soup, 157
    Manhattan-Style Clam
        Chowder, 156
    Minestrone, 149
    Mini Meatball Soup, 159–160
    Old Country Stew, 187
    Postholiday Turkey Soup, 155
    Smoked Sausage Gumbo, 175
    Split Pea Soup in a Hurry, 150
    Vegetable-Lentil Soup, 148
Sour cream
    Baked Beef Tenderloin with
        Brown Sauce, 181
    Chicken Fajitas, 173
    Chicken Quesadillas, 121
    "DE"licious Chocolate Chip
        Cookies, 290
    "fruity" mousse, 269
    Pepperoni Pizza Dip for Fresh
        Veggies, 268
    Spinach Party Dip, 118
    Summer Squash Casserole, 225
    Veal Stroganoff, 183
    Very Berry Crème, 282
Soy flour
    Butter-Rum Cupcakes, 274
    "DE"licious Chocolate Chip
        Cookies, 290
Spiced Apples, 285
Spinach
    Bacon Scallops with Baby
        Spinach, 211–212
    Japanese Pork and Spinach
        Soup, 160
    Mini Meatball Soup, 159–160
    Mushrooms Stuffed with Three
        Cheeses, 111
    Roma Tofu Bake, 198
    Spinach-Feta Pie, 194
    Spinach Party Dip, 118
    Tofu and Veggies, 199

Split Pea Soup in a Hurry, 150
Spreads. See Dips and spreads
Spring Vegetables, Fresh and
        Crunchy, 238
Squash. See Summer squash;
        Winter squash
Steak with Sherry Sauce, 178
Step One
    alcohol, 46
    Arrow Sheet, 38–39
    carbs to avoid, 40
    "Counter" carbs, 41–44
    fat-loss expectations, 25–27
    freebies, 37
    frequently asked questions, 47
    neutral fats, 35–36
    neutral proteins, 34–35
    neutral vegetables, 37
    rest and rehabilitation of
        pancreas and liver, 17, 31–34
    sample menus, 48–53
    slip-ups, 48
    sweeteners, 45–46
Step Two
    carb choices, 59–62
    "Counter" carbs, 63
    fat-loss expectations, 25–27
    frequently asked questions, 63–65
    reintroduction of carbohydrates,
        56–57, 58–59
    reminders and guidelines, 57–59
    reprogramming of pancreas and
        liver, 18, 55–56
    sample menus, 65–69
    slip-ups, 64–65
Step Three
    counting carbs, 71–78
    foods and portions, 80–85
    frequently asked questions, 86–88
    maintenance of health and
        weight, 18, 71
    sample menus, 90–93
    slip-ups, 86
    spreading carbs throughout day,
        79–80
Stews
    Old Country Stew, 187
    Smoked Sausage Gumbo, 175
Stock, Chicken, 151
Strawberries
    Chocolate-Strawberry Smoothie,
        103
    Fruit Pie with Coconut Crust,
        278–279
    Melon and Ricotta Salad, 136

one-carb serving, 270
    Very Berry Crème, 282
Stress reduction, 21
Stuffed Jalapeños, 110
Summer squash
    Basil Chicken with Vegetables,
        169
    Broken Noodles, 185
    Chicken and Wild Rice Soup,
        154
    Garlic Zucchini, 239
    Minestrone, 149
    Mini Zucchini Pancakes, 237
    Summer Squash Casserole, 225
    Tabbouleh with Grilled
        Vegetables, 233–234
    Vegetable Frittata, 250
Sun-dried tomatoes
    Easy Pesto Chicken, 165
    Mushrooms Stuffed with Three
        Cheeses, 111
Sunflower seeds
    Avocado Tomatoes, 115
    "Miracle" Granola, 260
Supplements, 19–21
Sweet-and-Sour Coleslaw, 230
Sweet potatoes
    Creamy Vegetable Soup, 146
    Grilled Sweet Potato "Fries," 228
    Mesclun and Sweet Potato
        Salad, 137–138
    Roasted Sweet Potato "Fries," 229
    Sweet Potato Latkes, 236
Sweeteners, 45–46
Swiss cheese
    Baked Cod au Gratin, 213
    Chicken Strata, 167
    Crustless Quiche, 253
    Easy French Onion Soup, 147
    Turkey Melts, 176

Tabbouleh with Artichokes, 133
Tabbouleh with Grilled Vegetables,
        233–234
Tea
    Ginger Chai Refresher, 106–107
    Ginger-Lemon Green Tea, 98
    Icy Melon Tea, 99
    in Metabolism Miracle program,
        21
Tex-Mex Eggs, 248
Tilapia Sandwiches, BBQ, 221
Tofu
    Bok Choy and Tofu Stir-Fry,
        201–202

Chocolate Mousse, 277
Roma Tofu Bake, 198
Tofu and Veggies, 199
Tofu Marsala, 200
Vegetarian Pot Luck, 196
Tofu noodles, in Shrimp Lo Mein, 210
Tomatoes
    Avocado Tomatoes, 115
    Baby Artichoke Salad, 131
    Broccoli-Mushroom Frittata, 251
    Chicken and Wild Rice Soup, 154
    Crab-Stuffed Tomatoes, 114
    Grilled Pork Kebabs, 188
    Grilled Snapper with Salsa, 217
    Italian Garden Salad, 135
    My Favorite Cobb Salad, 141
    Old Country Stew, 187
    Pesto Cherry Tomatoes, 113
    Tabbouleh with Artichokes, 133
    Tabbouleh with Grilled Vegetables, 233–234
    Tex-Mex Eggs, 248
    White Bean–Stuffed Tomatoes, 204–205
Tomatoes, sun-dried
    Easy Pesto Chicken, 165
    Mushrooms Stuffed with Three Cheeses, 111
Tuna
    Miracle Tuna Melt, 220
    Pantry-Ready Tuna Niçoise, 142
Turkey
    Mini Meat Loaves, 123
    Postholiday Turkey Soup, 155
    Savory Lettuce Bowls, 124
    Turkey Melts, 176
    Turkey Salad with Pistachios and Grapes, 140
    Turkey Waldorf Salad, 139
Turkey bacon
    Bacon Scallops with Baby Spinach, 211–212
    Bacon-Wrapped Pork Loin, 189–190
    Cheesy Chips, 266

Faux Breakfast Hash Browns, 259
My Favorite Cobb Salad, 141
Split Pea Soup in a Hurry, 150
Turkey sausage
    Broken Noodles, 185
    Old Country Stew, 187
    Pepperoni Pizza Dip for Fresh Veggies, 268
    Smoked Sausage Gumbo, 175

Veal Stroganoff, 183
Vegetables. *See also* Side dishes; Vegetarian entrées; *specific types of vegetables*
    Creamy Vegetable Soup, 146
    fresh veggie plate, 269
    Pepperoni Pizza Dip for Fresh Veggies, 268
    shopping list, 296
    Shrimp Lo Mein, 210
    Vegetable Frittata, 250
    Vegetable-Lentil Soup, 148
Vegetarian entrées
    Bok Choy and Tofu Stir-Fry, 201–202
    Eggplant Parmesan, 197
    Mushroom-Cheese "Burgers," 202
    Quick Broccoli Pie, 195
    Roma Tofu Bake, 198
    Spinach-Feta Pie, 194
    Tofu and Veggies, 199
    Tofu Marsala, 200
    Vegetarian Pot Luck, 196
    White Bean–Stuffed Tomatoes, 204–205
Very Berry Crème, 282
Vitamin E supplements, 20

Waldorf Salad, Turkey, 139
Walnuts
    Apple-Walnut Custards, 282–283
    Carrot and Oat Muffins, 254
    "DE"licious Chocolate Chip Cookies, 290
    "Miracle" Granola, 260
    Oat-Nut Muffins, 255

Pear and Goat Cheese Salad, 128
Sweet and Crunchy Nuts, 264
Tabbouleh with Grilled Vegetables, 233–234
Turkey Waldorf Salad, 139
Water chestnuts
    Snow Peas with Water Chestnuts, 244
    Spinach Party Dip, 118
Water consumption, 18
Watermelon
    Caribbean Watermelon Salad, 134
    Icy Melon Tea, 99
    Melon and Ricotta Salad, 136
    Watermelon Sorbet, 278
Weight loss
    evidence of progress, 23–24, 27
    fat-loss expectations, 25–27
Whipping cream
    Chocolate Mousse, 277
    "fruity" mousse, 269
White kidney beans
    Old Country Stew, 187
    White Bean–Stuffed Tomatoes, 204–205
Wild Rice Soup, Chicken and, 154
Winter squash
    Crustless Pumpkin Pie, 272
    Pumpkin Bread Pudding, 286
    Pumpkin Custards, 284
    Vegetable-Lentil Soup, 148
    Winter Squash Soufflé, 241

Zucchini
    Basil Chicken with Vegetables, 169
    Broken Noodles, 185
    Chicken and Wild Rice Soup, 154
    Garlic Zucchini, 239
    Minestrone, 149
    Mini Zucchini Pancakes, 237
    Summer Squash Casserole, 225
    Tabbouleh with Grilled Vegetables, 233–234
    Vegetable Frittata, 250

ABOUT THE AUTHOR

Diane Kress, RD, CDE, is a registered dietitian and certified diabetes educator with more than twenty-five years' experience in medical nutrition therapy. She is well known in the New York–New Jersey–Connecticut tristate area as a leading authority on innovative diet counseling. After years of practicing as a traditional nutritionist, she researched and developed the Metabolism Miracle program, specifically for those patients who could not succeed with traditional diets. The Metabolism Miracle program has already provided over three thousand of her private-practice patients with remarkable results involving permanent weight loss and decreased medications with improved blood sugar, blood pressure, cholesterol, and overall well-being.

Diane Kress's specialty areas include dietary treatment of morbid obesity, weight reduction, diabetes management and prevention, metabolic syndrome, and cardiac care nutrition. She has worked in the clinical settings of hospitals, has consulted for school systems, and currently owns and directs her own private practice, the Nutrition Center of Morristown, in Morristown, New Jersey.

Kress is a member of the American Dietetic Association, American Association of Diabetes Educators, and American Diabetes Association and has been affiliated with the Garden State Association of Diabetes Educators. She has authored articles for newspapers and is a well-known speaker at medical programs throughout New Jersey. She lives in New Jersey with her husband and two children.

For more information on the Metabolism Miracle program, author blogs, and group support, visit www.themetabolismmiracle.com.